Missed Signals on the
Western Front

Missed Signals on the Western Front

How the Slow Adoption of Wireless Restricted British Strategy and Operations in World War I

MIKE BULLOCK AND
LAURENCE A. LYONS

McFarland & Company, Inc., Publishers
Jefferson, North Carolina, and London

LIBRARY OF CONGRESS ONLINE CATALOG DATA

Bullock, Mike, 1939–
     Missed signals on the Western Front : how the slow adoption
of wireless restricted British strategy and operations in World
War I / Mike Bullock and Laurence A. Lyons.
          p.   cm.
     Includes bibliographical references and index.

     ISBN 978-0-7864-4937-8
     softcover : 50# alkaline paper

     1. Great Britain. Army — History — World War, 1914–1918.
     2. World War, 1914–1918 — Campaigns — Western Front.
     3. World War, 1914–1918 — Communications.   4. World War,
     1914–1918 — Technology.   5. Wireless communication systems —
     Great Britain — History.
     D546 .B85   2010
     940.4'1241 — dc22   2010023652

British Library cataloguing data are available

Front cover image ©2010 Clipart.com

Manufactured in the United States of America

McFarland & Company, Inc., Publishers
  Box 611, Jefferson, North Carolina 28640
   www.mcfarlandpub.com

To Brevet Lt. Col. Malcolm "Sandy" Sanderson,
a National Service "Pal" (M.B.)

To my brother, Charles Lyons (L.A.L.)

Acknowledgments

We would like to thank the following people and institutions.

Our long-suffering and patient wives, Frances Bullock and Jean Anne Lyons, who encouraged us to press on throughout the many years it took to complete this book.

Robin Bullock, who provided his exceptional information technology skills to help us complete the text and, just as important, to communicate across the ocean.

John Bourne, who supervised the thesis that led to this book and provided essential guidance to ensure the soundness of the book's conclusions.

Sanders Marble, who provided many important critiques of the ideas that form the core of the book's argument.

Peter Simkins, who commented on the book's concept and assisted in helping us with the Imperial War Museum.

Jeff Lynn, who helped us compile the index.

The staffs of the Royal Signals Museum, the Royal Engineers' Museum, the Imperial War Museum, the Public Records Office and the public library in Alcester, which provided outstanding assistance in locating and providing access to documentary material upon which this book is based.

The evaluations presented and the conclusions reached by the authors are entirely their own and they are solely responsible for them.

Table of Contents

Preface

This book has two goals. The first is to present the first comprehensive history of British signals in World War I since the pioneering work of R.E. Priestley, published in 1921.[1] Priestley's work, although benefiting from its immediacy to the war, is unfortunately extremely difficult to read and understand. It is organized more or less chronologically and treats various subjects as they come up in the course of the war. For example, the subject of protecting telephone wires from shellfire appears many times in his work with little attempt to present a coherent narrative of the evolution of approaches to the problem. His work does contain a reasonably good index and by following the references to a given subject it is possible for the reader to put together a clear picture, but it takes effort to do so. This book explores all of the aspects of British signals in the war, which Priestley attempted to do, in a clearer and more understandable narrative. It draws upon many more sources both contemporary and in the years subsequent to Priestley's work.

In the course of writing this history it became more and more apparent that the British Army's Signal Service singularly failed its parent organization by its inability to develop wireless communications to its fullest, though in most other respects it made heroic efforts to provide communications in the most difficult of circumstances. So the second goal is to demonstrate that the technology to provide lightweight portable wireless telephones (which could also have served as continuous wave [CW] wireless telegraphs) to the British Army was available early in 1915, could have been used on the Somme and certainly would have made a significant difference in the 1917 and 1918 battles.

The organization's failure to exploit contemporary wireless technology contributed to the inflexibility of British planning and execution both under static conditions and in the more open warfare conditions experienced in 1918. Had the technology been employed, from the summer of 1916 onwards, the military objectives of the British Army on the Western Front could have been reached more quickly and at far less cost in lives.

Introduction

History of British Signals in World War I

In meeting the first goal of the book the performance of the British Army Signal Service on the Western Front between 1914 and 1918 needs to be analyzed. The Signal Service was a separate and integral branch of the Royal Engineers.[1] It was required for the direction and control of the battle and the proper coordination of supply; in effect, it acted as the nervous system for the whole, and eventually vast, organism of the Army.[2] It is considered in the wider context of the extreme challenges that confronted the British Expeditionary Force (BEF), in which the scale of operations surpassed all previous experience. During the same period, the pace of scientific invention, of necessity, increased in intensity. Its results created further demands on resources and personnel that were already stretched to capacity.

In recent years, there has been a much-increased focus on the operational conduct of the war. This has added a new and overdue dimension to the historiography. Previously the balance of academic interest inclined towards a detailed analysis of leadership at the highest level, both political and military, and its effect on the prosecution of the war. This was augmented by a plethora of personal accounts and experiences from participants at all levels. As part of the recent trend, there have been a number of significant contributions.

Shelford Bidwell and Dominick Graham have studied firepower during the war, investigating its development and tactical deployment and highlighting the prevailing low level of all-arms co-operation and the significant difficulties which this presented for Signals, among others.[3] Martin Van Creveld has investigated the evolution of command in war and the increased demands made on command systems, highlighting the requirement for changes in command structures and technological developments. The importance of Signals in the conduct of the war and the way in which it influenced crucial decision-making is given particular emphasis.[4] Tim Travers has stressed the increasing and crucial importance of artillery and automatic fire and considered the ability of command structures, and the personalities involved, to deal with these complex issues.[5] Robin Prior and Trevor Wilson's contribution is important in its consideration of command at this key level and the development of battle tactics to match the emerging technology.[6] Paddy Griffith has analyzed tactics on the Western Front, particularly during the second half of the war, and considers the BEF's ability to adapt to the new technology available, principally in the development of artillery and automatic firepower. The study assesses the achievements of British staff officers and their subordinates, at an operational level, in the use of the new technology.[7]

There is general and unequivocal agreement by these commentators on three issues. Firstly, that the new generation of artillery, and its coordination with infantry action, exerted the greatest influence on battlefield conditions. Guns, which could inflict enormous damage to infantry as early as Mons in 1914, realized a far greater potential for suppression and destruction by the second half of 1917 and thereafter.[8] This was achieved by greatly increased efficiency in explosive power, range and accuracy of both direct and indirect fire. Secondly, that the development of automatic firepower, and its recognition as a vitally important infantry weapon, increased both the scale and, particularly, the intensity with which operations were conducted.[9] While there might often be wide disagreement as to its tactical deployment there is no similar debate about the extent to which it increased and complicated, to a significant degree, the logistical difficulties of the battlefield. Thirdly, that Signals had a vital and interdependent role to play in the coordination of the command structure with the new technologies.

The increasingly massive scale on which operations were conducted and the huge logistical problems that faced those whose task it was to support and maintain the British Expeditionary Force, tested to the utmost the adaptive qualities of all arms of the service. They were, in any case, already fully committed in terms of personnel and equipment. Some of the most recent academic work pays considerable attention to all of the above areas, fully emphasizing their importance and the extreme difficulties that they imposed.[10] This was nowhere more true than for Signals, with its wide ranging and increasing responsibilities, often with a high technical content. It is against this background that its contribution and achievement is to be considered.

Despite its importance in the war at both strategic and operational levels, it is astonishing that, apart from R.E. Priestley's immediate post-war review of the work of the Royal Engineers Signal Service during the war,[11] there has been no specific scholarly attention given to signals communication in the lengthy intervening period.[12] The reasons for this became clearly apparent as the research progressed, the challenges and difficulties of which it would be hard to overestimate. Priestley's work is invaluable for an initial understanding of the way in which Signals policy, and its subsequent organization and practice, had an impact on the overall conduct of the war. However, it is highly impenetrable and has required very detailed interpretation in the light of later and, arguably, more objective analysis. Nonetheless, it is the only significant and comprehensive contemporary source available. It is for this reason that it has provided an indispensable thread for the main text while, on matters of detail, its appearance with great frequency as a source in the footnotes is not only unavoidable but absolutely essential. Unfortunately, though not unusually for this type of immediate post-war first-hand account, the work contains no bibliography, or notes to the text, which would have been of the greatest assistance in highlighting other sources.

It is also significant that prior to his war service and later distinction as the unique reviewer of the work of the Signal Service, Priestley had been a highly respected scientific member of both Shackleton's (NIMROD) and Scott's 1910 to 1913 expeditions to the Antarctic and later completed a distinguished career as a Vice-Chancellor of both Melbourne and Birmingham universities, in addition to receiving a knighthood. Against this background, it is not surprising that, while his work has long awaited detailed analysis and comparison with both contemporary and later sources, it has now successfully withstood the rigors of detailed research, despite considerable difficulties of interpretation.

What is beyond doubt, however, and constantly reinforced within the academic community, is the urgent need to fill this gap in the historiography.

In considering the relevant historical material available, it is acknowledged that writing on the war generally tends to fall into two very distinct categories. The first is mainly official or personal accounts published immediately after the end of the war. They portray the mixed emotions that followed the end of the conflict and reflect views at all levels, from those of the High Command through to those involved in the front line, in all its adversity. The second is a wide range of books, by modern scholars and historians, written mostly from 1980 onwards, though with a few published to mark the 50th anniversary of the end of the war. Those written from 1980 onwards, particularly, have had the distinct advantage of being able to take a more measured and detached view of events, with considerable benefit to a clearer understanding of the issues involved. They have been able to exploit the full range of source material with a much more wide-ranging brief than the strictly narrow military interpretation of earlier writing.[13]

Signals has proved to be no exception to this general rule, though the source material available is both extremely scarce and fragmented and hidden in a wide variety of locations. This is not unexpected. Signaling during the war, while primarily the responsibility of the Royal Engineers, had an impact on all formations and units within the BEF, at all levels. While it has been possible to overcome these difficulties, developing a coherent and comprehensive view has been extremely challenging.

The research started with the Military Establishments that would be able to make a primary contribution: the Royal Engineers, the Royal Signals, and the Royal Artillery. Difficulties were immediately apparent because of the transfer of Signals responsibility from the Royal Engineers to the Corps of Signals in 1920 (becoming the Royal Corps of Signals in 1921). This resulted in a corresponding transfer of some, but by no means all, of the archive material relevant to the study, which was done on a somewhat random basis. Detailed analysis and comparison of the sources available was, consequently, made more difficult, but through the co-operation of their archivists it has been possible to overcome these difficulties. The information available in both areas provided valuable source material relating to signals organization and the means and development of signals technology.

Source material available from the Royal Artillery proved to be even more elusive and fragmented, though crucially important because of the vital link that Signals provided for Artillery, more than for any other arm of the service.

The extensive collection of manuscript diaries and papers held at the Imperial War Museum has provided an invaluable, though in Signals terms fairly limited, source. It has, however, opened up further lines of investigation.

The research extended to The National Archives: Public Record Office at Kew, which provided extensive information on the development and growth of wireless that was championed, almost exclusively, by the RFC within the Army, for the majority of the war. Material for the case studies of the battles of the Somme and Cambrai, which appear at the appropriate points in the text, was also readily available from this source. Of paramount importance was a detailed study of selected papers of the High Command, including those of Field Marshal Sir Douglas Haig and, particularly, those of the Director of Army Signals, Lieutenant-General Sir John Fowler. The extensive series of Circular Memoranda, produced by the latter, have been invaluable in tracing the development of signals policy and practice throughout the entire period of the conflict. They varied in content from those dealing with important matters of policy to many concerned with relatively trivial administrative affairs. They have also served to reinforce views developed from a variety of other sources.

The Liddell Hart Centre for Military Archives, King's College, London University, the Liddle Collection, Leeds University, and Churchill College, Cambridge, also furnished useful supporting information, as did visits to various regimental museums.

A fundamental element of the research has been a comprehensive and detailed study of a wide variety of other books, papers, diaries and personal accounts detailed in the bibliography. These have been divided between both the immediate post-war and later historical categories. They have been particularly significant in an appreciation of wider operational issues and their effect on signals strategy and policy. Some, written by specialists, have contributed towards a clearer understanding of signals practice.

In the book, it is not the intention to look in detail at the development of signals technology, with the exception of wireless, the understanding of which is crucial to the book's conclusions. Even by the end of the war the technology was unimaginably primitive by today's standards, but some consideration of the means of communication available has been necessary. A close examination of signals policy and practice has been essential, however. This has provided a clear understanding of the problems faced by the personnel involved in its daily implementation. It has also illustrated its effect on decision making at all levels, from GHQ downwards.

An essential starting point has been the consideration of the basic requirements for a good system of signals communication during the war that was simple in concept but proved exceedingly difficult to implement. General Staff Instructions describe these as reliability, speed in transmission and the ability to meet the demands of constantly changing conditions.[14] The latter was, arguably, the most demanding because of the need to satisfy a wide variety of circumstances from static trench warfare to, eventually, a rapid advance in open warfare. The requirements proved formidable in the circumstances of the massive scale, and confusion, of operations in the war.

Three fundamental questions arise. Firstly, to what extent did the High Command have a clear understanding of the requirement for a comprehensive policy for signals communication throughout the war? Secondly, to what degree was the Signal Service successful in meeting the extensive demands placed upon it to provide an effective system of communications during the war? Thirdly and specifically, did the Signal Service exploit wireless technology to its fullest capability, recognizing its potentially revolutionary impact on command and control? In the answers to these questions lies a fuller appreciation of the specific effect of signals communication on the prosecution of the war.

With these questions in mind, an important example to consider has been the use and development of wireless during the war and its influence on the overall strategy of the High Command. There is wide military recognition that, although available at the outset, it never reached its full potential, even though it was used extensively by 1918. Van Creveld has no doubt that, because of their limited aspirations for wireless, GHQ often constructed operations in such a way as to make them controllable by wire.[15] He would go so far as to say that it was this limited approach that led, directly, to the strategy employed at the Battle of the Somme. John Terraine gives support for this view in contending, similarly, that command in battle was restricted to what the telephone lines permitted.[16] He extends this further to the more general need for having what he describes as "an audible voice in battle," which in his view was never solved satisfactorily throughout the whole of the war. From this he draws the conclusion that control of the battle was lost, more often than not, for this very reason. Van Creveld endorses this in his unequivocal judgment that the network of communications that is vital to the functioning of modern warfare was absent from Great War battlefields.[17]

To place the development of signals policy and practice in context, it is necessary to consider it in relation to the chronological progress of the war.[18] In 1914 the BEF was equipped for a rapid trial of strength and its equipment reflected this. It relied heavily on visual, dispatch riders, orderlies, liaison officers and telegraph. With the advent of static trench warfare in 1915 different means of communication were appropriate. Visual was both dangerous and vulnerable in these conditions and was replaced by telephone. As artillery fire increased in intensity, telephone became vulnerable even though cables were buried at ever increasing depths. In 1916, to counteract these difficulties, other means, such as wireless, were used on a limited basis and by 1917 the power buzzer and Fullerphone were employed for the same reasons. It was only in 1918, in circumstances of mobile, open warfare, that wireless approached its full potential. The way in which each means of communication developed will become apparent in the operational sections of the book.

The most compelling feature of the war was the increasingly massive scale on which it was conducted. It was within this environment that the unsophisticated and limited signals technology had to operate. It is important to recognize its predominance as a factor, particularly in relation to signals, and is worthy of further consideration, at this stage, though it will be clearly apparent throughout the main text. Griffith is instructive at this point.[19] After the slow build-up of 1914, the remorseless advance of trench warfare saw a huge proliferation of personnel, artillery and other military developments over a wide front. The effect of this, combined with often atrocious weather and its effect on the battlefield conditions, and concerted enemy action, took a tremendous toll on signals manpower and equipment, the demand for which outstripped its supply for the remainder of the war. He is in no doubt that Signals, which played a vital role in every battle, had to shoulder some of the heaviest responsibilities with the slenderest of manpower and materials, while at the same time having to assimilate radical technological changes and improvements in equipment.

There is no doubt that, given the scale of the conflict, the potential for serious communications difficulties was only too apparent. Indeed, with the limited technology available they were almost insurmountable. In the final analysis they were overcome, and only then to a degree, by the dedicated service of the whole of the Signal Service. Griffith supports this in arguing that it is not too much to suggest that the BEF's most successful battles, whether in the relatively static warfare of 1917 or in the mobility of 1918, owed a great deal to this dedication, coupled with the expertise, of the Signal Service.[20]

An appreciation of signals organization is important in any assessment of their overall performance. This is especially true for that most crucial and difficult area for signals — the front line in the heat of battle. There are myriad examples recorded of extremes of difficulty in this area through the chain of command to the artillery, to the Royal Flying Corps, or with other units. The overall and constantly recurring theme is one of a blurred or non-existent picture of events.

Three examples serve to illustrate this, at this stage. Firstly, Prior and Wilson, in considering 1915 generally, conclude that the whole communications system for artillery registration could fall down when enemy fire severed the telephone link between the Forward Observation Officer and the batteries.[21] Secondly, Travers contends that during the German Spring Offensive of 1918, the destruction of communications resulted in the almost complete disintegration of the command structures of the Third and Fifth Armies.[22] Thirdly, Travers — among many examples — cites the specific circumstances of the 38th Division attack on Mametz Wood; in this instance, it was reported that communications were very poor with Division, non-existent with the Artillery, and the High Command literally did not know what was going on. [23]

It is against this background that the book evaluates the comparative success or failure of both the High Command and the Signal Service to provide effective communications during the war. This is its primary purpose. A summary of the composition of the Signal Service, year on year, is provided by Priestley.[24] This was an evolving and by no means orderly process, however, moving expediently to meet the demands of an Army organization that expanded exponentially and beyond recognition by the end of the war. The way in which the Signal Service responded to these demands, and the constant changes required in both its structure and size, unfold as the main text progresses.

Wireless

It is commonly recognized that the immense casualties suffered in World War I infantry actions were in part a consequence of the inability of commanders to control their forces once they were committed to action. Commanders carefully planned actions in detail prior to engagement but were unable to influence events when the battle was joined. They did not learn of success or failure until it was too late to reinforce the former or terminate the latter. Staff officers were not aware of uncut wire, heavy casualties and unreduced enemy strongpoints until it was too late to do anything about them. The inability of commanders' staffs to control a World War I battle with the unprecedented size and geographic dispersion of the forces involved was a direct result of the inadequate communications available in 1914 to 1918. The lack of adequate communications restricted the quantity and timeliness of information flow within and between formations (company, battalion, regiment, division), between units and their commanders, between infantry and artillery and between artillery and air observation. The Entente and Central Powers armies tried many alternative means of communication to meet operational requirements but no single means possessed the capacity, flexibility, transportability and resistance to destruction and intercept needed for the World War I battlefield environment. One, wireless, showed promise of satisfying these requirements but did not fulfill its promise in this war. The U.S. Signal Corps Official History summarizes the consequences: "The high combat casualty rates of World War I can be partly attributed to the lack of a reliable wireless communications system. Once soldiers went 'over the top,' they found themselves isolated. During deafening artillery barrages a commander could not control his men with his voice, and vision became limited amid the fog of battle. In order to maintain contact, soldiers tended to move in groups that made them easy targets for enemy machine gunners. Although wire lines were portable they could not last long under constant and withering artillery bombardment that chewed them to bits; what the shellfire spared often fell victim to the treads of tanks or other vehicles. With their communications cut off, attackers found it difficult to call for reinforcements or artillery support." [25]

Only later, in subsequent twentieth century conflicts, would the promise of wireless be realized. Why this occurred, and why wireless was not employed to a greater extent in World War I seemed odd to one of the authors, who, as an electrical engineer and radio amateur, was very familiar with the history of early radio and with technical developments prior to and during the conflict. In particular, the dramatic expansion of commercial radio in America and Britain, which began in 1920, appears to contradict the widely held view that wireless was too technically immature to have an effect on the conduct of the 1914 to 1918 war.

In his history of the First World War John Keegan states this widely held view as follows: "Radio communication, wireless telegraphy as it was then known, offered a solution to the difficulty [of the direction of firepower] in theory, but not in practice. Contemporary wireless sets, dependent on sources of energy too large and heavy to be useful militarily outside warships, were not practicable tools of command in the field. Though wireless was to play a minor strategic role early in the coming war, it was to prove of no tactical significance at any time, even at the end.... In retrospect, it may be seen that a system existing in embryo, though promising to make effective all the power available to combatants in their quest for victory, lagged technically too far behind its potentiality to succeed."[26]

As will be seen in this book, wireless not only offered a solution to command and control difficulties, as Keegan stated, but: contemporary wireless sets, wireless telephony in particular, could have been practicable tools of command in the field, but little engineering effort was exerted to achieve this goal early in the conflict; wireless telegraphy actually did have tactical significance at the end of the war, under conditions of mobile warfare; tactical wireless was not in embryo, as a prototype of a working wireless radiotelephone (which could also have served as a CW wireless telegraph) had been built in 1915 and demonstrated to the High Command in 1916; and, crucially, tactical wireless did not technically lag too far behind its potentiality to succeed — what was missing was the vision to appreciate it as a vital tool and the will to develop it.

This book will prove that the reason wireless was not used as early in the war as it could have been was a significant institutional bias against it in the British Army which had its origins before the war and which was reinforced by the crude wireless sets with which the army began the war. Technical immaturity was not the reason; after the initial shock of hostilities the Royal Flying Corps (RFC) drafted Marconi's best engineers, who then proceeded to develop and install a working airborne radiotelephone set during the summer of 1915. The set was demonstrated to Lord Kitchener in February 1916. Had such a lightweight, low power set been placed in mass production and made available, not only to the RFC, but also to the entire British Expeditionary Force by the end of that year, for example, the battles of third Ypres and Cambrai would have had a better outcome. Moreover, if prototypes of such a set had been distributed to the Army in early 1916, the battle of the Somme could have been fought with fewer casualties because of better control of the artillery; indeed the whole strategic planning for the battle would have been provided with far greater flexibility with a marked and historic effect on the final outcome. The book will examine these and similar actions and develop reasonable "what if" scenarios based on reliable, survivable communications between units, between units and commanders, and between ground or air observers and artillery. In so doing it will demonstrate that the earlier introduction of wireless would have had a profound influence both on tactical operations and on the entire strategic conduct of the war. Instead of basing plans on the stationary and highly vulnerable telephone system, as happened at the Somme, the staff planners would have been freed to implement what made sense militarily. Operations would have been based on achieving mission objectives instead of being designed around the layout of the fixed communication system.

The Organization of This Book

To fulfill its objectives, the book is organized as follows: Chapter 1 discusses the status of wireless development before 1914 and demonstrates not only that the Royal Navy was far ahead of all the world's navies in its application of wireless technology, but also that the British Army lagged dismally behind the Navy in its appreciation of wireless and plans for its use. Chapters 2, 3, 5, 7, and 9 discuss operational signals during the war. Apart from their importance as a long outstanding addition to the historiography, these chapters are also an essential prerequisite for Chapter 11, which evaluates the performance of the Signal Service in providing the third key element, together with command and control, of success in modern warfare — effective communications. Chapter 4 is crucial to understanding that the RFC had not only developed a working model of a lightweight radio telephony set (and CW wireless telegraph) in 1915, but had the engineering talent to carry the development further and thereby revolutionize army communications, if the will to do so had existed in the Signal Service. Chapters 6, 8 and 10 are counterfactuals on five key engagements of the war, which hypothesize the benefits that a reliable tactical communications system would have provided in these engagements, not only leading to success where failure prevailed, but also, and fundamentally, in minimizing British casualties. Chapter 12 is devoted to a discussion of intercept, encryption and jamming, key issues for a wireless communications system. The chapter notes that while fear of intercept or overhearing severely limited the development and application of wireless during the war, intercept was not only a problem for wireless, but also was common to all forms of communication, sometimes with disastrous results. Chapter 13 summarizes the actual use of wireless during the war, with particular reference to its significance in the overall strategy adopted by the General Staff. Finally, the Conclusion assesses the comparative success of the Signal Service in meeting the demands placed upon it throughout the war while highlighting its virtual indifference to wireless as an effective element of communications.

CHAPTER 1

Military Wireless Before the War

In 1873 the Scottish physicist James Clerk Maxwell published four partial differential equations which combined all that was then known about electricity and magnetism. Maxwell's equations were mathematical expressions of the experimentally derived laws known as Gauss's law for the electric field, Gauss's law for the magnetic field, Faraday's law and Ampère's circuit law. Gauss's law for the electric field relates the flux of the electric field through a closed surface to the charge contained within the surface. Gauss's law for the magnetic field states that the net flux of the magnetic field through a closed surface must be zero. Faraday's law states that a current will be induced in a wire moving through a magnetic field. Ampère's circuit law states that a current flowing through a wire produces a magnetic field. In order to make Ampère's circuit law consistent for a circuit which includes a condenser (a circuit element that stores electric charge), Maxwell had to introduce the notion of displacement current, which states that a magnetic field can be produced by a time-varying electric field. This was a crucial addition to Ampère's circuit law. Mathematical manipulations of Maxwell's equations with this modification produce the wave equation, which describes the propagation of electromagnetic waves. Therefore in 1873 Maxwell predicted that electromagnetic waves moving at the velocity of light could be produced by time-varying currents in conductors such as wires or surfaces. This prediction was made purely as a mathematical consequence of the equations he had derived from known phenomena. It was the greatest achievement in physics in the 19th century.

Experimental verification of Maxwell's equations would not occur until 1886. The German physicist Heinrich Hertz designed an experimental apparatus which would generate an electromagnetic wave and a device which would detect it. He generated the wave by creating a spark between two conducting hemispheres and detected the wave by seeing a spark in the gap between the two ends of an interrupted loop of wire placed in the vicinity of the two hemispheres. Hertz's laboratory equipment was the basis of radio communications to come. It included a source of sparks attached to a length of wire to radiate electromagnetic waves and a loop of wire to detect and receive the waves. As a communication system it had severe limitations. Greater sensitivity was needed in the receiving apparatus and a solution to this was soon to follow. More significant, however, were the limitations imposed by using a spark discharge as a source of energy. As discussed in Appendix A, the rapidly damped pulses were very wasteful of spectrum space and a significant source of interference when more than one transmitter attempted to transmit. Despite refinements in later spark gap designs these drawbacks could never be eliminated since they were inherent in using spark discharge to communicate. Both of these drawbacks eventually placed significant restrictions on both the commercial and military use of spark wireless.

A young Italian, Guglielmo Marconi, saw the potential of using electromagnetic waves to communicate. Though lacking in technical education, Marconi had an intuitive sense of the elements needed to achieve a viable communication system and the persistence and resources to perform exhaustive experiments until he had perfected each of these elements. Following Hertz, he used a spark between two conductors to generate the waves. He recognized, however, that the waves would be generated more efficiently if the energy from the spark were fed into vertical or horizontal wires of varying lengths and of varying configurations, called antennas. He also felt that the detector used by Hertz was inefficient. After trial and error he settled on a glass tube filled with fine iron filings, which would align and conduct in the presence of a magnetic field. He called this device a coherer. The spark transmitter and the coherer were the basis of the wireless telegraphy system Marconi first demonstrated to the British government and subsequently developed into a successful commercial enterprise. This wireless telegraphy system, with incremental engineering improvements, such as more efficient coupling of the spark energy to the antenna and magnetic or crystal detectors to replace the coherer, was the dominant wireless communication system in the world for approximately 30 years, from 1890 to 1920. It is important to emphasize that this system was a telegraphy system and was used to transmit the dots and dashes of Morse code. The continuous wave (CW) technology needed to accomplish wireless telephony and also capable of transmitting messages and music, would not begin to appear until after 1910. (The basic technical distinctions between spark and CW wireless sets are discussed in Appendix A.)

The possibility of improving communications in war by using wireless telegraphy, and later, telephony, was first perceived as early as the last decade of the nineteenth century. Its employment in naval warfare seemed its most appropriate application at that time. The Royal Navy began its investigations of wireless at the same time as Marconi, but independent of him. Its leading proponent was Henry Bradwardine Jackson, a man of extraordinary brilliance and vision, who later became an Admiral of the Fleet and was First Sea Lord for the first two years of World War I. In 1887 he observed that Hertzian waves (as electromagnetic waves were then called) might be used to help defend against enemy torpedo boats. In 1895 when he was named as commanding officer of HMS *Defiance,* he had an opportunity to acquire apparatus to conduct experiments with Hertzian waves. With this apparatus, in August 1896, he succeeded in transmitting and receiving Morse code signals at a range of 50 m., the maximum available from the ship. At the end of August he also met Marconi. He learned that "the principles on which Signor Marconi's apparatus were constructed were similar to those employed by *Defiance*, but [were] more fully developed and the instruments themselves were much more sensitive."[1] Jackson also informed Marconi that he had been working on similar apparatus but put Marconi's mind at ease by telling him that he had no intention of patenting his work.

Jackson became a firm champion of Marconi's invention within the Navy. After trials of Marconi's equipment were conducted on Salisbury Plain, Jackson sent Marconi a general specification for a shipborne set: "I think personally that your apparatus is worth a trial and would be of use to the service, if the signals can be made over 3 miles, without reflectors: all round lenses would be permissible. The size of the transformer would not be of importance but I would state roughly 4 cubic feet (0.11 cubic meters) and a weight of 2 cwt (101 kg) should not, if possible be exceeded. The power available would be a continuous pressure of 80 volts of which 5 horsepower (3730 W) would practically not be much felt and be always available. All parts of the apparatus would have to be protected from wet and capable of standing rough usage and heavy shocks from the firing of guns."[2]

After receiving equipment developed according to his specifications Jackson organized a series of trials using torpedo boats and HMS *Defiance.*

Successful transmission of signals over a range of 3 miles was achieved. Jackson also determined that the wireless apparatus was rugged enough for sea duty and did not require any more attention than other electrical devices on board. He did, however, identify the problem of interference, noting that it was impossible for two ships to transmit simultaneously.

In 1897 Jackson was assigned as Naval Attaché to the British Embassy in Paris, which ended for a time his direct involvement with wireless telegraphy. He continued to enthusiastically support Marconi and the development of naval wireless. When the opportunity presented itself he returned to wireless: "In 1901, Captain Jackson joined the Mediterranean Fleet, ostensibly to take command of HMS *Vulcan*, but in fact to continue his development of tunable wireless sets away from radio interference in the United Kingdom caused by commercial transmitters."[3]

At the end of 1898 Marconi and Jackson had demonstrated the following[4]:

1. a wireless telegraph system could operate over land and water and could work particularly well between a shore station and ships;
2. the range of working was much greater than could be achieved by either a conductive or inductive electrical telegraph system;
3. wireless telegraphy could be used at night as well as during the day; and was unaffected by bad weather such as rain, fog or storms — provided the insulation of the antenna was not degraded;
4. the interposition of hills and trees did not prevent communication between a sender and a receiver;
5. the apparatus could be used by any telegraphist after a short induction period;
6. the system that comprised the transmitter and receiver was not costly, though the installation of a high mast and associated antenna might be expensive;
7. the dimensions of the various units, with the exception of the antenna and mast, were such that the units could easily be accommodated on board ships and large yachts; and
8. wireless telegraphy had many applications.

Based on further tests and on an operational trial conducted in 1899 the Navy ordered 32 Marconi sets to be delivered in mid–1900. These were distributed to various squadrons, schools, ports, signal stations and individual ships. The Navy ordered 19 additional sets designed by then Captain Jackson, invoking the right of the government to manufacture and use a patented invention if it was in the national interest. Captain Jackson was careful to duplicate Marconi sets as closely as he could to assure interchangeability of the government equipment with Marconi's.

The Navy continued to follow Marconi's achievements closely and applied them with enthusiasm to meet its needs. In December 1901 Marconi electrified the world by sending a message across the Atlantic. He had built a powerful transmitter at Poldhu in Cornwall and claimed he had received a signal in Newfoundland. There were skeptics then and later.[5] Based on what we know of radio propagation today, the frequency used was too low for good reflection off the ionosphere and, more significantly, Marconi made his observation when the entire propagation path was in daylight. As has been known since the 1930s, radio waves travel much further at night, when the ionosphere is lower. Since 1900, attempts have been made to duplicate Marconi's experiment by transmitting on the same frequency in daylight, without success.[6]

In January 1902, to answer his critics, Marconi arranged for the Cunard liner *Philadelphia* to be equipped with a receiver so that it could listen to Poldhu on its voyage from Britain to the United States. The captain of the ship certified that the receiver picked up the Poldhu signal from 700 miles out by day and 1550 miles out at night. These results, of course, were of great interest to the Navy.

Sir John Fisher was appointed First Sea Lord in October 1904. "Fisher at once invested in a Navy-owned shore-based wireless network and hastened the fitting of all ships with the new 1.5 kilowatt (and for battle cruisers 14 kilowatt) transmitters…. Superimposing the wireless chain atop the existing cable network surmounted limitations in transmitter range. By 1906, without recourse to civilian transmitters the Royal Navy could keep two-way ship-to-shore contact with large warships operating within 500 miles of the triangle formed by Gibraltar and Malta at the base and Cleethorpes in the United Kingdom, at the point."[7] In addition to these improvements in the wireless network the Royal Navy, under Fisher, created a war room capable of tracking the daily movements of all warships and fast merchant steamships in the world, based on information gathered from regional intelligence officers, customs, consular and diplomatic sources and obtained through special arrangements with Lloyd's.[8] In 1905, for example, the War Room helped the Royal Navy to track the progress of the two Russian squadrons on their journey from the Baltic to their fateful end at Tsushima.[9] By the end of Fisher's tenure, in January 1910, the War Room enabled the Admiralty not only to direct fleet movements but also to control operations. In March 1910, Fisher's successor, Adm. Sir Arthur Wilson was able to remotely control the movements of the battle fleet off the Spanish coast using War Room plots and wireless.[10]

Parallel with naval developments, the Army had been researching wireless separately as the specific responsibility of the Royal Engineers (REs). In fact, it had seen limited use in the South African War. However, owing to the primitive nature of the equipment used and especially interference from climatic conditions, it had demonstrated little success as a viable means of communication.

It quickly became apparent that the Army was making little progress and that there was no real momentum in its wireless development program. Consequently, a parliamentary committee was formed in August 1912, under the chairmanship of Sir Henry Norman, an individual having marked interest in new technologies, notably the wireless and the automobile, with the brief "to consider the utilization for military services of wireless telegraphy and telephony with special references to recent developments in the science and to report."[11] Interestingly, this committee was formed coincidentally with the first appointment of a Director of Army Signals, but no cause and effect relationship, either way, seems to have occurred.

The committee held 24 meetings, examined numerous documents, witnessed demonstrations and received testimony from 27 witnesses including Col. George Squier, the American Military Attache in London, holder of one of the first Ph.D.s in electrical engineering awarded in the United States (from Johns Hopkins University), who was later to command the United States Army Signal Corps. In its 1913 report, the committee determined that the state of wireless telegraphy in the Army was "so inefficient as to be unreliable, and therefore practically valueless in time of war."[12] Practical tests on two wagon sets and two pack sets "showed failure in every respect." "We gathered from witnesses who appeared before us that grave doubts [were] generally felt by senior officers as to the reliability of Army wireless as at present organized and that they would not feel safe in time of war unless an alternative means of communication were provided."[13]

The committee made recommendations regarding "the general organization of wireless equipment and service in the Army; wireless instruction; technical equipment; future policy with regard to equipment; wireless telephony; Army wireless procedures in signaling; and wavelengths."[14] The committee also recommended the purchase of Poulsen arc equipment, which was the only continuous wave transmitter available in 1913. Danish inventor Valdemar Poulsen had used the property of an electric arc to oscillate at a single frequency as the basis of his design. The resulting transmitter required significant power, however, and had to be transported by a vehicle capable of carrying its weight and providing the necessary power. To its credit the committee did recognize the advantages of continuous wave equipment in making this recommendation, giving as reasons "considerable possibilities of immunity from interference, especially in combination with the heterodyne receiver; immediate change to any one of a great number of wavelengths, including very long ones, far longer than could be produced with the spark set with a given aerial, which facilitate working over mountainous country, and render tapping by the enemy more difficult."[15] Despite this clear understanding of technical issues, remarkable for its time, and its grasp of the actions needed for the Army to exploit the new wireless technology, the overall influence of this committee on the future of Army wireless was overwhelmingly negative for the following reason.

The committee's major and overriding conclusion, based on concerns about overhearing (intercept), which had massive and adverse future implications, was that "the state of wireless in the Army was such that it would be better to abandon it altogether as *an inefficient wireless service in war would be a constant source of doubt and danger.*"[16] Further discussion of this unfortunate conclusion is presented in Chapter 13. In the event, the specter of overhearing, with only limited justification, was to haunt its full acceptance by the General Staff and, apart from a select number within the Signal Service, the Army generally until mid–1917.

The Navy continued to take advantage of technical improvements to wireless. After his transatlantic experiment, Marconi, searching for a more efficient way to inject the spark energy into the antenna, found that by using a transformer to couple the circuit containing the spark gap to the circuit containing the antenna he could increase the radiated power. In so doing he achieved an unexpected but welcome benefit. Previously, when the spark gap was directly connected to the antenna the radiated power was concentrated around a single frequency, known as the resonant frequency of the antenna. In the new configuration, the radiated power was concentrated around two resonant frequencies, later called Tune A and Tune B. Even better, transmissions on Tune A did not interfere with transmissions on Tune B, and Poldhu did not interfere with either.[17] Later, sets were designed which could operate either on Tune A or Tune B. The Admiralty was eager to use these new sets and replaced all existing transmitters with them in 1904.

By 1905 the British had decided that wireless was to be standard equipment in all ships larger than destroyers. They introduced the Standard Wireless Installation 1905 which used a separate transmitter and receiver for Tune A and for Tune B. The sets were powered from the ship's electrical system rather than batteries and used Marconi's new magnetic detector instead of a coherer.[18] "There is little doubt that from every point of view the Royal Navy at this time had the most efficient wireless communication system in the world. They had introduced three channels of communication, had standardized their equipment and by a blending together of specialized naval requirements and the genius of Marconi had produced the best material. To this was added a high technical competence of the officers and men of the torpedo branch and the backing of senior officers who saw the great possibilities of wireless communications. It is interesting that in this innovation Royal Navy was ahead of other countries. With other new devices such as the submarine and aircraft the reverse was the case. The reason is clear. Submarines and aircraft, if anything, threatened to weaken sea power as applied with a battlefleet strategy, whereas wireless telegraphy aided it."[19]

Interference and frequency congestion continued to be a problem. Tunes A and B of the Royal Navy were also used by merchant ships with Marconi equipment, so naval vessels not only suffered interference from each other but from normal maritime traffic. Clearly future wireless developments were dependent on the ability to use many different frequencies to reduce interference.

In 1906 an International Radio Telegraphic Conference was held in Berlin to facilitate the communication between commercial stations and ships and to standardize the procedures for sending and receiving wireless telegrams. "It made provisions also for the allocation of wavelengths which affected warships. It established two wavelengths for the public commercial service which were 300 m. (1000 kc/s) and 600 m. (500 kc/s); all public coastal stations were required to operate on one of these frequencies and 300 m. (1000 kc/s) was established as the normal wave for all ships and on which they were required to be able to work."[20] Ships were allowed to use other frequencies above 500 kilocycles per second; small ships could use frequencies above 1000 kilocycles per second. The Royal Navy called the 1000 kilocycles per second frequency P tune, and the 500 kilocycles per second frequency Q tune. The Navy assigned four other tunes (frequencies), R, S, T and U, for use by naval vessels larger than destroyers. Four additional tunes, C, D, V and W, were added later. "In 1907, too, the 'Instructions for the Conduct of W/T Signaling' were issued by the British Admiralty. They included an organization allocating the various wavelengths or tunes to various purposes. A fleet at sea in Home waters would keep in touch with the shore by listening to broadcast routines from Poldhu. Tunes were allocated for sending messages back to commercial or naval shore stations and another tune was reserved for the flagship to keep in touch with scouting cruisers or any other detached ships. A fleet at sea would maneuver and communicate between ships by visual signals and as each ship had only one wireless set a system of what were known as wireless guardships was instituted. In a fleet a separate guard ship would be detailed to listen on each wave. Messages received by these guardships would be passed by them to the flagship by visual signal."[21] These procedures are the first known instance of a frequency management system that is an essential element of the military use of wireless.

As a result of these efforts the Royal Navy possessed the most efficient wireless communication system of all the world's navies by 1910. Technical improvements in wireless such as the quenched spark and Poulsen arc transmitters and Marconi's crystal detector were installed in naval vessels as they became available. The Royal Navy also exercised the wireless system extensively during the annual naval maneuvers, learning how to exploit the new communication capability and to identify its shortcomings. One of the main objects of the naval maneuvers of 1911 was to test wireless communications. The Home Fleet was the Red Fleet and the Mediterranean and the Atlantic Fleets were the Blue Fleets. The Red Fleet tried to engage one of the Blue Fleets before they could combine. "Communications were therefore of most importance to the Blue fleets in order to effect their concentration. Red decided in consequence to do their best to jam them. The Blue fleets communicated on T Tune and the *Dreadnought*, the Red flagship, talked to her cruisers on R Tune with U Tune reserved to report the enemy battlefleets. The Red fleet decided to try and jam T tune at three-quarters power continuously so as to prevent it being used even for very short signals; in the event the Blue fleet operators got used to the jamming note and by varying their own note slightly found they could read signals through it. The Red fleet subsequently believed they should have waited until Blue started a signal before trying to jam. Continuous jamming was not in any case believed to be practicable in war as insufficient would be known about the characteristics of the enemy wireless sets. It was also noted that it was never evident what effect jamming was having on the enemy. In fact jamming as a wireless counter-measure was to be little used in the future for with the introduction of a larger number of wireless channels, with musical notes and aural reception it had lost its potency. Throughout these maneuvers wireless worked perfectly and there was little interference."[22] By keeping up with technical progress and by constantly exercising its capability, at the start of World War I the Royal Navy had a wireless communication system whose equipment, organization and training were superior to that of any other nation.

CHAPTER 2

Operational Signals — Pre–war and Early Mobile Warfare

The Royal Engineers were first given responsibility for operating a Signal Service for the British Army during the Crimean War of 1854–56. The task was to enable the military headquarters in the Crimea to communicate with their governments in England and France by means of submarine cable and cross-continental lines while, at the same time, providing field telegraphs in the forward operational areas.

In 1867 a British Army conference at Chatham reviewed the whole subject of signaling in the field. As a direct result, the School of Military Engineering, Chatham, established a Signal Wing in 1869 for the instruction of all army personnel in electrical and visual means of communication. In 1870 a Telegraph Troop, Royal Engineers was formed and equipped. For the following thirteen years it provided detachments for a number of campaigns including the First Ashanti War (1873–4), the Zulu War (1877), the Transvaal War (1881), and the Egyptian War (1882). In 1884 the Telegraph Battalion, the Royal Engineers was formed and, at the same time, the General Post Office (GPO) formed a nucleus of volunteers and a Supplementary Reserve. The telephone was first used in the field during the Egyptian War (1882). It was, however, during the Second South African War that the Signal Service of the army was greatly extended.

When the British landed in South Africa in 1899, its forces had a Telegraph Division of 100 linesmen and telegraph operators, mainly composed of GPO personnel, who went on to do excellent work.[1] As Boer resistance was gradually overcome and the British advanced, communication with General Headquarters (GHQ) was maintained by cable and airline with great success and played a significant part in the eventual

25

outcome. The comments of Lord Roberts, the Commander-in-Chief, bear this out: "The main line telegraph was extraordinarily well done and the way repairs were made, lines renewed and new lines started was quite admirable throughout."[2]

This was the first official recognition of the value of the Signals arm as a separate entity in the modern army.[3] It therefore follows, and is entirely logical, that the experience of the South African War was used as the basis for the Signals element of the re-construction of the British Expeditionary Force (BEF), which took place during the years immediately following the South African conflict. Indeed, signal personnel were vitally affected by the overall re-construction of the BEF that led to the eventual formation of the Signal Service in 1912. Consideration of the steps leading up to this formation is important in an appreciation of the establishment of the Signal Service that went to France in 1914.

In 1906 a committee was appointed to report on intercommunication services. It strongly recommended a central organization of all means of existing communication under one controlling authority. There were four principal recommendations: that one overall Director of Signaling be appointed; that communication units for each army formation be controlled by the General Staff of the formation; that communication services take over artillery signaling as far forward as battery HQ (a forward looking recommendation, later reversed by the 1911 committee — see below); and that large increases in expenditure be made on the development of a Signal Service over the next few years — inevitably, a balance between the cost of the minimum services felt necessary by the General Staff and the expenditure defined as appropriate by its controlling body, the Army Council.[4]

In 1911 a further committee was formed, again with the brief to report on intercommunication services, but to take account of the 1906 committee's recommendations. These had been generally accepted. However, the decision to take over artillery signaling was reversed, which was to have serious repercussions during the early days of the war.

The historic consequence of the 1911 Committee's final report was the creation in 1912 of a separate Signal Service as a branch of the Royal Engineers. A Director of Army Signals was appointed.[5] (This was Lieutenant-Colonel J.S. Fowler, who served in this key post, with great distinction, until the end of the war, by which time he had attained the rank of Lieutenant-General.) His responsibilities were defined by an Army Order as follows: "The Director of Army Signals was made the Supreme Arbiter of the Signal Service and given power to communicate direct with his representatives on all matters of administration and technical detail connected with the Army Signal Service."[6]

The duties and responsibilities of the officers within the new Signal Service were also defined. The Director of Army Signals had as his immediate subordinates, the commanders of the GHQ, army, corps, and divisional headquarters signal companies who acted as technical advisors. Under the Director's orders, they were responsible for the general organization, maintenance and efficiency of the Signal Service. Separate regimental signaling organizations were laid down — effectively, they were to provide communications between themselves, superior commanders, neighboring units and their own units.

Two crucial issues with far-reaching consequences flowed from the new policy. Firstly, regimental signals personnel would provide their own communications outside the jurisdiction of the Signal Service. The need for some sort of liaison function was immediately apparent to provide a vital link if communications were to be controlled in a cohesive way.[7] To this end an important decision was made to second specially selected junior officers with the task of linking up the communications of regimental units with the new Signal Service. This created the necessary liaison between the various formations in the chain of communication.

Secondly, while signaling in battalions, regiments and artillery batteries continued to be their own responsibility, this was firmly based on the understanding that signalers were infantry soldiers first and that their signals duties took second place. A potentially very dangerous situation was created, with implications that will become apparent later.

The chronological development and detail of the means of signals communication is to be considered later. It is important, however, to consider the basic types of communication available to the Signal Service that had developed up to the outbreak of the war as the result of a fundamental review and re-organization of intercommunication services. These were: telephone and telegraph for work in forward areas as essential equipment for all cable units (their greater prominence will be seen later); motorcycle dispatch riders, mounted orderlies, runners and carrier pigeons; flag and other means of visual communication, including various types of lamps designed for day and night signaling, using semaphore and Morse; wireless, though this was limited in concept and confined almost entirely to cavalry operations — its lack of development and use influenced greatly the later overall strategy of the way in which the war was conducted and will be considered later.

Motorcyclist dispatch rider in Feuchy, 5 June 1917. (IWM No. Q-5468)

Although the means available were limited, there was an urgent requirement from all arms of the service for much improved methods of communication. Tremendous demands were imposed on the 75 officers and 2,346 men who constituted the Signal Service up to the Battle of the Marne. This was particularly the case because, while in theory at least, their prime responsibility would be to provide communications from Base on the French coast up to battalion HQs, in practice they would be called upon to supervise, and often carry out, the work of signalers right up to the front line. The serious and far-reaching implications of this policy will become more apparent as this study of operational signals proceeds.

Appendix B illustrates the establishment strength of the various elements of signals personnel with the BEF in August 1914 before embarkation for France.[8] Each was at a different stage of training and readiness and need to be considered individually.

The regular Signal Service units, though inadequate for requirements, must be considered, by any standards, as exceptionally well trained and efficient. Within the numerical constraints imposed upon them, their performance was exemplary up to and including the Battle of Mons and continued through the difficulties of the retreat to the Marne. However, based on what was later to be considered necessary on a comparative basis in 1917–18, their numbers were totally inadequate to the task before them.

In 1914 available signals personnel were thinly spread.[9] They formed 1 Line of Communications Signal Company, 1 GHQ Signal Company, 2 Army Corps HQ Signal Companies, 6 Divisional Signal Companies, 13 Cable and Airline Sections, 4 Signal Troops together with 1 Signal Squadron to serve the Cavalry Division and 1 small Wireless Section.

Their responsibilities often extended right up to the front line. This was an extension of their duties never intended and for which their establishment was entirely inadequate, in both numbers and equipment.

There were, also, two characteristics common to BEF Signals in 1914 that set it apart from the later, more developed service. Firstly, there was an almost complete reliance on telegraph and delivered messages for all purposes. Secondly, a looseness of organization reflected by the lack of anything remotely approaching a workable chain of command. In theory, the Director of Army Signals exercised control over all the units under his supervision, but with a small staff he could not keep in touch effectively with the number of diverse formations involved. In practice, the officers in charge of signals units were responsible only to the staff of their formation for the technical work and efficiency of their unit.

The difficulties were exacerbated by an almost total reliance on telegraph coupled with a strong antipathy towards using telephone. It is relevant to consider why this antipathy existed. This is particularly the case when it had already become an important means of commercial communication outside the army and had been developed and used by the French and German armies with some success.

In fact, the reluctance to use telephone arose for two reasons. Firstly, the concept of mobility, which underpinned the general strategic approach of the General Staff in the early years of the war and which they were loath to abandon despite the compelling realities of the extended period of, more or less, static warfare that continued until early 1918. Secondly, an overemphasis on the dangers of enemy overhearing. Consequently, concern for these issues overruled the considerable advantages of convenience and opportunities for personal exchanges that the telephone would have provided.

The result was that at the outbreak of war, the Army was reliant, almost entirely, on telegraph for the transmission of orders, reports and urgent information through the higher formations. Forward signalers had a crude design of telephone but its efficiency was undermined by its lack of easy portability. Better-designed and more effective telephone sets were to be a feature of future years, to be considered later. For the moment, the telephone was unpopular with the General Staff who preferred to do without conversation altogether despite the shortcomings in operational decision-making and control that this implies.[10] Therefore, telegraph was used for all urgent messages throughout the BEF, while cyclists, mounted orderlies and motorcyclists were used for less urgent communication.

When the BEF landed in France, it quickly became apparent that telegraph alone could not cope with the demands placed on it, which led to the creation of the Dispatch Rider Letter Service (DRs) and the use of visual methods of signaling over short distances. However, no personnel were specifically allocated to visual signaling above battalion level. As a result, cyclists and mounted orderlies had to train in the use of visual, over and above their already heavy responsibilities, using the basic means available of heliograph, night lamps and flags. Consequently, telegraph predominated from GHQ to battalion HQs supplemented by DRs.

However, within battalions — not technically controlled by the Signal Service for which they had, nonetheless, tacit responsibility — signalers were proficient in visual only. This created serious difficulties in maintaining signals efficiency. It was important therefore that far-sighted battalion commanding officers recognized this deficiency and overcame it, to a degree. They reinstated the discontinued role of battalion signals officers, which helped to ensure the greater efficiency and smooth running of the battalion signals organization. Effective commanding officers went still further in recognizing the need for maintaining signals effectiveness by equipping the signals section with cable and telephone, entirely at their own expense. They undoubtedly reaped the benefits of this approach later as static trench warfare developed. There is no doubt that battalions with well trained and supervised signalers performed most effectively under these conditions.

By this time it was abundantly clear that numbers within the signals units with the BEF were based on absolutely minimum requirements. Moreover, the available reserves were nowhere near sufficient to maintain and support even existing numbers, partly as a result of pure miscalculation, but more as the result of casualties sustained.

The reserves in question (see Appendix B) consisted of 103 officers

Capture of Chipally Ridge by 58th (London) Division. FRA signalers with heliograph, etc., in a German trench captured on the previous day, 9 August 1918. (IWM No.Q-9191)

and 2,893 men of the Territorial Signal Service, who were only partially trained. There were also a number of Indian Army telegraph units that had greater difficulty in adapting to the new conditions of the Western Front. In addition, a divisional signals company with the 7th Division was in process of formation.

Over and above these was the potential reserve of the signals companies of the University Officer Training Corps (OTCs). They were considered mainly as reinforcements for DRs, where their intellectual skills would be of considerable value. Many would also illustrate their suitability for officer training. Finally, and certainly of no less value as reserves, were the engineers and telegraphists provided by the GPO, though these would require training in Army discipline and procedure.

On 20 August 1914, therefore, the BEF landed with its Signal Services complete in establishment but deficient in the ways described. Initially, under almost peacetime conditions, the communications required through the chain of command could be dealt with effectively by DRs during daylight and by telegraph by night, when DRs were less effective.

By 22 August 1914 the BEF was deployed on the line of the Conde —
Mons — Biche canal and contact established with the enemy. The Signal
Service had by then had sufficient time to create a reasonably effective
communications system. Forward signals was particularly well placed as it
operated in an area already well connected by an efficient and complete
telegraph and telephone system.[11] In fact, forward communications did
not reach this level of efficiency again until much later in the war.

Farther behind the lines, permanent existing communication systems
were also used, though their value was not recognized immediately. Overall,
there is no doubt that the establishment of a good line system was a distinct
advantage when visual signaling, in enclosed country, was impossible except
over small distances. Although lamps and flags were used in a limited way,
telegraph provided the backbone of an effective system.

With the hurried retreat from Mons to Le Cateau no attempt was
made to provide line communication, which proved impossible because
of continued harassment by enemy cavalry and artillery. In any event, no
supplies were available from Base and, crucially, the first indications of
cable shortages, which restricted signals effectiveness continually over the
ensuing years, became evident. Consequently, greater use had to be made,
once again, of the French permanent line system. Some improvements in
liaison and co-operation were made by the commendable intervention of
the Director of Army Signals.[12] Nonetheless, DRs remained the mainstay
of communications in retreat, with very little assistance from cable where
potential headquarters locations could be accurately accessed in advance.

When, on 26 August 1914, the British Expeditionary Force held its
line at Le Cateau, there was insufficient time to create an effective communication system. In addition, as the fighting, on this occasion, took
place in open country there were less established French lines, particularly
forward of division. Where cable was laid it had to be done at great speed,
from diminishing stocks and with only vague information as to its best
location to serve potential headquarters.

It is significant to recognize in this situation the early indications of
a problem that was prevalent in the early days of the war. Lack of accurate
information caused messages to go astray, personnel of all arms were
exposed to avoidable risk and reserves utilized, on occasions, in ineffective
ways. This was one of the first lessons of the war for the Signal Service
accompanied by a second of even more compelling significance.

This related to the increased power and weight of enemy artillery. It
was concentrated on Allied forward lines with disastrous effect for the first

time, to become thereafter, the predominant feature of the First World War battlefields. The first effect of this was that cable, where used, was extensively cut — later a problem of much higher proportions. Despite courageous and dedicated commitment by Signal Service personnel, it could not be maintained to provide an adequate system. Fortunately, the rolling nature of the countryside allowed visual to be used more extensively. To avoid the inherent difficulties of operator exposure, some ingenuity in camouflage was required.

On 25–26 August 1914 the British Army's retreat resumed until withdrawal to the Marne was complete. The tide then turned and an extended period of static warfare, interspersed with battles of attrition, occupied the ensuing three years.

Two features are important and of particular relevance to this phase of the war. Firstly, it has to be realized that the retreat to the Marne was unique compared with later experience. It took place over undamaged country with a friendly population, a situation not repeated except partially in 1918 when, however, the range of enemy guns and bombing added a highly significant new dimension. Secondly, with the difficulties of cable supply, use and reliability, the signals medium of greatest value was the DR.[13] DRs, having been recruited from the university OTCs, with the benefit of some field work experience and a good intellect, illustrated that they were able to adapt effectively and quickly to changing conditions. They had the ability to think for themselves and to gain maximum value from information gathered in the course of duties. This proved a distinct benefit to the BEF as a whole. An added advantage was that their future potential as officers was enhanced and recognized. Above all, their unfailing courage was the hallmark of their success operating, as they did, for long hours in atrocious weather, over difficult country with poor maps and locational information. The cost in human terms was immense as casualties among DRs increased dramatically. As a result, other signals means such as wireless had to be used, albeit sparingly.[14]

For the moment, on 5 September 1914, the British Army established its final defensive position on the Marne followed by its advance to the Aisne. Thus started a prolonged period of predominately static warfare interspersed with battles of attrition, which created immense new problems for Signals, during which the experience gained from the retreat proved of vital importance.

CHAPTER 3

Operational Signals — Static Warfare in 1915

This chapter begins consideration of the prolonged period of static warfare between late 1914 and early 1918 interspersed by battles of attrition. They were fought on a massive scale, with levels of intensity entirely beyond any previous experience of conflict, creating huge difficulties for Signals.

Following the retreat to the Marne, a short pause enabled corps and divisional signal companies to regroup and to replenish stores which had been severely depleted by either destruction or abandonment. In the main, this was completed satisfactorily.

Consequently, the advance started with Signals in a good state of readiness. Although the German Army in retreat destroyed much of its permanent line, which the BEF had used with great success on previous occasions, the destruction was minimized by the speed of the advance. Thereafter, a general policy of exploiting the enemy's system was developed and practiced. This was helped further by good cable route selection. Consequently, reliable communications were established in the shortest time possible with the minimum of signals personnel and casualties sustained. As a result, an effective link between divisions and General Headquarters (GHQ) was created and maintained.

Where necessary the line system was augmented by the use of visual communication and dispatch riders (DRs) with varying degrees of success.[1] Visual was often made difficult by the generally wooded and undulating nature of the countryside over which the advance was made, although the few landmarks available were used successfully. Initially, with the enemy in relatively slow retreat, DRs were particularly effective over the short distances between divisional and brigade HQs. However, as the enemy's retreat quickened they faced the triple dangers of straying within range of British artillery fire, overshooting HQs and coming under opposing machine-gun fire. In spite of these difficulties, DRs again provided a superb service but suffered heavy casualties to both men and machines within units which were already seriously depleted. Nonetheless, messages were delivered promptly and clearly. Early references, at the highest level, to the use of wireless as a means of successful communication between airplanes and artillery for target spotting also begin to appear at this time.[2]

This was an occasion when there was also a very limited use of carrier pigeons, again with mixed success.[3]

The overall effect of the change from retreat to advance had improved Signal Service morale, in line with the whole of the Army. All ranks of the Service had performed well even when, on occasions, they were drawn into the line as infantry. More will be said of this serious and continuing misuse of Signals' personnel later.

By 14 September 1914 the enemy retreat halted in well prepared defensive positions on the Aisne, strongly supported by artillery (at least in the context of this period of the war). Thereafter, a footing on the north bank of the Aisne was achieved by the Signal Service only with great resolution under heavy and accurate enemy artillery fire. Lines were established, on occasions, by Signals personnel swimming across the river carrying them, the major priority being the establishment and successful maintenance of forward lines.

Though the conflict on the Aisne was to be prolonged, the British Army's role concluded when its troops were withdrawn, after relief by the French, on 19 October 1914.

Thereafter, the BEF was deployed around Ypres-Armentieres-La Bassée, with its GHQ at St. Omer facing numerically superior enemy forces. The objective of the opposing armies was to achieve a quick breakthrough with the intention of cutting communications but neither remotely succeeded in the short term. The result was the formation of a rigid line of opposing forces across northern France and Flanders and trench warfare set in, interspersed with intense battles of attrition.

The study of the stalemate that followed forms the main basis of this section, but it is an important prerequisite to dwell briefly on the vital lessons for Signals which followed from the retreat to the Marne and the subsequent advance to the Aisne.

The lessons learned, in reality, formed the basis on which future organizational structures and signals practice developed to meet the new and vastly increased demands placed on the Signal Service. However, it is recognized and accepted that, despite the advent of generally static warfare and the considerable time — measured in years — for which this prevailed, previous experience was seldom repeated. This was because of the vastly increased scale and intensity of the war and the problems associated with the development of essential new technology.

The paramount lesson for Signals in both retreat and advance had been the need to provide the means of receiving early information on the movement and positions of formations. While this may appear self-evident, in the context of the 1914 general command and control situation it was capable of great improvement. This was coupled closely with the need for a considerable enhancement in signals training throughout the whole of the BEF. Paradoxically, the incidence of static warfare provided the opportunity for a review of all aspects of training as part of a wider general revision of signals practice in new circumstances.

The march from the Aisne to the north was completed using DRs for communication by day and cable spurs, to what was only a semi-permanent line system, by night. When contact was eventually established with the enemy and static positions assumed, communications to the south of the line posed particularly difficult problems, most especially for visual. The surrounding countryside was flat and visual means were impossible, except over short distances, because of exposure to enemy observation.

A series of German attacks followed around the area Ypres-Wyschaete-Messines and later Armentieres-Bethune against an exhausted BEF, which nonetheless held its line. During this brief spell of action, DRs distinguished themselves once again as illustrated in a dispatch by Field Marshal Sir John French of 20 November 1914.

> I am anxious in this despatch to bring to your notice the splendid work which has been done throughout the campaign by the cyclists of the Signal Corps. Carrying messages at all hours of the day and night in every kind of weather, and often traversing bad roads blocked with transport, they have been conspicuously successful in maintaining an extraordinary degree of efficiency in the service of communications. Many casualties have occurred in their ranks but no amount of difficulty or danger has ever checked the energy or ardour which has distinguished their Corps throughout the operations.[4]

Overall, the Signal Service contribution was highly significant at the First Battle of Ypres in maintaining communications. During the battle no intricate system of trenches yet existed. Maintenance by day was virtually impossible and only achieved to any significant degree through considerable and courageous loss of life. The huge increase in artillery fire, especially before and during enemy attacks, made maintenance of lines in the crucial area forward of brigade HQs exceedingly difficult at a time when good communications were vitally important. Lines were constantly broken and heroic efforts to keep them open resulted in yet further losses of signals personnel.[5]

Thereafter, British forces grew sharply with a commensurate increase in the size and number of formations within the British Expeditionary Force. The role, size and technical complexity of signal formations developed accordingly to accommodate the increases. The subsequent signals evolution, with its new and increased responsibilities, will be a continuing theme throughout the remainder of this section of the book. It heralded many innovative approaches to communication problems, of which some failed, others succeeded but all contributed towards valuable experience for future development. It is appropriate, therefore, at this point, to examine the circumstances that drove this innovative approach, and its initial development, at this early stage of the war, particularly during the period around the First Battle of Ypres and continuing through into the winter of 1914–15.

As it became evident that the conflict was to be of a much more prolonged and static nature than anticipated, radical changes in signals practice were required to accommodate the new circumstances. The necessity for a system of relief for infantry in trenches meant that Signals personnel needed to be relieved on a regular basis, particularly in forward areas. Also, the pressing need to maintain communications, despite heavy and accurately ranged artillery fire, required the duplication of routes from division forward. In addition, the destruction of buried lines, despite deep buries and constant attention from linesmen, highlighted the requirement for alternative means of protection. Lines were laid across country well away from roads and buildings, using covered ways where available and in ditches and trenches not in a direct line between HQs. The establishment of lateral lines between battalion HQs to left and right allowed critically important information to be passed directly rather than through brigade HQs with greater chance of successful communication. Finally, the introduction of motorcycle linesmen cut down significantly the repair times for broken lines, though it was an extremely hazardous occupation. The system that evolved is well illustrated by Priestley at Plate IV.[6] This provides a picture of the highly intricate nature of signals communication routes throughout the BEF after only a few weeks of static warfare.

The developing system required a substantial increase in the use of permanent deep buried lines from division rearwards and a more frequent use of telephones at battalion and brigade HQs. In these circumstances, the inherent danger of enemy overhearing was disregarded under the pressure of maintaining communications at all costs. The provision of alternative lines over frequently and heavily shelled country became an absolute necessity. Where these could not be provided or maintained, dispatch riders were used.[7]

It is important to note, at this point, that lines forward of brigade, and often division, were laid above ground. As the result of static warfare they were highly vulnerable to enemy artillery fire as well as from the wet and muddy conditions that prevailed, and the general passage and living conditions of the occupying troops. The constant breaks in the line had to be repaired under very difficult circumstances, more often than not under fire. Wet and mud particularly affected insulation of lines and hurried repairs were only of a temporary nature.

To alleviate this situation, the remedy was an entirely new type of system with lines raised above ground level. By the end of September 1914 all units had been instructed to pole their cable routes in this way, though poles were in short supply. But poled cable inevitably drew enemy fire and consequently had to be set at the lowest level possible, within the fast developing trench system. It does not require a high degree of imagination to conjure up a picture of its chaotic proliferation. Yet again, the provision of a new system taxed signals personnel severely. Nonetheless, the new arrangements were of great value and increased efficiency enormously, compared with those that they replaced. Good and more reliable telephone conversation was made possible again. In addition, the constant cutting of lines, as the consequence of trench traffic, was much reduced. The effect of shell blast on loosely slung cable was much less devastating than on that laid at ground level. As a consequence, linesmen were able to cope more easily with circuit maintenance for the first time since the dramatic increase in enemy artillery fire had started. Of vital importance, DRs could now take an urgently needed and well-earned rest.

Furthermore, as a result of static warfare and indeed by its very nature, visual means of communication became both less appropriate and effective. The predominance of training, to date, had concentrated on this method. However, during trench warfare in close proximity to the enemy, flags and lamps were not only ineffective but also extremely hazardous in use, the former being too prominent, and the latter noisy — noisy to the extent that it might be overheard by the enemy. The outcome was a large increase in the scale of casualties to both battalion signallers and infantry. Hence this method of signaling ceased almost entirely, although with serious ongoing implications for the Signal Service. Because the majority of training for infantry signals had been in mainly visual means, there were immediate implications. There was a lack of available trained personnel in other means, particularly telegraph and telephone. The effectiveness of battalion internal communications was reduced significantly and the Signal Service was required to extend its activities much farther forward towards the front line. Most concerning of all, infantry signalers, without relevant training, were absorbed into the firing line.

There followed two major and often conflicting implications for new signals developments designed to meet conditions of static warfare.

The first was a reduction in the use of visual communication where this could, in some instances, have continued to be employed to good effect. Indeed, in some extreme cases battalions sent their visual equipment home. However, more farsighted signals officers recognized the value of visual communications in special circumstances and looked for ways in which it could be improved using less conspicuous and more effective implements; for example, signals discs and shutters, which could be used from cover, and periscopes for signals observation, in similar circumstances. Silent electric signaling lamps with a greater range and smaller, and hence safer, light dispersion than their predecessors, also proved of value, with better use of the local topography. They attracted the minimum of enemy fire compared with signaling flags that had been used, when communications were vital and other means were inappropriate or not available.

The second, adopted for static warfare, was the increased and extended use of telephone in forward positions that required the appropriate training. This caused a variety of problems. Paradoxically, signalers no longer required to operate inappropriate visual means of communication, having been drawn into the firing line as infantrymen, were not immediately available for retraining. The situation was exacerbated by many having become casualties. In any case, training in the field was slow and often not fully effective because of the prevailing conditions. This was made worse by fewer signalers being trained at home bases as their instructors were, of necessity but with serious future implications, being absorbed into battalions serving in the front line.

The inevitable consequence of the foregoing was that, while the line system of communication was the ideal for battalions in early 1915, there were insufficient signalers available for initiation into cable laying and maintenance. This was at a time when the line was considered vital by battalions as the link between battalion and company HQs, to lateral battalions and between neighboring fire trenches. This situation was almost always made much worse when there was no appointed battalion signals officer to coordinate, supervise and obtain the best results from the limited personnel available. The result in practice was that brigade signals officers, members of the Signal Service, had to assume responsibility for providing the line communication system right up to the front line, even though this was completely outside the scope of their duties. This proved to be a virtually impossible task in view of its complexity and an ever increasing though essential demand for an efficient line system.

Thus at this early stage of the war there are the first indications of the need, though certainly not the capacity, for the Signal Service to take battalion signalers under its control.[8] This proved a matter of controversy throughout the remainder of the war. As it progressed, the overriding decision remained that battalion commanders had responsibility and control of signals personnel within their ranks. In practice, however, the powers of both divisional and brigade signals officers increased in this area with the paramount need for the development of a command system for signals. A vital element of this was an efficient and all-embracing rear organization for the supply of stores, administration and, crucially, reinforcements. Indeed, Priestley contends that well coordinated signals contributed as much to success in battle as courageous fighting and good leadership.[9]

But the problem remained that the original establishment of the BEF, geared to a short sharp trial of strength, had made little provision for any substantial increase in the size of the Army as a whole. The Signal Service proved no exception to this, especially so far as stores and reinforcements were concerned. Vitally, some improvements were achieved later, in 1917, by a general review of communications in the field that will be covered in detail later in this section.[10]

Consequently, there were two urgent problems that the Director of Signals had to deal with immediately and which were to have to have a continuing significance for the remainder of the war.[11] The first was the supply of reinforcements to the various signal units in the field, and the second was the provision of technical and other stores required for the maintenance of effective communications throughout the BEF.

In view of the crucial importance of both these issues it is important to consider them in greater detail at this stage. Beyond doubt, the more pressing of the two was the provision of reinforcements, where considerable difficulties had to be overcome to provide even partial remedies.

The provision of reinforcements, pre-war, was based on a fixed percentage of original field strength. Signals personnel, of all trades, were held at the Royal Engineers (REs) depot in this proportion. But the technical complexity of signals work often resulted in a mismatch between available specifically trained personnel and field requirements; the much-increased demand for permanent linesmen for static warfare is a typical example. The Director of Army Signals, at this time, was particularly concerned about reinforcements being "*sent up all wrong*" for divisional signals companies with the provision of men of unsuitable trades and training.[12]

A remedy that was partially successful was the establishment of a dedicated signals unit within the RE depot in early 1915. This had responsibility for the final equipment, in all aspects, of reinforcements for active service and the specific allocation of personnel. By far the most significant outcome of this policy was the promotion of a Signal Service esprit de corps, a vital element in its acknowledged and continuing success.

Almost as pressing, at this stage of the war, as the supply of trained reinforcements was the provision of technical signals stores in sufficient quantities and specifically appropriate for static warfare. A special signals depot at advanced base at Le Havre was established in the early months of the war that delivered requirements direct to individual units.[13] With increases in demand as the Army evolved, however, some decentralization became essential and signals stores were set up at army HQs. These achieved two important objectives. The first was that stores were allocated in relation to the specific need of armies in the field according to their technical requirements; the second was that a much broader and informed view could be taken to avoid inappropriate allocations.

In general terms, the policy of stores provision and allocation proved adequate for day-to-day requirements, apart from cable. The demand for this entirely outstripped supply, for the remainder of the war, owing to an exponential increase in its use.[14] In other respects, there were initial shortages at this period of the war. However, the increased output of factories at home, coupled with organizational improvements for dealing with design, production and distribution of technical stores, brought about a significant increase in available supplies.

As cable shortages became more widespread with the consolidation of static warfare, DRs and particularly the pigeon service were used more extensively. The pigeon service started from very small beginnings, when it was generally used for Intelligence purposes. However, it became an important means of general communication during the battles of 1915 and, indeed, for the remainder of the extensive period of static warfare up to the beginning of 1918.[15]

Before moving on from the early days of static warfare during the winter of 1914–15 to deal with the battles of 1915, it is important to mention two factors which were immensely important for the Signal Service as the war developed. The first was the relationship between the Artillery and the Signal Service. This was to have an immediate and thereafter increasing significance associated with, and influenced by, the growth of the telephone system to a position of prime importance for forward signals. The second was the early development of wireless for use with artillery.[16] Even more significantly, this foreshadowed the continuing controversy, which surrounded its use for this and other areas of communication, which will be evident as this section develops.

Artillery signals, up to this point, were not the specific responsibility of the Signal Service. This reflected a serious omission in the pre-war reorganization of the Signal Service. Nonetheless, in practice, the General Staff and artillery commanders held the Signal Service responsible for any inadequacies in their establishment of appropriately trained signals personnel. The problem was exacerbated by a sharp increase in the number of artillery units and the difficulties that this imposed in providing adequate signals communication between the infantry and its supporting guns. A separate system of command communications was urgently needed. The established conventions were deep seated and artillery commanders were not yet ready to give up their freedom of action for greater efficiency. However, something had to be done. At first, this was exemplified by unofficial cooperation between artillery and signals officers. As new artillery units were established, the unofficial arrangement tended to become the accepted norm. The consequent benefits to artillery were enormous, not least in providing them with a degree of priority for the future provision and maintenance of signals equipment.[17]

The increased demand for signals facilities, and particularly telephone, by forward units — which will become more apparent in studying the battles of 1915 — had a major significance in the more extensive reform and evolution of signals responsibilities. According to Priestley, it marked the beginning of an endless expansion of signals activity and revolution in staff methods as great as any that has occurred in war.[18]

Alongside the requirements of artillery for a more effective link with infantry had been the development of wireless during the early part of the war, which although considered in more detail later, requires clarification at this point. In fact, its primary uses up to this stage of the war had been the interception of enemy wireless messages[19] and its use for spotting by the Royal Flying Corps (RFC) for the direction of artillery fire — acknowledged as its vitally important and primary role.[20] Good, though not generally recognized, work was carried out in intercepting enemy transmissions relating to the dispositions and movements of its forces. Furthermore, those officers intimately involved with the development of wireless had great enthusiasm for their task and worked hard to gain a greater degree of acceptance for its use. While they were to be rewarded for their efforts at a much later stage, it is generally accepted that from this point in its development wireless never reached its full potential throughout the entire war. There is also a convincing argument, as discussed in other chapters of this book, that had it reached its full potential, the overall strategic and operational conduct of the war would have been affected, with beneficial and, perhaps, historic effect.

It was against this background that the British Army prepared for action following the winter months of static conditions in 1914–15. The predominant feature of signals evolution had been the universal rise in popularity of the telephone system. The General Staff had not only overcome its antipathy to its use but also demanded telephone lines for all purposes. As a consequence, alternative means of communication were not used to advantage in appropriate circumstances.[21] This philosophy underpinned its approach to communications in the battles in which the BEF was principally involved in 1915: Neuve Chapelle (March), Second Battle of Ypres (April), Aubers Ridge and Festubert (May), and Loos (September). The full and heroic role of the Signal Service, in these battles, is universally acknowledged.

For the Signal Service the single most influential feature of 1915 was the massive increase in both the caliber and intensity of enemy artillery fire. At this point, the German Army led the field (though the British Army was quick to follow with the introduction of 60 pounders and 4.7" guns, which together with field guns and 4.5" howitzers grew steadily in number as the year progressed). The immediate effect was that unprotected cable linking front line infantry with their superior HQs and artillery could not survive intact, despite valiant efforts by signals linesmen to repair breakages.[22]

The inevitable consequence was that, without adequate cable protection, communications were totally disrupted, accompanied by extensive casualties among signals personnel. Of vital and ongoing significance, their scarce skills were lost with them. The solution of a shellproof buried cable system was accepted as the only viable remedy but would take time to achieve. Temporary measures had therefore to be taken.

Visual communication was definitely discredited in these vulnerable circumstances.[23] Wireless was effectively still in its infancy. Runners, though more reliable, were inevitably slow in the prevailing conditions and very costly in terms of casualties. As a result, pigeons were used as the main, though inadequate, alternative when cable failed.

However, the overriding demand for buried cable continued and increased. Greater depths near to the front line were demanded, because of its immunity to shrapnel, shell splinters and human traffic though not always to high explosive shells. As the demand became universal it presented extreme difficulties for already over-stretched signals personnel. They required help from both pioneers and infantry to achieve anything approaching the required system. With some justification, the extra work was badly received by the latter, who felt that they were already hard pressed.

The effectiveness of buried cable was severely tested at the Second Battle of Ypres. It was buried, at depths of between 2 feet 6 inches and 3 feet, in waterlogged ground between the rear limit of the area in which frequent shelling was anticipated and as far forward as battalion HQs. In general, the buried cable stood up well to the enemy's artillery assault. However, a serious new problem emerged where multiple cables were used to ensure continuing signals communication, despite individual breakages. Problems occurred because a multiplicity of earthed lines, through induction, increased the danger of enemy overhearing. This will be dealt with as a discrete, though crucial, issue later in this section of the book.

There is no doubt, however, that the most revolutionary and demanding aspect of the development of buried cable was its spread, in armored form, towards and in the front line trenches. Even though buried at depths as shallow as 6" below the bottom of the corners of trenches, it was much more secure as a means of reliable communication, though incredibly difficult to maintain. In any event, it was entirely preferable to the existing poled arrangements, which caused intense irritation to infantry. In fact, they were often a major contributory factor in reducing the effectiveness of the system by their deliberate misuse of cable. Priestley covers this point well.

Infantry officers and men censured the Signal Service as they stumbled about the trenches by day and by night, falling over wires stretched knee high across the bottom of the trench, or recoiling from breast-high or neck-high obstacles of a similar nature. Signals officers equally blamed the infantry when lines went down and examination proved that they had been torn down, deprived of insulation by fires lit in the bottom of the trench or maliciously cut.[24]

It cannot be said, however, that burying cable overcame the difficulties of maintaining the trench communications system intact altogether. This was particularly the case, owing to the Flanders mud in which it was concealed. Buries were often lost and much effort was expended in supervising routes, tracing those which were lost and educating front line troops in their preservation.[25]

Many valuable lessons were learned about the limitations of cable communications at the Second Battle of Ypres, which held good for the remainder of 1915. Not least was the pressing need to re-examine the case for providing alternative means of communication that could be readily available when cable failed during an enemy bombardment.[26] Frequently, the life of forward lines could be measured in minutes only. Good communications between battalion HQs and the front line, by cable, were very much the exception rather than the rule.

This illustrated the need for a means of communication whose reliability did not depend entirely on an unbroken link from the front line rearwards. One solution, yet again, was the provision of some sort of visual means of communication. But as this had fallen into disrepute previously, its resurrection could not be easily accomplished, primarily because the equipment and personnel to use it were not now available.

A possible solution was to use flags, periscopes, disks and shutters from sheltered positions by day and the new silent electric signaling lamps by night, from positions that minimized light dispersion, least likely to trigger an enemy reaction.[27] However, the limitations that had frustrated their previous use continued to apply. They depended entirely upon good weather conditions for successful employment and were easily disrupted by the smoke and dust of an enemy bombardment.

Another remedy, not subject to the limitations of either cable or visual means of communication, was the use of wireless. However, its development as a viable alternative continued to be retarded by its lack of recognition by the majority of formation commanders. Fortunately, the same did not apply to those involved in its immediate development. Certainly,

wireless was not adapted in any way for trench warfare until some experimental work took place in the summer of 1915.[28] This marked the first
faltering steps in its eventual establishment as the mainstay of signals communication by 1918.

The reappraisal of wireless as an alternative to cable coincided with
a continuing rearward extension of the area affected by enemy shelling.
With the consequent destruction of cable, wireless could have been its
ideal back-up at corps HQs. Unfortunately, no suitable set was readily
available. Forward of corps HQs, the Marconi pack set could be used but
its range and power were, paradoxically, excessive. This made it susceptible
to enemy jamming and interception as it came within a wavelength of the
front line, and effectively, ruled it out for forward work.

Practical considerations therefore dictated the need for two types of
set. One was required for use near the front line and at battalion and
brigade HQs and their supporting artillery batteries. Another, more powerful set, for use by corps and heavy artillery, could provide communications further to the rear.

Some experiments under active service conditions were already taking
place under Signal Service supervision. A good example of its early success
is well illustrated by Priestley. This refers to an occasion when enemy shells
destroyed six from a total of seven available cables with serious casualties
incurred while attempting their repair. Meanwhile, a wireless station maintained communication broken only by its aerial being shot away. This was
easily replaced.[29]

Overall, progress with wireless development had reached the stage
where, by August 1915, a design had been completed for a suitable forward
set. It allowed for a minimum of training and was reasonably foolproof.
Hence, not unnaturally, it was designated the BF set! Later, more appropriately, it was known as the British Field Set (BFS). It was intended to
replace the existing and cumbersome combination of a Sterling transmitter
and a shortwave receiver that were in current use between the RFC and
artillery, for spotting purposes. The combination, when used by troops on
the ground, required five men for transport, with no guarantee that all the
component parts would arrive either together or intact. Conversely, the
new BF Set, with combined transmitter and receiver, was sturdily built
and better designed to withstand the demanding conditions of forward
work.

The problem of providing a set with more power and greater portability, for use down the line, also needed to be solved. This was achieved,

to a reasonable degree of satisfaction, by the Wilson transmitter used in conjunction with the Mark III service shortwave receiver. These allowed adequate communications to be established, in combination with the BFS, over a ten mile range.

Finally, at the Battle of Loos in September 1915, the BFS demonstrated its value and was used successfully under testing conditions. A set was erected in Loos after its capture by British forces and achieved excellent results. Despite being under constant threat from the enemy's shrapnel and high explosive bombardment, communications were maintained where other means had failed. Three examples from Priestley illustrate this emphatically.[30] During the battle, firstly, a wireless message prevented a potential disaster when cavalry might have been ordered through the line under the misapprehension that it had been broken when, in reality, it had not. Secondly, a withdrawal when hard pressed was contemplated but prevented when a wireless message was received illustrating that reinforcements were on the way. Thirdly, a wireless message achieved redirection of friendly fire by British artillery that was unaware that the position it was shelling was now occupied by British forces.

But problems with and resistance to wireless by commanding officers remained. Some were real while others were based on misconceptions. There was overriding and justifiable concern that wireless was insecure and likely to enable the enemy to locate British positions with greater accuracy. The codes and ciphers used to overcome insecurity were both inadequate and troublesome to use when hard pressed in action. Perhaps of greatest significance, the Signal Service itself, apart from those immediately concerned with its development, had reservations about the effectiveness of wireless, which discouraged acceptance elsewhere. The technical failures, inevitable in a new venture, frustrated its acceptance still further.

Wireless was now, therefore, at the crossroads of its development. The way in which this progressed, and overcame real difficulties and prejudices, will be a continuing theme throughout the remainder of the book.

The other significant rival to visual and wireless as a means of communication to bridge forward areas, when cable was difficult or impossible to maintain, was the pigeon service. There is no doubt that the service achieved a greater degree of acceptability by corps and divisional signal units when it was used in May 1915 during the Second Battle of Ypres. It achieved considerable success in bringing back reports on, and requests for, artillery fire to rear commanders. This marked the beginning of a rapid growth and acceptance of the pigeon service. Thereafter, it was regarded as a legitimate alternative means of communication in appropriate circumstances, though it had limitations in use.

The pigeon's major strength was its speed and reliability over distances far greater than could be covered by, for example, contemporary wireless facilities. Pigeons were not unduly affected by shellfire and normally flew above the effects of gas attacks. They were difficult to disable in flight and could be more easily replaced if hit than, for example, runners or DRs. Above all, pigeons were popular with front line troops as they could generally be relied upon to pass messages quickly and at minimal risk to their handlers. But logistical difficulties affected the overall success of the pigeon service. Lofts had to be kept well back from enemy observation, which meant that normal channels of communication often had to be bypassed. Messages from battalions and the front line, rerouted through divisional and even corps HQs, were delayed in reaching brigade HQs, for which most were intended. However, such messages were given top priority rating by signals offices in the chain of command. The average message time was between 10 and 20 minutes, dependent on the distances travelled.[31]

Difficulties were also experienced in the handling of pigeons. Those involved required specific training in the stringent requirements for feeding, watering and general care. If carried out inappropriately, these could detract seriously from the pigeons' performance, resulting in lost or delayed messages. However, efficiency in performance improved rapidly, so that by the autumn of 1915 pigeons were a regular and highly valued method of communication. The pigeon service, hereafter, moved from local control to the Director of Army Signals.[32] The effectiveness of the service was demonstrated strongly at the Battle of Loos in September 1915 when, during the first two weeks of the offensive, an increasing number of messages were passed using pigeons. Many casualties were avoided as a result. In addition, good transmission times were achieved and information passed accurately.

Before summarizing Signal Service developments during 1915 generally, and passing on to its performance during 1916, there is a final and important issue that was causing considerable and justifiable concern, at that time — that of enemy overhearing and intelligence. This first manifested itself, to any significant degree, during the summer of 1915, when it became clearly apparent that the enemy was extremely well informed, in advance, of British Army plans and movements.[33] Planned raids and even minor attacks were met with enemy fire, accurately directed and precisely timed. Trench reliefs were shelled at the exact times of changeover.

Replacement artillery, machine guns and trench mortars all received immediate enemy attention, despite vigorous attempts to conceal their arrival. Fresh troops entering a sector for the first time received welcoming shouts from enemy trenches using precise identification. Priestley provides an extreme example when, on one occasion, a well-known Scots battalion, arriving as a relief, was welcomed by the enemy playing its regimental march! [34]

The incidence of the above happened too regularly and with too high a degree of accuracy to be coincidental. The results were demoralizing for British forces although, no doubt, a great boost to enemy morale. In addition, it caused serious disruption and increased casualties.

It quickly became apparent that the enemy's intelligence emanated from a variety of sources, although mainly through line tapping and earth induction. Messages were intercepted by the enemy through British multiple cable installations and conduits of sound provided when lines were laid, for example, along railways, pipelines and water channels. Wireless and power-buzzer messages (to be referred to in greater detail later) were, at this stage of the war, also vulnerable when speech could often be picked up at distances of between 100 to 300 yards. [35]

It therefore became clear that changes in both policy and procedures were urgently required. It was imperative to instill in all ranks awareness of the dangers and consequences of enemy overhearing. Changes had to include much improved insulation of cable systems and grounding arrangements. This had to be aligned with the absolute requirement for meticulous telegraph and telephone procedures, even in the most pressing of circumstances. Special regard had to be paid to names, times, movements, artillery instructions and locational information being properly coded or, better still, passed by a more secure means of communication.

The subject of enemy overhearing is one that will be referred to repeatedly as the book progresses. Certainly, it became a matter of even more significance and concern from 1916 onwards. This was because, despite innovations designed to prevent it, these proved inadequate as the British Army signal system grew in size and complexity, in line with the general growth of the BEF as a whole.

Taken overall, however, by the end of 1915, the Signal Service had become a much more cohesive force within the British Army with a now well-developed esprit de corps. All ranks involved in signals activities, at every level, had a distinct identity of which their proudly worn blue and white armband was a symbol. [36] This applied equally to senior signals officers from army HQs forward, who now had enhanced powers to coordinate signals activity within a more workable chain of command.

Even more significantly, the first signs were now apparent of a general realization that an elaborate system of signals communication, which was essential to success in warfare, was beginning to permeate the High Command. Unfortunately, and all too infrequently, this was not carried forward into positive action. Further forward, there was still some mistrust of the signals hierarchy and individual units wished to retain strong control over their signals element. A typical example is again provided by Priestley in connection with reliefs in the line.[37] Incredibly, the prevailing practice had been for the outgoing units to remove cables, lines, instruments and terminals, which incoming units then had to reconstruct. At best, this caused unnecessary expenditure of time and, at worst, additional casualties from those involved in the reconstruction. By the end of 1915, however, a degree of trust and co-operation between ingoing and outgoing units had developed and systems had begun to be left intact. By 1918 this had become standard practice. This had received support from an army and corps signal conference held in the autumn of 1915. It was then agreed that improved cooperation was required and that moves of equipment should be reduced to the minimum necessary.[38] In any event, it was quite evident that buried cable could not be moved easily. Where it was, rebuilding entailed many nights of laborious work with large parties at risk.

Thus, by the end of 1915, a signals system that could cope, at least adequately, with conditions of static warfare had been established. The system required certain indispensable elements. Vital to its success was the general introduction of telephones as the predominant means of communication throughout the BEF, coupled with improved protection of forward lines. This required the support of alternative means to vulnerable cable facilities in the area of heavy enemy shelling from the front line rearwards. These proved to be, principally, pigeon and some wireless. In addition, it was necessary to establish defined areas of signals responsibility with a more specific chain of command and continuity of signals policy.[39] Other essential elements were improved systems for the reliefs of signals personnel and coordination of training,[40] reinforcements, equipment and stores[41] throughout the Signal Service. The foregoing illustrates a greater awareness of the importance of good communications and the Signal Service's role in providing them.

The system was impressive but marked only the first and, at times, faltering steps in an evolutionary process of signals development. This had to be substantially refined and increased to meet the demands placed upon it during the momentous events of 1916.

The major task for the Signal Service in 1916 involved, principally, the supervision of signals facilities from division forward to the front line, in preparation for the opening of the Battle of the Somme. Nonetheless, its defined responsibilities still precluded the forward areas in advance of battalion HQs.[42] This was a huge task. The experiences of 1915, and the huge increases in enemy artillery fire, which marked the early months of 1916, indicated that a reappraisal of all means of communication was required. This was especially true of buried cable, which would be required to meet the demands placed upon it in the forthcoming conflict.

In 1915 experience illustrated that, where shallow buries had been used towards the front line, they had proved adequate for protection against shell splinters, shrapnel and human traffic. However, they were still vulnerable to serious damage by high explosive shells. Certainly, by the beginning of 1916, owing to the intensity and caliber of enemy artillery fire, shallow buries, surface and poled lines were entirely inadequate for the provision of anything approaching a system of acceptable reliability. This was particularly the case in the Ypres Salient which faced the heaviest barrage and even 3 foot buries could not withstand the onslaught. Indeed, there were occasions in early 1916 when on some divisional fronts all surface and airlines were cut. The result was that surface laid cable became obsolete, except where used for emergency crossings or beyond the range of enemy shelling range. The days of poled cable were also numbered.

A major innovation was that armored cable, which had been experimented with and used in small quantities in 1915, was now more widely available and employed. It was intended for use as buried cable but the exigencies of previous situations had often resulted in its use as unburied trench cable. In these circumstances, while it could better withstand the passage of human traffic, it was still vulnerable to shell splinters and shrapnel. A degree of protection was still required even if, on occasions, this was no more than that provided when, as a last resort, it was laid below duckboards.

A variety of armored cables were tested amongst which steel, brass and lead covers predominated. All had disadvantages in use. Steel was liable to kink and become difficult to handle. Brass was even more easily damaged than steel with similar consequences and lead was easily distorted, even by its own weight. However, all if handled with care were more efficient than unprotected cable.[43]

It was clearly evident, however, that by the early spring of 1916, burying at increasing depths was the main requirement and safeguard for a
reliable signals system, as the weight and intensity of enemy artillery
increased. The enemy's 5.9 howitzer, especially, with its high trajectory,
was a particularly potent weapon against anything but deep buried armored
cable. Even then, this did not always provide protection against a direct
hit.

The overriding demand for deeper buried cable forward of divisional
HQs created immense problems for the Signal Service.[44] Scarcity of labor
was the most serious. Experience showed that by increasing depths by
small amounts, say from 3 to 4 feet, this gave little extra protection and,
paradoxically, made repair more difficult. Consequently, a significant
increase in depth with a target of 6 feet became the ideal realistic requirement. However, shortages of labor meant that a fewer number of routes
could be completed, if they were to meet the essential depth required.

The continuing problem of earth induction providing intelligence
for the enemy prevented the concentration of multiple cables in a restricted
number of deep buried routes. This would have been the ideal arrangement. However, a major breakthrough came with the introduction of
twisted cable, which dramatically reduced induction problems and made
concentration of routes more feasible. The available labor force was then
able to provide, more adequately, the required number of 6 foot buried
routes that could withstand the enemy barrage more effectively. This situation prevailed until the more general use of 8 inch guns by the enemy
rendered even 6 foot buries inadequate for protection. Further problems
for the Signal Service, that was in any case under great pressure, were created in both the Ypres and Kemmel sectors of the British front.

At Ypres, an intricate cable system was required because of the soft
and muddy nature of the terrain. Shallow buries had a very short life
expectancy as did the linesmen attempting to repair and maintain effective
communications.

At Kemmel, because of its uniqueness as a valuable observation point,
a comprehensive signals system was required. This would exploit, to the
full, its advantage for enemy observation and relaying of information to
artillery. In fact, the Canadian Corps, in its area of responsibility alone,
laid 400 miles of buried armored cable. As 1916 progressed, similar systems
were planned for the whole of the southern portion of the British front
that would require vast amounts of work to complete.[45]

CHAPTER 4

1915 — The RFC
Invents Wireless Telephony

The three services had varying viewpoints about wireless. The Royal Navy recognized wireless as being of high strategic importance. Conversely, the Army's High Command viewed it with mistrust. To a degree this was understandable as its lack of confidence centered, almost exclusively, on its perceived insecurity and the consequent danger of enemy overhearing. The availability of codes and ciphers did not provide sufficient reassurance that it would not be misused.[1] The outcome was that, by the outbreak of war, there had been only limited development of wireless in the Army. Certainly, it was not considered as a viable alternative in the communication chain. Its only enthusiastic support came from the Royal Flying Corps (RFC) and the Royal Engineers Wireless Section. It is to their inestimable credit that they pursued the development of wireless to the point where its value both to the strategic planning and operational success of the Army could not be ignored, even if belatedly. Because the RFC was part of the Army, however, the responsibility for wireless resided with the Royal Engineers (RE), an Army organization whose management was considerably less enthusiastic than the RE Wireless Section.[2]

The RFC's driving force was Major Charles Edmund Prince, assisted by Major Robert Orme, serving as a wireless officer, in January 1915, at No. 1 Reserve Aeroplane Station, Farnborough. Prince, before joining the RFC, had been one of Marconi's lead engineers. Before the war he had served with the Westmorland and Cumberland Yeomanry, where he had been fortunate to have a receptive and technically minded commanding officer in Major H.C.T. Dowding — later Commander-in-Chief, Fighter Command during World War II.

Dowding, in April 1915, formed and assumed command of No. 9 Experimental Squadron at Brooklands. Before the war Brooklands had been set up by the Marconi Company as an experimental station. It was taken over by the RFC at the beginning of the war. At Brooklands Dowding was joined by Prince and Orme, who were assigned military ranks, and, shortly following, by a small section of NCOs and other ranks, devoted to wireless development.[3] In relation to wireless, Brooklands had three main functions: the training of wireless operators, the testing of wireless material and methods already available, and experimental work towards improving apparatus. There was, inevitably, rivalry amounting to conflict between the REs, with responsibility, but no real budget, for research and Brooklands. There is no doubt, that at this point in the development of wireless, the REs contribution was at an amateur level by comparison with the RFC's professional approach.[4]

However, with RFC wireless administered by the REs Prince found it difficult to obtain equipment for his work, having to "beg, borrow or steal instruments due to there being no proper experimental establishment."[5] As a consequence, wireless was not used extensively by the RFC until May 1915 at Festubert, when pilots observed the battle and reported back using wireless telegraphy. However, the development of wireless continued to prosper, driven by Prince's enthusiasm. Army wireless progressed at a much slower pace owing to the clearly apparent lack of enthusiasm, from the High Command downwards,[6] with the exception of those, within the RFC and REs, with specific responsibility for its development. Consequently, while the powerful but very cumbersome Marconi Pack Set was available for use to the rear, nothing suitable was adapted for trench warfare until the summer of 1915. The available Marconi Pack Set was overpowered for use in forward positions and, as a result, subject to both jamming and overhearing by the enemy.

The promise of airborne wireless was recognized early.[7] It could correct artillery fire, put the guns on fleeting targets, send tactical information such as the movements of friendly and enemy forces, report activity behind enemy lines, allow communication between aircraft, inform air patrols about enemy aircraft, and alert antiaircraft batteries about approaching enemy aircraft. While conducting experiments at Brooklands intended to produce a continuous wave (CW) vacuum tube transmitter simple and practical enough to be used in the air by unskilled personnel, Prince saw that wireless telephony was the key to realizing that promise. It was clear to him that "a fleeting target would be more quickly indicated, or a location described by word of mouth, than by a system of slow and laborious telegraphy and map references."[8] Wireless telegraphy not only required the pilot and observer to be trained in Morse code but also required them to be sending it when they were likely to be very busy flying the plane, observing the ground and defending themselves against hostile fire. Prince also saw that exploiting vacuum tubes for CW voice transmission was more promising than improving spark transmission and crystal reception for wireless telegraphy. He also knew that the transmitter for telephony needed to be simple for use by unskilled personnel and durable enough to function in the airborne environment.

In the summer of 1915 Prince and the Brooklands engineers built a vacuum tube airborne transmitter that enabled wireless speech to be received from an airplane for the first time. This technical achievement cannot be overstated. The transmitter had to work in an environment of intense noise, vibration and often violent air disturbances in which the human voice is unable to speak to the human ear over a greater distance than a few inches. In this environment speech had to be converted to current modulations, these modulations radiated, received, rectified, magnified, reconverted into sound and again heard by a human ear. In the early stages the difficulties of the reception of speech in the air was so great that only transmission from air to ground was attempted and the first practical set evolved was a transmitter capable of employing *either speech or CW telegraphy.*[9] In February 1916 wireless telephony from an aircraft to the ground was demonstrated to Lord Kitchener at a distance of 40 miles.[10] Conditions were not ideal, the aircraft was flying through a snowstorm, but speech from the aircraft was heard clearly. At the same time, the signal was also heard by another receiver 100 miles away.

The microphone in the aircraft amplitude modulated (just as in today's AM broadcasting) the CW generated by a vacuum tube oscillator by changing the antenna's resistance to ground. The airborne set weighed 10 lbs. without batteries. The dry cell batteries needed to supply the high voltage (600 volts) required for the vacuum tube weighed 36 lbs. The transmitter used an antenna reeled out of the aircraft that was 250 ft. long. The frequency of transmission was 1,000 kilocycles per second or 1 megahertz (MHz), roughly in the middle of the US AM radio band. The working limit of range was about 20 miles for telephony, 35 miles for telegraphy. The 250 ft. long antenna is a quarter wavelength at 1 MHz, which is the optimum length for that frequency. Shorter antennas can be used, but require somewhat higher power from the transmitter to achieve the same range. This is one of the many design trade-offs to be considered in producing an operational radiotelephone, as will be discussed below.

In view of the difficulty of receiving speech in the air (because of the environment described above) it was decided that transmission from the ground to an aircraft would initially be by wireless telegraph. In the autumn of 1916 Prince designed an airborne vacuum tube receiver that was capable of receiving signals from a one-half kilowatt spark transmitter on the ground at ranges of from 30 to 50 miles. Later on intelligible speech, transmitted from the ground, could be heard in the air over this same receiver, but the receiver was difficult to adjust and the difficulties of hearing speech in the air limited its use until a set requiring less adjustment could be built and a flying helmet with built in earphones and microphone could be designed.

In his description of the airborne radiotelephone Prince notes that "the overseas forces, nevertheless, did not for a long time make any use of air to ground telephony, although just before the Armistice, a meeting of the Higher Commands recommended its introduction for reconnaissance and similar work, *as originally suggested in 1915.*"[11] He does not comment about the applicability of the radiotelephone to ground combat, but the same observation is of course true for that military application as well. In fact, when in 1918 the CW radio was finally introduced to support ground forces, it was used for telegraphy only. Even then, the benefits to the ground forces to be gained from radio telephony were not appreciated or understood.

In modern terminology Prince and his team had accomplished proof of concept, which means that they had proved that it was possible for an airborne transmitter to communicate speech to the ground and had developed a prototype or first device capable of doing so. The next step in the development process would have been to produce a number of similar devices to accomplish this same end and submit them for testing under a variety of conditions. This being wartime it would have been appropriate to test them in the field, as well as in more controlled environments. The results of this testing would have enabled the engineers to improve the initial design, such as enhancing speech intelligibility, extending the range of transmission, reducing power requirements, increasing durability and ruggedness for use in the field and making the transmitter easier to operate.

At the same time that the airborne transmitter was being evaluated, the possibility of using it as part of a ground communication system could also have been explored. Since it was capable of transmitting either voice or telegraph, developing a dual use transmitter could have been considered. As noted above, the simplest design for this would have been to switch the modulating device between a microphone and a telegraph key, but more sophisticated methods could also have been tried. Also, for the ground application, the transmitter power versus antenna length design trade-off mentioned above would have been carefully evaluated. The military advantages of a shorter antenna are clear. It was well known that the tall mast required for the early spark sets was an inviting target for enemy artillery. Not only would increasing antenna power reduce the length of an antenna, but the antenna's orientation could be changed from vertical to horizontal, further reducing its profile. Although a vertical antenna is best for transmission and reception on the ground, a horizontal antenna would be satisfactory for transmission if driven by sufficient power and for reception if the receiver is sufficiently sensitive.

A further advantage of submitting the transmitter and receiver to the field for initial testing would have been that the field units would have had an opportunity to employ them under actual military conditions and to determine what the strengths and weaknesses of the units were for military operations. In so doing the field units would also be training themselves in the use of wireless telephones and CW telegraph sets, determining how best to use the new technology. An added benefit would have been that the field units could have employed these preproduction units at the Somme. What this could have meant for that battle is discussed in a subsequent chapter.

Once this period of controlled and field testing was completed, the engineers working on the project would have absorbed the considerable amount of data collected and would have proceeded to refine the design and produce a truly militarized radio suitable for installation in observation aircraft and for use on the ground. Progress toward developing a simple, durable set after the initial success would have depended on obtaining reliable high vacuum tubes (or hard valves). But this occurred when the French TM (Telegraphie Militaire) tubes were placed in mass production by British manufacturers in 1916 and became known as R-valves.[12] By the end of 1916 Prince and his team of engineers could have designed and placed into mass production a reliable lightweight radiotelephone and CW telegraph set suitable for use not only in the air, but on the ground as well. In modern terminology the prototypes would have been dubbed first-generation. The units incorporating the lessons learned from controlled and field testing

and placed into mass production would have been called second-generation. The process does not stop, particularly in wartime. As further refinements of the design are produced later, based on data gathered from
operational use in a variety of circumstances, they would have been called
third generation, fourth generation, and so on.

This is not a far-fetched sequence of events. Such a process, in fact,
was followed in the design and production of tanks in the same time
period. The potential of marrying a heavily armored vehicle to caterpillar
tracks was recognized by visionaries in the British Army such as Colonel
Ernest Swinton.[13] Once the Western Front had settled into stalemate it
was clear that such an armored vehicle could enable the infantry to cross
no man's land by engaging the machine gun defenses which were otherwise
difficult to suppress. Swinton persuaded influential individuals such as
Maurice Hankey and Winston Churchill to back this idea.[14] Churchill
provided funds from the Admiralty, questionably, some say illegally,[15] dub-
bing the machine a landship to justify funding the development. A demonstration in June 1915 showed that such a vehicle could cut through barbed
wire and advance through no man's land. After this demonstration the
tank, as it was christened in December 1915 to disguise its military application, began development. As Prince did for the radio, Swinton developed
a set of requirements to be met by the vehicle; today they are called specifications. Requirements included a speed of 4 miles per hour, a 5 foot obstacle to be surmounted, a 5 foot wide trench to be crossed, a 20 mile range,
a weight of about 8 tons, an armament of at least two machine guns and
one quick firing gun and a crew of 10 to operate it.[16] "Little Willie" (soon
followed by "Big Willie") was the first tank built to the specifications but
it did not meet them. Speed was very low and it could not cross trenches.
Despite these difficulties Col. Swinton pressed on and oversaw the development of the first combat tank in January 1916. In other words the tank
proceeded from proof of concept to the delivery of a prototype in six
months. The Mark I tank, as this prototype was called,[17] was placed in
mass production and entered combat in September 1916 at Delville Wood
on the Somme. A second-generation production tank, the Mark IV,
appeared early in 1917.[18] A third generation production tank, the Mark V,
appeared in 1918. Based on information gathered and lessons learned on
the battlefield, these later generations of tank incorporated improvements
in engine power, armor protection, reliability, battlefield adaptability, i.e.,
the ability to cross trenches or shell holes, speed, and range.

Another example of fast-track development was the fighter. This had progressed from individual aircraft firing small arms at each other to aircraft equipped with machine guns in a very short period of time. Aircraft were developed on both sides that had to meet the competition. When Anthony Fokker developed a fighter capable of firing through the propeller,[19] the Eindecker, the allies rushed to develop fighters that could counter it.[20] Improvements in engine power, such as the rotary engine,[21] maneuverability, range and armament continued throughout the war as each side sought to outdo the other. Prototypes were followed by second-, third-, and fourth-generation aircraft within months. Cost was not a constraint. Considerable sums were spent by both sides to ensure that the air services were equipped with the most up-to-date aircraft.

Method of releasing a carrier pigeon from a porthole in a tank. (IWM No. Q-9247)

The development and application of the radiotelephone did not proceed on this fast track, or indeed on a slow track, as shall be seen. Certainly cost was not a consideration. The costs associated with the development of more capable radios would have been a fraction of the resources spent on the development of the tank or of the combat aircraft. A number of suggestions are offered in this book as to why this happened. In retrospect, it does appear to be obvious that an armored vehicle capable of withstanding small arms fire, able to cross shell pocked ground and traverse trenches, cutting through barbed wire as it does so, would be enormously useful under the conditions then prevailing on the Western Front. Even to the

Information of a target received by RFC Wireless Artillery Officers in front of Menauban July 1916. (IWM No.Q-4036)

most obtuse Army officer or politician such a capability could be a stalemate breaker or even a war winner. Similarly the advantages of developing combat aircraft superior to that possessed by the other side are equally obvious. On the other hand, while a lightweight portable radiotelephone would prove to be vital to ground combat in future wars, its immediate benefits in 1915 were far more subtle than those of the tank or of an improved aircraft. Poor communications had not been identified as a key cause of battlefield failure and high casualties. A remedy for the inability of commanders to communicate with subordinates, for the inability of infantry units to communicate with each other, for the inability of the infantry to communicate with the artillery and for the inability of aircraft to communicate with the infantry or the artillery was not a high priority in 1915.

The task which Prince and his team addressed was an obvious problem for aircraft. There was literally no other way for aircraft to communicate with the ground other than wireless. Crude methods such as displaying panels on the ground or in the case of the aircraft, firing flares or waving flags, were only marginally acceptable. So this application for the use of wireless was identified early, just as the Royal Navy had clearly seen that the only way ships could reliably communicate with other ships and the shore was through wireless. Put another way, an invention that meets an obvious need is going to be backed more readily than one which requires a degree of subtle understanding.

So why wasn't the radiotelephone recognized as a major breakthrough for the area for which it was designed, namely communication between aircraft and ground units, specifically artillery? The need for such a capability was clear. Unfortunately one can only surmise that in this case the good was the enemy of the better. There was in fact a means of communicating from an aircraft to ground, as mentioned earlier in this book. Spark transmitters had been installed in aircraft early in the war and a complicated means of communication had been set up whereby aircraft could observe the fall of shot and correct artillery fire. The procedure went something like this: Wireless communications were one way, from aircraft to ground. The observation aircraft held two men, the pilot and the observer. When a shoot was planned the observer would tell the pilot to put the aircraft in a position where he could see the muzzle flashes of the guns and he would send an order to fire by wireless. Then the observer would tell the pilot to move to another position where he could see the shells falling.[22] Both the observer and his counterpart on the ground possessed a card on which was marked symbols used to correct the battery's fire. The observer would transmit via wireless a symbol that would tell his ground counterpart whether the shell impact was short, long, left, or right of the target and by how much. The process would continue until the shells landed consistently on the target. (Interestingly the card upon which this process was based used a clock code[23] similar to the clock code used by allied bombers in the Second World War to identify the azimuthal directions of incoming enemy fighters.) Under static war conditions where the firing battery and the target were stationary this system worked. It worked well enough to be used throughout the war. Note, however, that this is only the first of the seven benefits for air to ground communication identified early in the war. This system could not engage fleeting targets, identify movements of friendly and enemy forces, report activity behind enemy lines, allow communication between aircraft, and warn air patrols or alert AA batteries. Needless to say, when conditions changed to mobile warfare in 1918, this system could not meet the new requirements.

It is plausible to suggest that this same mindset is what prevented the use of the radiotelephone by ground forces. As this book shows in considerable detail a number of different communication methods were used. None of them were particularly satisfactory but they were good enough to meet the immediate requirements. When the requirements changed and the first method broke down a different but equally unsatisfactory method was tried until it too broke down. Thus, dispatch riders were used until the nature of the ground conditions close to the front limited their mobility. Telephones were the next step, but they were subject to overhearing by the enemy and were unable to function when shells cut the wires. Then the wires were buried up to 6 feet, which of course meant that they couldn't be moved. The power buzzer became popular, particularly for troops who had advanced, but its inability to carry much information severely limited a commander's ability to get a good picture of the battle and it too was intercepted by the enemy. The Fullerphone prevented interception but was dependent upon wire. If they got through, pigeons could provide information but not much of it and there were considerable delays in passing the information to the appropriate recipient. On the ground wireless telegraphy only came into its own when there was literally no other way to communicate, namely in the conditions of mobile warfare experienced during the German Spring Offensive in 1918 and the Hundred Days counteroffensive. Wireless telephony, the radiotelephone, was never used on the ground.

Reverting to the story of the development of the airborne radiotelephone, Prince's great engineering accomplishment was not exploited by either the RFC or the Army. According to Prince, "An urgent demand arose, however, for telephonic communications between machines in the air, and all energies were devoted to solving this far more difficult problem."[24] As noted, the Army did not grasp the superiority of air to ground telephony over telegraphy for artillery observation and other functions. Instead, the Brooklands engineers were redirected to address the problem of air to air communications.[25] In addition, in 1916 all experimental work at Brooklands ceased and all personnel were assigned to Biggin Hill.

The design goals for air to air were similar to those for air to ground. The sets were to be operated by unskilled persons or by those who could receive minimal training. Both the transmitter and the receiver had to require very few adjustments. Telephony was strongly favored over telegraphy. Neither pilot nor observer could receive enough training to understand Morse code automatically and subconsciously. Nor could they be

A motorcyclist dispatch rider in snow, St. Pol, December 1917. (IWM No.Q-6389)

expected to use Morse when many other tasks demanded their attention. Therefore, although it would have been much easier to provide aircraft with radiotelegraph equipment, the equipment would have been useless. In addition, there was no requirement for two-way communications. Only the flight leader needed to be equipped for transmission. The aircraft in the rest of the formation were equipped only for reception. Each plane was to be fitted with a 100 ft. trailing antenna that was to be reeled in or jettisoned when combat became imminent. Power for the sets was to be provided by air driven generators with battery backup.

The chief design challenges had to do with the microphone and the reception of voice transmissions. Vibration and engine noise required a microphone sensitive to voice but not to surrounding noise. This was accomplished by designing an insensitive microphone that had to be shouted into. Another aspect of the design that presented a challenge was to determine where in the transmitter the electrical signal from the microphone should be applied. The most obvious point appeared to be at the grid (see Appendix A) of the vacuum tube in the oscillator circuit. This proved to be impractical, however, because the transmitter using this design required considerable adjustment by the operator to work properly. The final design applied the signal from the microphone to the grid of a second vacuum tube, called the control valve by Prince,[26] whose amplified signal was then applied to the anode circuit of the vacuum tube in the oscillator circuit. This design, called choke control by Prince, provided a transmitter circuit requiring no critical adjustments anywhere and stable under the most extreme environmental changes. It thus was suitable for use in the air or on the ground, in benign or harsh environments. The final design of the transmitter required no adjustments; the user had to do no more than switch on the unit and talk.

The first transmitter used dry cell batteries to provide 600 volts to the vacuum tubes. This was superseded by a small air driven generator in the production unit which provided not only high-voltage to the vacuum tubes but also 6 volts to heat the cathode filaments.

The receiver designed by Prince to prove the concept of air to ground communication used a single vacuum tube. It required careful adjustment to operate successfully either in the air or on the ground. Designing an adjustment free receiver for air to air communication proved to be a design challenge. The solution, suggested by Capt. H.J. Round, another able Marconi engineer, who had designed the Admiralty's intercept stations (see chapter 12), was the cascade amplifier, in which the output from one vacuum tube was fed into the input of a second vacuum tube and the output from the second tube was fed into the input of a third tube. This three stage amplifier provided constant amplification over a large range of wavelengths and required no adjustments. Finally, a flying helmet incorporating a microphone and earphones was designed that blocked out much of the background noise so incoming voice transmissions could be heard.

The skills of the design team solved these and other problems and by mid–1917 the air to air telephone system was ready for production. The choke control transmitter and the three stage receiver were at the heart of the system. The transmitting aircraft trailed 120 ft. wires and the receiving aircraft trailed 80 to 100 ft. wires. The wires were to be reeled in or jettisoned when combat threatened. Normal range for transmitting from aircraft to aircraft was about 4 miles, but was often exceeded. The range to a ground station from the transmitting aircraft was 20 to 30 miles. Training in the use of this equipment was instituted under Capt. J.M. Furnival, who had been one of Prince's earliest associates. About 36 pilots per week were trained in the use of this equipment, with particular attention given to proper articulation in the air. Other officers were trained in the maintenance of the equipment. An entire organization was built up as wireless telephony quickly superseded all other methods of communication for aircraft.

Wireless telephony was first used by squadrons engaged in home defense. A chain of ground stations was constructed, using transmitters of similar design to the aircraft transmitters but transmitting at higher power. At distances up to 100 miles these were used to warn patrols of the approach of enemy aircraft. As time went on the aircraft, because of their elevation, were able to communicate to the ground stations at roughly equivalent distances.

Two squadrons on the Western Front were also equipped with radiotelephones. Flying over enemy lines was prohibited to prevent a set from being captured and copied. Despite this prohibition, a set fell into enemy hands and resulted in the following German Directive[27]: "The enemy has secured a distinct advantage in his successful use in aeroplanes of CW apparatus, which possess great superiority over the spark apparatus. It is of the greatest importance to us to salvage further enemy apparatus equipment of this description. In this way millions of money will be saved, as we have not so far been successful in constructing a continuous-wave apparatus for aeroplanes, which can work without certain disadvantages." Clearly the enemy appreciated and was greatly concerned with the engineering achievement this represented.

This chapter reflects a lost opportunity. Both the RFC, later the RAF, and the BEF came to appreciate the value of CW wireless only much later in the war. The BEF did not make use of air to ground telephony until, just before the armistice, higher commands recommended its use, as originally suggested in 1915 by Prince. The BEF never made use of radiotelephony for the ground to ground communications. A lightweight wireless telephony set could have been mass produced for Army use by the end of 1916. Prototype versions of the set could have been used in the battle of the Somme.

CHAPTER 5

Operational Signals
on the Somme

The Battle of the Somme, as a whole, requires a separate case study not only because of the extreme and unique experience which this presented for the Signal Service, but also because of the foundations that were laid down for future Signals policy and practice.

By early 1916 the main demand for Signal Service activity had moved to the Somme area to assist in the preparation for the forthcoming offensive. An adequate and secure communications system within the British sector, from which the attack was to be launched, had to be provided. This was, in every way, a mammoth task. It had to be completed in the relatively short time available before 1 July 1916. In addition, a communications bridge across no-man's-land had to be prepared for use during the assault as it progressed. This was essential to carry forward the main line system with the attack, together with the appropriate alternative communication systems to be used as the situation developed.[1]

Both of the above presented a huge challenge to the Signal Service. This was particularly the case as the French experience at Verdun, in the earlier part of the year, had illustrated. Only cable buried at a depth of 6 feet would be relatively invulnerable in the assault area. A colossal amount of labor to build a secure line system, which was the principal communications requirement, would be required. During the battle this would involve the provision of 7,000 miles of buried cable in the forward areas alone. This would be made many times more difficult by the fact that the work had to be carried out in forward positions. Priestley is most apposite. "It was no question of steady work carried out under congenial conditions and Trade Union rules in the comfort and safety of home surroundings!"[2]

The reality was that the work had to be carried out day and night, in all weathers, often under enemy fire and working to full capacity with the minimum of rest. The reward for this labor proved, later, to be an effective system that reflected great credit on the Signal Service for its skill and well directed organizational success. It also provided a fundamental lesson for both the General Staff and the Signal Service. This was that, with sufficient quantities of labor using deep buried armored cable, a secure and effective communications system could be achieved immediately behind battalion HQs both in static warfare and also during the early stages of an attack.

However, to achieve good forward communications during an attack in semi-mobile conditions, with the need for an extension in the communications chain under battle conditions, different considerations applied. These had to be designed to meet the novel situation which now faced the BEF, which had never before prepared for a battle of such potential scale or intensity. Meanwhile, the enemy had been preparing its position for more than a year. This comprised a series of four defense lines with self-contained forts, which could provide enfilade fire, with a first line defense of barbed wire, 45 yards in depth. The British artillery had to breach and seriously diminish the enemy's defenses with a thorough bombardment. The infantry would then be able to attack against weakened, if not obliterated, positions. The Signal Service role was to ensure that signals personnel were equipped and ready to follow behind the advancing infantry to provide an effective line system. It would need to be augmented by alternative means of communication, appropriate to situations arising.

In the event, the reality of the situation when the first attack took place on 1 July 1916 was far removed from that predicted and hoped for, despite the intense preparations that preceded the battle. The advancing troops, and those providing the signals system which followed closely behind, met an entirely different enemy response from that anticipated. The attack that had been expected to meet with rapid success faltered almost immediately as it attempted to make progress over ground battered by both British and German artillery. The well-prepared enemy had, in the main, retained its forces intact despite the ferocity and unprecedented strength of the British artillery bombardment. The Signal Service shared the intense and unexpected difficulties that resulted from attempting to provide an effective line system. The way in which this was prepared and developed is considered now.

The battle developed, from the first attack on 1 July 1916 until it finally closed down in November for the forthcoming winter, in very specific ways. From the first day, the predominant characteristic was one of slow moving siege warfare with repeated attacks. This involved the BEF, at all levels from corps downwards, in not always, by any means, specific objectives. Each attack required detailed preparation and was followed by semi-static warfare, interspersed with occasional and generally unsuccessful German counterattacks. The overall result was one of very slow forward progress by the British Army in the face of heavy enemy resistance and organized withdrawals. Eventually, the onset of winter and the need for an exhausted British Army to regroup brought all movement to a close.

The role of the Signal Service was to provide a variety of communications solutions to the problems that flowed from the above, to cover, principally, two situations. The first would be for individual and carefully prepared surprise attacks with strictly limited objectives. The predominant difficulty for Signals, in these circumstances, was the movement, mostly unspecified, of HQ locations. The second would be for slow moving siege warfare. This would require reliance on less reliable line communications than the deep buried system left behind. The need for alternative means of communication, as the situation dictated, would then be the priority.

In both situations the Signal Service had the task of supporting infantry across no-man's-land. Communications could then be maintained with Brigade and Divisional HQs for the provision of reinforcements and ammunition. In addition, facilities were required for artillery formations. Instructions for the direction of supporting fire were essential while the infantry dealt with already bombarded enemy positions. Of equal importance, battalion HQs needed vital information concerning counterattacks.

For almost all situations the telephone remained the preferred method of communication. Inevitably, however, alternative means suited some situations better. They included visual, pigeons, mounted orderlies, runners, wireless and, occasionally, earth induction sets. The latter were untried at this stage of the war but gained much prominence later.

The overriding objective was to provide a comprehensive and reliable communications chain between the advancing infantry and brigade and divisional HQs. The keys to success for forward signals organization, in the confusion of battle, were flexibility and adaptability. The measure of its success in achieving this objective at the Battle of the Somme is well covered in an official tribute in dispatches.[3]

> The Signal Service, created a short time before the war began on a very small scale, has expanded in proportion to the rest of the Army, and is now a very large organization. It provides the means of intercommunication between all

the armies and all parts of them, and in modern warfare requirements in this respect are on an immense and elaborate scale. The calls on the service have been very heavy, often under most trying and dangerous conditions. Those calls have invariably been met with conspicuous success, and no service has shown a more wholehearted and untiring energy in the fulfillment of its duty.

The way in which this success was achieved, even if perhaps overstated by the official tribute, is best illustrated by reference to one of the most typical situations in which forward Signals was called upon to meet its organizational objectives. This was for an attack on a brigade or divisional front with limited objectives, involving a number of critical factors.

The enemy's defenses were first subjected to heavy bombardment for anything from a few hours to a number of days. This was followed by an infantry assault with limited territorial objectives of usually no more than a mile. An essential preliminary to the attack was that the cable head of the deep buried cable was established as near as possible to the front line. For this careful planning was required. The provision of alternative means of communication, if this could not be achieved to the required level of security and reliability, would be a priority.

Another imperative for Signals was that no moves of HQs were anticipated during the attack, though battalion and even brigade HQs might move up after the attack was consolidated. A further assumption was that no counterattack was expected. The deep buried cable system could then be carried forward by organized parties and not in the heat of battle. A wide circulation of the positions of signals offices, cable heads, pigeon posts, wireless stations and all other means of communication available was absolutely essential from brigade commanders down to front line officers and selected other ranks.

The greatest problem to be overcome was the maintenance of line communication from the cable head up to and in the trenches. The obvious solution was to provide as much protection for cable as possible. In the trenches this was often achieved with some degree of success by placing cable in a shallow undercut on the side facing the enemy. This would usually provide good protection, even when the trench was virtually destroyed. Multiple cables were used as a solution for maintaining communications from the trenches to the cable head, preferably using routes least likely to be shelled by the enemy. In the attack, however, enemy artillery retaliation was heavy and lines virtually impossible to maintain, so the tendency was for all descriptions of communications traffic to converge on the safest route available. This, at least, provided a partial remedy.

Ground lines, used in the immediate follow-up to an attack, were even more difficult to maintain.[4] Even if they withstood the enemy bombardment, they were still vulnerable to destruction. This was caused by the walking wounded, stretcher bearers, reinforcements, orderlies, wagons and other of the BEF's support functions, which churned up the strongest cable.

When ground lines were partially or completely destroyed, communications could still be maintained from the fighting line back to battalion and brigade HQs. Runners would be used initially. If, however, casualties were high, then visual means or pigeons would be tried though mist, smoke and dust from the enemy's bombardment could render both ineffective. Visual means were often effective over the short distances involved in attacks with strictly limited objectives, where they might still be able to operate, even in the most adverse conditions. Pigeons, in short supply at this point of the war, were mostly retained by hard-pressed commanders for use as a last resort in a real crisis.

Where attacks were to be made on a much larger scale, with the objective of seriously breaching the enemy's line — 1 July 1916 provides the most outstanding example — additional and more extensive considerations applied. What differentiated a major offensive from a limited attack were the much greater distances to be covered and the constant movement of HQs. The solutions to these specific communications problems were only partially solved after taking into account a combination of factors. A system of sound buried cable forward to the cable head, which should be as near to the front line as possible, was an essential prerequisite to an attack. In fact, on 1 July 1916, for example, insufficient time was allowed for this to be fully completed. Consequently, where inadequate shallow buries remained, the line was broken inevitably and communications as far back as division failed. This was the case even when multiple routes through brigade HQs were used. Therefore reliance had to be placed on visual means or trench wireless, both of which were subject to serious limitations.

In the early stages of a major battle communications forward of the deep buried system were virtually impossible altogether, even though forward parties were allocated to carry the line forward with the assault. Casualties were, inevitably, high and communications difficult to establish. This proved the case, even when careful preparations were made from a study of the enemy's defenses, assisted by aerial observation. Following the preparatory barrage, the whole nature of the countryside over which the

Trench wireless set in use in captured German trench, location unknown. (IWM No.Q-7230)

attack was made was liable to change and consequently only the broad aspects of the original plan survived. The pragmatic solution was to wait until the situation had settled. Then a new line system could be established in lulls in enemy bombardments and when battalion HQs had moved forward.

Interior of a forward wireless station, location unknown. (IWM No. Q-27120)

The necessity remained, however, for some means of communication to bridge the gap between the first stages of an extended attack and the successful re-establishment of the line system. On these occasions, a combination of DRs, runners, pigeons, wireless and visual means could be used from divisional and brigade HQs. They had, of course, the same limitations to which all were subject in these circumstances. Because of the perceived danger of providing intelligence for the enemy, visual means, particularly, were not always used to advantage when they might have been. This was particularly the case when, in the early part of an offensive, the enemy's attention was likely to be distracted. In any case, with the introduction of the new and quiet Lucas daylight lamp with minimal beam dispersion, the chances of significant enemy detection were much reduced. This was confirmed when it was used successfully during the Battle of the Somme.[5] Finally worthy of mention, in large-scale attacks, was the value of airplanes in maintaining contact with the infantry. This was provided on a fairly extensive scale and supplied up-to-date information for brigade and divisional HQs. Visual means of communication were employed to

Battle of Arras. A Pioneer battalion's signal station using daylight lamp on the railway track near Feuchy, May 1917. (IWM No. Q-5257)

pass on observations, the best results being achieved when pre-arranged formulae were used.[6]

There is no doubt whatsoever, whether during large scale or limited attacks or in the long and arduous periods of static warfare which intervened, that the brunt of signals work fell on battalion signalers, although with some compensations.[7] They certainly played a crucial role in the success or failure, not only of signals communication during the Battle of the Somme, but also in the final outcome.

Battalion signalers sustained by far the greater proportion of overall signals casualties. All aspects of forward signals work including line maintenance, message delivery by hand or visual means carried high risks. Casualties were often as high as 50 percent in a single action.[8] Many occurred in their continuing misuse as infantry. The result was an organizational change that flowed directly from the high casualty rate. The decision was made to hold back a significant proportion of battalion signalers in brigade reserve. These could be used to replace casualties or to assist in improving forward signals, as an action developed. As an added benefit, while in reserve they were able to improve their training, particularly in visual means of communication, which had been badly neglected. This enabled them to fulfill the battalion signaler's function to the full.

Nonetheless, during the Battle of the Somme, signals communications as a whole must be judged as less than satisfactory. This was so, despite heroic efforts by Signals personnel to whom many tributes were paid by the High Command.

A fundamental mistake had been made in the abolition of the role of the battalion signals officer. This was part of a general re-organization at this level, including the infantry platoon, an element in the learning curve of the BEF. This led, inevitably, to some deterioration in training and general signals organization in battalions. In fact, in many battalions, unofficial battalion officers continued to be appointed. This anticipated proposals made during 1916 for the re-establishment of the role that led to a marked improvement in signals efficiency. This was an important consideration in the general review of intercommunication in the field, formalized in March and November 1917 and referred to later, in detail.[9]

Experience illustrated that the ideal for an effective forward signals unit was a committed contingent of battalion signalers, officers and men with first hand experience. They required a good working knowledge of signals and sound technical training. Training, particularly, was vital and received a boost from the rejuvenation of divisional signals schools. During rest periods, or on a quiet sector of the front, infantry and artillery signalers could be trained in all aspects of signaling. This included the most recent innovations such as power buzzer-amplifiers and, to come, Fullerphones.[10] Both were significant developments in signals communication in 1917, and of vital importance in preventing enemy overhearing, which will be re-examined as an issue later. The whole emphasis for successful signals communication continued to be speed and reliability. It was generally accepted that, during the years of trench warfare, the divisional signals schools played a significant part in helping to achieve these essential aims.

Taking the Battle of the Somme as a whole, a number of crucial lessons had been learned by the Signal Service. Not least, and most difficult to accept, was that within the zone of heavy shelling by the enemy — an ever increasing area — no means of communication was infallible. All were vulnerable eventually. The deepest buries could not withstand a direct hit from an 8-inch shell. Visual communication could not be maintained, with any degree of continuity, because of atmospheric conditions. Wireless sets had masts and aerials shot away and pigeons were effective only during daylight hours. The pragmatic solution was a combination of all means of communication, dependent upon specific conditions. As a last resort, DRs and runners could be used, although high casualties, especially over long distances, were an inevitable consequence.

The situation was often made even more difficult. While the Signal Service was fully aware of the limitations of the means of communication at its disposal during a heavy battle, Staff at all levels expected the same level of services as were available during static warfare. They paid little regard to the difficulties involved. The facilities anticipated could not be provided without sufficient labor. This was simply not available to push forward the deep buried cable system. Even if it had been, the inevitable level of casualties, in these circumstances, could not be justified. In the event, in the absence of buried cable, wireless sets were pushed forward with assaulting troops towards the end of the campaign. However, it proved impossible to establish effective wireless communications with the equipment available, not least because a party of several men was needed to carry the set and batteries[11] required.[12] The long aerials in use at the time were also vulnerable to shellfire. Nonetheless, as a last resort, wireless was occasionally successful in passing operational messages.

Compelling evidence for the more urgent development of wireless was beginning to accumulate. At this time, it would have been invaluable as brigade and battalion HQs moved ahead of the deep buried cable routes. However, the mistrust of wireless, by the majority of staff officers, was a complete hindrance to its development, despite professed enthusiasm.[13] The Battle of the Somme provides a typical example of the way in which a more perceptive and less inhibited use of wireless could certainly have had a marked effect on the entire way in which the battle was planned strategically and carried through operationally.

As the Battle of the Somme ground to a close in November 1916, the Signal Service had the essential opportunity to review its performance during the battle. There had been shortcomings in its general ability to provide a comprehensive communications system for the BEF that were, mainly, a legacy of its original establishment. A re-appraisal of the service was certainly overdue and led, eventually, to the publication of *Forward Inter-Communication in Battle* in March 1917 and *Inter-Communication in the Field* in November 1917 — both seminal documents for the Signal Service.

CHAPTER 6

A Counterfactual — The Somme with Wireless Telephony

In the summer of 1915 Prince had produced a working model of a vacuum tube radiotelephone transmitter. It was light enough to be carried on an aircraft and could be heard at ranges of 30 to 50 miles. The transmitter for the unit weighed about 10 pounds and the batteries an additional 36. He had also designed a vacuum tube receiver whose weight was not specified but would have been less than that of a transmitter. Both transmitter and receiver could use the same battery set. So, with no further improvements, a radiotelephone set weighing about 55 pounds was available for use both with the ground forces and with aircraft. While 55 pounds was more than one man could comfortably carry, it was considerably lighter than the 150 pound weight of the current spark set and could easily be carried by two men. Had the effort been put into it, Prince's initial model could have been turned into a series of other models incorporating refinements in the design, including weight reduction and a reduction in the size of the antenna, so the 55 pounds could have been reduced significantly. Regarding the antenna size, in 1918 CW sets were fielded that used a loop antenna[1] whose dimensions were considerably smaller than the 250 foot length employed in Prince's design. Reduced antenna size meant that the vertical mast that made spark wireless sets such an inviting target for enemy artillery was no longer needed.

As previously noted these prototypes or first generation models could have been produced in reasonable quantities early in 1916, once reliable vacuum tubes became available. Though far from perfect the prototypes could and should have been sent to the field for testing and educating personnel in how to use them. For example, when CW radios were finally sent to the field in 1918, their "delicacy" was noted[2]—that is, they were subject to failure under rough field hand handling and they were also difficult to operate, requiring careful adjustments by field personnel who lacked training. It is to be expected that the first units of any product incorporating new technology are going to have flaws that need correcting. In our own day no matter how much testing a software developer does, the first version of new software is going to contain many bugs which are commonly identified by the first users and then corrected in subsequent versions of the software. The sooner the new product, in this case, Prince's radiotelephone, was submitted both for controlled laboratory testing and for field testing, the more quickly the flaws in the design could have been found and corrected. It would have been to the advantage of the developers and the Army to place many, say 250 or more radiotelephones, in the hands of field personnel as soon as possible. It is therefore entirely plausible that in 1916 these prototype units could have been allocated to the divisions on the Somme, perhaps as many as 20 per division. The number actually in use would likely have been determined by how many of these could be used in a division without interfering with each other. Although mutual interference by these CW sets was minimal compared to that of spark sets, the technique of frequency planning to minimize interference was in its infancy in the Army. Frequency planning also permits re-use of frequencies when sets using the same frequencies are sufficiently distant from each other. As previously noted, the Navy employed frequency planning as early as 1910, by allocating the tunes of its spark sets to various types of ships and restricting use of the same frequencies when vessels were in proximity to one another.[3] It's fair to say that if radiotelephones had been distributed to the ground forces in 1916, frequency planning would have been well understood and routine later in the war.

In constructing a counterfactual for the Somme battle, it is unreasonable to assume that the place and date of the battle would have been changed because radiotelephones were available. These devices would have been too new and untried. Van Creveld asserts that the plans for the battle were built around the existing communication system[4] instead of the communications for the battle being built around the plans. The truth of this assertion is hard to verify because the enormous effort expended in building a large fixed communication system guaranteed that it could not be easily adapted to changes in the battle plan. If the new radiotelephones had been numerous and reliable, then communications might have been sufficiently flexible to support changes in the battle plans as new information became available regarding enemy strength, vulnerability to shellfire and ability to launch counterattacks. The engagement therefore might have taken place somewhere other than the Somme and on another date, but that is unlikely for the reasons quoted.

So the counterfactual is constructed based on the 1916 offensive occurring on the Somme in July. The new radiotelephones would not have been sufficient either in quantity or reliability to replace the communications planned for the Somme battle, but they would have been an invaluable supplement to the fixed communications system. The buried cable communication system behind the British front line almost certainly would have been built. Planning for the battle would have assumed the existence of such a system. Similarly, planning for communications to be carried forward with the advancing troops would not have relied on radiotelephones, and would have been a mix of visual, pigeons, mounted orderlies, runners, wireless telegraphy and prototype power buzzer methods. Radiotelephones would have been viewed as a supplement to these older methods. The following is an analysis of several parts of the battle where even a small number of radiotelephones would have made a huge difference.

1 July 1916

The approach taken here is to follow the progress of the battle during the first day, in sectors from north to south.[5] The assault was unsuccessful in the northern part of the battlefield but achieved its greatest success in the south. In each sector the preliminary bombardment had lasted for seven days, although there were variations among sectors. In some sectors some form of lifting or creeping barrage was planned to move ahead of the infantry to keep the defenders' heads down and prevent them from manning their trenches.[6] The fundamental flaw of the Somme creeping barrage was that it was to begin at the defender's front line and move back to the second and third lines as the battle progressed. The underlying assumption was that the seven days' barrage that preceded the assault would cut the barbed wire and obliterate the defender's front line and no more shells need be assigned to this task — a fatal misconception. The creeping barrage was planned to move ahead on a fixed schedule, indeed to be synchronized with the ability of the infantry to move forward. The Army adopted this method because, during the battle, commanders had no means to determine either (a) the position of their own troops or (b) the locations of defensive positions, machine gun emplacements in particular, holding up the advance. In the absence of information about how the assault was progressing this was the best support that could be provided to the infantry. In the counterfactual scenario radiotelephones provide this information. Thus, in the best case, there's no need for the ammunition wasting creeping barrage; the shells are better used on identified targets. If the creeping barrage is used, then it can be called back to fire on identified targets. In each case the artillery is used to destroy the defensive obstacles and the enemy's artillery.

Although radiotelephones were not actually employed, the effect of their employment can be estimated by what happened in the XII Corps' (18th and 39th divisions) sector, at the extreme south of the assault.[7] In this sector, the British artillery had very successfully neutralized the German artillery prior to the advance, so the assaulting troops were not subjected to intense shellfire, as happened elsewhere. In addition, the planning for the 18th Division's attack had the part of the barrage provided by the heavy artillery move forward, as elsewhere, but had the barrage provided by the field guns move back toward the German front line to stop or slow down the German machine gunners climbing out of their dugouts. The 18th's neighboring division, the 30th, did not split the barrage but instead was supported by six concealed Stokes mortar batteries, whose fire also severely hindered the machine gunners. This was the most successful attack on the first day of the Somme. If prototype radiotelephones had been used by all units this success could have been duplicated elsewhere on the battlefield.

North of the main Fourth Army attack part of the German defenses bulged to the West, around the village of Gommecourt. A diversionary attack, intended to draw attention from the main attack, was to be carried out by the VII Corps; the 56th (London) Division would attack the salient from the south and the 46th (North Midland) Division would attack the salient from the north. When the attack went in the first waves of the two British divisions were decimated by German machine guns whose crews had survived the British preliminary bombardment in deep dugouts and by the German artillery which had not received British counterbattery fire.[8] At this point the following waves of the attack should have been held up while the British artillery engaged the German machine guns and the German artillery. But that didn't happen because the first waves had no communications with division headquarters and could not report that they had been caught in the open and slaughtered. Nor did they have any means of communicating the position of the German machine guns or that the German artillery was responsible for high casualties. Under the counterfactual scenario prototype radiotelephones are with the first waves or directly behind them. They communicate the status of the attack to the commanders and the commanders suspend the following waves until the British artillery can remove the threat. Instead of a failed attack where the 46th lost 2455 casualties and the 56th Division lost 4314,[9] and gained no ground, each division reaches its objective with lower casualties.

The northern flank of the main attack was the responsibility of the VIII Corps of the Fourth Army. The attack included detonating a mine under the Hawthorn Redoubt 10 minutes before the attack began. The attack plan called for a creeping barrage which would move forward at the rate of 100 yards per minute,[10] starting at the German front line. When the mine detonated most of the barrage moved back to the German second and third lines. Most of the German artillery had survived the preliminary bombardment. When the attack went in the German machine gunners, warned by the explosion of the mine, had exited their deep dugouts and manned their weapons. The result was a disaster. The 31st (Pals) Division, on the left, suffered 3600 casualties[11]; the 4th Division, on the right, suffered 5752 casualties.[12] Neither division gained any ground. To the right of the 4th Division the 29th Division was assigned the Hawthorn Redoubt and the village of Beaumont Hamel. Following the detonation of the Hawthorn Redoubt mine the German infantry emerged from their deep dugouts and took up defensive positions. The creeping barrage had moved on behind them. The main attack faced devastating machine gun fire and shellfire from untouched German batteries. The 29th Division suffered 5240 casualties.[13] Again under the counterfactual scenario prototype radiotelephones are with the first waves or just behind them. They report intact defenses to their commanders who halt subsequent waves and call back the barrage to deal with the intact defenses and with the German artillery. The divisions reach their objectives with lower casualties.

Immediately to the south of the VIII Corps was the X Corps, charged with capturing the Leipzig Redoubt, the Schwaben Redoubt and Thiepval village. The barrage supporting the attack was to move in front of the attacking infantry according to a preestablished schedule. When the attack went in intact machine gun positions prevented forward movement even as the barrage moved on. Only the 36th (Irish) Division achieved brief success, overrunning the Schwaben Redoubt, but was isolated and eventually forced back.[14] The 36th Division suffered 5104 casualties and the 32nd Division 3949.[15] In the counterfactual scenario radiotelephones are with the initial assault waves and the barrage is called back to deal with the German machine-gun positions and German counterattacks. The divisions again reach their objectives with lower casualties.

To the south of the VIII Corps the III Corps were assigned to attack the fortified villages of La Boiselle and Ovillers, a formidable defensive position further strengthened by the Schwaben Hohe and Sausage Redoubts. The 8th Division on the left of the attack had some initial success but then was unable to advance against machine gun fire from both flanks. The troops who had advanced to the German front line were forced back by strong counterattacks. At the same time German artillery concentrated on the British front lines and no man's land, preventing the movement of reinforcements. To the right of the 8th Division the 34th Division was assigned the task of pinching out the fortified village of La Boiselle. The detonation of two huge mines beneath the German position wiped out the defenders above the mines but left the rest of the defenses intact. Once again the British barrage moved on and the attacking troops were forced to advance against interlocking fire from the German machine guns whose crews had ridden out the preliminary barrage in deep dugouts.[16] The attack gained little ground at high cost. The 8th Division suffered 6380 casualties and the 34th Division 5121.[17] Once again, in the counterfactual scenario, higher headquarters is quickly notified by radiotelephone that the attack is held up by German machine guns and the barrage is called back to deal with them. Both divisions have a much better chance of reaching their objectives and do so at less cost.

South of III Corps the XV Corps faced the Fricourt and Mametz Spurs off the Pozières Ridge. The Germans had converted these into formidable fortresses with an extensive trench system and deep dugouts. On the left of the attack the 21st Division was to assault Fricourt village. The assault was supported by the detonation of three mines. Except for those immediately above the mines, the defenders survived the primary bombardment, climbed out of their dugouts and manned their machine guns. The assault managed to capture part of the German front line at high cost. To the right of the 21st Division the 7th Division was assigned to take Mametz village. They too were assisted by the detonation of six small mines. Once again the German machine gunners survived the bombardment. Although the first waves managed to cross no man's land with few casualties, they were worn down steadily when the machine gunners took their positions and subjected them to lethal crossfire.[18] They were unable to advance beyond the German front line. The XV Corps was more successful than its neighbors to the north, primarily because the British artillery was more successful in suppressing the German artillery. Even so the 21st Division suffered 4256 casualties and the 7th 3380.[19] In the counterfactual, radiotelephones allow the frontline troops to communicate with their commanders, call back the barrage and direct artillery fire on the positions holding them up.

The British assault farthest to the south was carried out by the XIII Corps. It proved to be the most successful of the attacks, primarily because the British artillery, augmented by French artillery of the French XX Corps, dominated the German guns. Successful counterbattery fire prior to the assault virtually eliminated German artillery fire on the attacking troops. The 18th Division on the left was assigned to take the approach to Montauban village. The barrage supporting the attack was made up of a barrage creeping forward carried out by the heavy artillery and a barrage creeping backward carried out by the lighter field guns. This kept the Germans from riding out the barrage in their deep dugouts and emerging unscathed by artillery fire.[20] As a result the initial attack was fairly successful and penetrated the German front line. By the end of the day the 18th Division achieved its objectives. To the right of the 18th Division the 30th Division was to attack Montauban village. The excellent support provided by the British artillery was augmented by six concealed Stokes mortar batteries whose fire kept the Germans in their dugouts until it was too late to emplace the machine guns. The 30th Division achieved all their objectives and then some. Their success came at a high cost, however: the 18th Division suffered 3115 casualties and the 30th Division 3011.[21] In the counterfactual, use of radiotelephones enables the assaulting infantry to identify the obstacles holding them up much more quickly, allowing the field guns or Stokes mortars to eliminate them. Since each division achieved its objective, the main contribution of the radiotelephones is to reduce casualties.

During most of 1 July 1916, the high command had little awareness of what was occurring on the battlefield. General Sir Henry Rawlinson, the Army commander, was able to stay in touch with his corps commanders, but they had little or no idea what was happening to the troops.[22] German shells had cut most of the telephone lines and thereby prevented communication between Corps headquarters and their divisions, let alone to subordinate elements. Even the pilots of the RFC were unable to distinguish between a firmly held British position and a position held by stragglers and about to be cut off.[23] False reports indicated greater British success than had been in fact achieved. The command structure had little knowledge of battlefield reality and therefore could not command or control their formations. In the counterfactual, through radiotelephones commanders are well aware of the well defended obstacles and shellfire holding up the advance; they are able to take action, holding back subsequent waves of infantry until they can redirect the artillery to target the obstacles and engage the German artillery.

2–13 July 1916

The failure to take the Thiepval Spur and Pozières Ridge meant that the main German defense system remained intact. Capture of these two prominent geographical features would have dislocated this system and possibly led to a rapid advance. Rather than attack them again and suffer large losses Haig decided to build on the success in the south. In doing so he infuriated Joffre, who felt that the importance of these positions justified attacking them regardless of loss.[24] Despite this objection, the next fullscale attack took place in the south on 14 July.

Between 3 July and 13 July approximately 50 attacks were launched on Contalmaison, Mametz Wood and Trones Wood, ostensibly to gain better positions for the main attack. Commanders carried out these attacks without coordinating with neighboring units and in many cases without consulting with their superior officers. As a result the enemy was able to divert artillery resources from unthreatened sectors to those subject to attack. The failure of one attack was followed by launching another. Enemy artillery isolated British battalions in no man's land and were not engaged by British batteries. Flanking machine guns prevented advance or retreat. Cumulative losses from these attacks added up to 25,000 casualties.[25]

The counterfactual for this period assumes that some but not all of these attacks would have been supported by radiotelephone sets. When the attacks were held up, either by artillery or by machine gun nests, the radiotelephones would have allowed commanders to be notified and artillery directed at enemy batteries or individual machine gun positions. The result would have been more objectives gained and fewer casualties incurred.

14 July 1916

In contrast to the piecemeal operations that preceded it, the 14 July attack was meticulously prepared. The artillery was concentrated to destroy barbed wire, trenches, strongpoints and enemy artillery. The frontage of the attack was limited to 6000 yards, rather than the 22,000 yards of the 1 July attack, so the concentration of shellfire on the enemy defenses was substantially higher than the earlier attack. A comprehensive counterbattery plan was developed to suppress the German guns. A true creeping barrage was employed, lifting 50 yards every one and a half minutes to keep pace with the advancing troops. The attack was launched at night to gain the advantage of surprise.[26] The result was a complete success. The 9th Division captured the village of Longueval and reached the outskirts of Delville Wood. To their left the 3rd Division reached the main Bazentin Ridge, breaching the original German second line.

Once the initial objectives were gained, the plan called for the artillery to engage the deeper objectives, which had not been as heavily bombarded. Gun batteries sent forward observers to follow closely behind the initial waves of infantry. When observation posts with a good view over the German lines were established the observers attempted to communicate with their batteries, using signal flags either because telephone wires had not been laid, or, if they had, had been cut by shellfire. The signal flags were very visible to the Germans and few of the signallers survived the incoming shells, preventing the accurate direction of British artillery.[27] By this time the Germans had fresh troops available to launch counterattacks and thereby halted any further advance.

The attack on 14 July, known subsequently as the battle of Bazentin Ridge, was a success in that it had captured the original German second line. The plans for the battle, however, had envisioned a breakthrough, like the plans for the first day of the Somme. As before, cavalry was held in readiness to continue the assault once the enemy's defense system had been breached. It was assigned to capture High Wood, Flers and Eaucourt Labbaye once the infantry had seized Delville Wood and the village of Bazentin-le-Petit on Bazentin Ridge. The infantry did not reach these objectives, so the cavalry assault did not occur.

The counterfactual for this battle assumes that the signalers mentioned above possess one or more radiotelephone sets. From their observation positions they are in direct contact with the supporting batteries. There is no need for them to make themselves conspicuous by waving flags and there is nothing else to identify their position, so they survive. They are immediately able to direct artillery fire on the counterattacking Germans, who, caught in the open, without access to preconstructed defensive positions, suffer devastating casualties. The British infantry are not stopped by the counterattacks and manage to capture Delville Wood and Bazentin-le-Petit. The cavalry attack is launched. Perhaps the cavalry reaches all its objectives, but the odds are against it. A more likely success is the capture of High Wood, less than a mile from Bazentin-le-Petit. In actuality, during the next months, the British were to expend countless lives to capture Delville Wood and High Wood and other objectives close by. These objectives could have been attained on 14 July.

Subsequent Events

Success on 14 July was followed by frustration at Delville Wood, where the battle to clear the wood lasted from 15 July into September. Both sides brought up more and more artillery until the wood was unrecognizable. Units who fought there were shattered, the South Africans in particular.[28] The close quarters of the battle would have minimized the importance of radiotelephones other than to report back and occasionally call for artillery support.

The next major attack was scheduled for 23 July. The target was village of Pozières on the Albert-Bapaume road. It was strongly defended as part of the original German second line on the Pozieres Ridge. Although the attack was poorly coordinated the 1st Australian Division captured most of the village.[29] The inevitable German counterattack, preceded by an intense bombardment by German guns which had not been subjected to counterbattery fire at the outset, did not retake the town, but inflicted 5000 casualties on the division.[30] On 29 July the 2nd Australian Division attempted to resume the advance but was halted by German artillery fire and machine guns. The counterfactual for these engagements resides again in the ability of forward observers equipped with radiotelephones to report battlefield conditions back to commanders. Even though it was too late for thorough counterbattery fire, once the 1st Australian Division in Pozieres was counterattacked, an attempt could have been made to engage the German guns. Better artillery support for the 2nd Australian Division advance, both counterbattery fire and direct fire on enemy strongpoints, might have prevented its failure. In each case casualties would have been reduced.

The battle of the Somme dragged on into November. The British Army continued to suffer high casualties for little gain. The introduction of a new weapon, the tank, on 15 September, failed to change the dynamic of the battle. The use of the radiotelephone throughout this battle, even in small numbers, would have made a significant difference. For the first time on the Western Front commanders would have known where their troops were after they had gone over the top. For the first time commanders could have affected the course of the battle by reacting to battlefield conditions. Instead of developing elaborate plans for an attack, including detailed timetables for the application and advancement of artillery barrages, and then being helpless to influence the course of the battle once begun, commanders could call back the artillery to engage appropriate battlefield targets and direct counterbattery fire to be applied to the enemy guns holding up the attack and killing their men. Command and control, possible in the 19th century but so far unattainable in the 20th, would have been restored to the battlefield, with nothing but positive results.

CHAPTER 7

Operational Signals in 1917

Following on from the experiences of the Somme battle, this chapter reviews, briefly, the factors that had inhibited the growth and effectiveness of the Signal Service to provide a communication system commensurate with the demands placed upon it, to date. Thereafter, it reviews the progress and reforms of 1917. These took place during a period of static or slow moving warfare interspersed with battles of attrition on an epic scale. The Third Battle of Ypres, while perhaps the outstanding example, does not in any way diminish the heroic contribution of the British Army in 1917 during the battles of Arras and Vimy Ridge (April), Messines (June) and Cambrai (November) or the problems which these presented for the Signal Service.

Before studying 1917, however, it is important to refer again to the now critically serious problem of enemy overhearing, first encountered in 1915. The principal culprit that made enemy overhearing easily possible was cable. The other was wireless, to a lesser degree, though only because of its relatively limited use. A stark demonstration of the advantage that the enemy could derive from overhearing is illustrated emphatically by Priestley. He cites the example of an occasion when a complete copy of an Operations Order for one British army was discovered at the HQ of a German brigade captured at the Battle of the Somme.[1] It was later proved conclusively, from interrogation of enemy prisoners, that details of the order had been overheard via British cable communications during a call from a brigade major to a battalion HQ. The result was the decimation of its troops as they left the trenches at zero hour. This provides an appalling, but by no means untypical, example of the extreme consequences of a lapse in procedure. It also underlines the inherent vulnerability of the cable system. New initiatives to assist in overcoming this vulnerability had been proposed and developed in 1916 with some success. The Fullerphone, a device that virtually guaranteed message security over the telephone line, provided a vitally successful breakthrough. Its widespread use during 1917 will be considered in detail later.[2]

The British Army had made its own attempts to benefit from eavesdropping on the enemy. In fact, there had been little tangible progress until it was able to adopt a reasonably portable French wireless listening set with a range of 6 to 10 miles. Initially, and not surprisingly, the sets were unpopular with the operators, linesmen and interpreters who had to work them. This was because they could be used to best advantage only as far forward as possible, in vulnerable saps or disused trenches. The most alarming feature of intelligence gained in this way was the extent to which the enemy could benefit from a lack of British Army cable and telephone security. There was an immediate reaction to this discovery. Security procedures were tightened with dire penalties for those who transgressed. Telephone conversation was heavily restricted and later banned within 3,000 yards of the front line, i.e., back to brigade HQs. This created serious disruption to the communications chain, for which a solution had to be found. It was already clearly apparent that no circuits could be considered entirely safe except, perhaps, when twisted cable was used. However, this was entirely inappropriate for installation in the front line owing to its bulk and weight.

Real benefits could flow from the knowledge that specific information on British Army strategy and operational orders was in enemy hands. It could be used to good effect in counterplanning although the extent of enemy overhearing was truly alarming by late 1916. Indeed, the extent to which this was true leads Priestley to contend that the German Army could probably have worked out the whole constitution of the British Army and anticipated its every move.[3]

However, by December 1916 the British Army's policing of enemy overhearing, together with the tightening of procedures that followed, had reduced the problem significantly. An awareness of the dangers of overhearing gained general acceptance throughout the BEF. Battalion commanders began to accept advice on this issue, from battalion signals officers, as being both vitally important and authoritative. Against this background, it was battalion signals officers who championed the early use of the Fullerphone. Its adaptation, particularly for trench use, ensured that messages could be sent with virtually complete security right up to company HQs.

Before moving forward to consider the events of 1917 as they affected the Signal Service, it is important to pause to evaluate the factors that influenced its general effectiveness as it approached this phase of the war. This has to include the limitations imposed upon it.

There was a general awareness, through the entire chain of command, that the war would now be prolonged. Generally static warfare would prevail. Nonetheless, the overriding principal that the BEF, and thus the Signal Service, must form its strategic planning on the basis of mobile warfare remained paramount. Furthermore, while the British Army had to rely on Empire resources alone, anticipation of a prolonged conflict, in which neither side had sufficient men or guns to break the deadlock, was inevitable. The logical sequel to this line of reasoning was that resources would have to be very carefully conserved and apportioned. The Signal Service was certainly no exception to this general rule. All requests for increases in establishment were rigorously scrutinized and agreed to only when circumstances proved absolutely necessary.

In reality this meant that the resources available to the Signal Service, in both men and equipment, did not come even close to matching the needs of its operational deployment. This applied, particularly, to the provision of telephone facilities, the development of wireless and the requirement to cater for an exponential growth in the Army as a whole. The most pressing area for increases in Signal Service establishment was undoubtedly that of the artillery. Serious deficiencies in its ability to provide adequate facilities had been clearly apparent at the Battle of the Somme. However, as the Signal Service was constantly evolving and never for any length of time static during the war, the appointment of Deputy Directors of Signals at both army and corps HQs, in 1916, laid the foundations of an authoritative voice for the Signal Service, which became more apparent in 1917.

In addition, by this stage of the war, the Signal Service had expanded to meet new responsibilities. These included the provision of signals facilities for the RFC, kite balloons, anti-aircraft batteries, survey and tunneling units, trench mortar batteries and a growing number and variety of other services. All required an effective and often complicated communications system.

The artillery, however, continued to place by far the greatest demands on the Signal Service. It required considerably more communications systems than had been available to the entire BEF in its original establishment. The allocation of resources to the Signal Service came nowhere near to matching these requirements, as will be seen in 1917.[4]

In addition, the Signal Service retained tacit responsibility for communications right up to and including the front line. Proposals had been made on a number of occasions for the Signal Service to take over responsibility, formally, for battalion and battery signals but this had always been strongly and successfully resisted. Inevitably, signals performance was adversely affected by this blurred chain of command. Though Signals units had to be modified to accommodate the new and increasing requirements this had to be done without, in any way, detracting from the mobility of the army, corps and divisional companies forming the nucleus of the Signal Service. They continued to be strictly limited by the overall restriction placed on establishment increases throughout the Army.[5] It was not until April 1917 that any concessions were made to this policy to meet the overriding realities of the situation.

However, there were some valuable additions to Signals personnel and equipment from non-military sources at the end of 1916. The Signal Service was allowed to recruit, from the GPO, men over the age of 45 — the upper age limit in force within the Army at this time. They brought with them existing skills and training as linesmen and operators. The GPO, meanwhile, continued to provide invaluable help with the provision and development of signals equipment from its engineering department. Its services were placed at the disposal of the Director of Signals. These were particularly helpful relating to telephone and wireless. Its personnel had also been involved in active service visits to France and at the army signals schools, established in July 1916. This added greatly to the training that could be provided and the spread of best practice throughout the Army. Training in the BEF had been intended originally to take place under field service conditions but the extent and complexities of innovations made this impractical. One beneficial paradox of static warfare, which itself created the need for more intensive training, was that it also provided the opportunities for this to take place.

Best practice was spread still further by the appointment of liaison officers on the staff of the Director of Army Signals. By the end of 1916, they were visiting both the French and Belgian armies to study practice and innovations as well as traveling throughout the BEF for the same reasons. A most constructive outcome was the establishment of a Signal Service committee whose sole purpose was to coordinate signals research and the spread of best practice.

The factors that influenced the effectiveness of the Signal Service up to the end of the Battle of the Somme form the background against which the book now considers its contribution during 1917 and into the winter of 1918 prior to the German spring offensive. For the British Army it was to be a period of grueling but progressive attrition. The Signal Service was called upon to play a crucial and full part.

The British Army entered 1917 in a reasonably strong position. This was based on the late offensives of 1916, as a consequence of attacks made on the south of its line between the Ancre and the Scarpe. The sequel was a slow but general retreat by the German Army starting in March 1917. For the Signal Service the year was to be one of huge development. Operations would be on a massive scale affecting its units from corps forward to the front line and beyond. Army signals, however, remained comparatively unchanged.

The result was that, for a short period, the war became semi-mobile again across most of the southern front against a well-planned German withdrawal. The immediate and urgent task was to establish a new and appropriate communications system to follow up the advance. The German Army had comprehensively destroyed its own systems that were not therefore available for use by the Signal Service, even temporarily. New reliable, mainly buried, cable routes had to be laid quickly. This requirement tested both the experience and training of the Signal Service to the full from corps through to the front line. It also presented another challenging opportunity for wireless. This was the only really effective means available when the advance temporarily out-ran the cable. In these circumstances, flags and lamps could be employed again, though with only limited chance of success, on the rare occasions when the conditions were favorable, together with limited use of pigeons.

The circumstances changed again for the Signal Service when the enemy's resistance stiffened and its artillery was established in strength behind strong and well-positioned defenses. The result was that, by the end of March, static warfare resumed and the Signal Service was able to consolidate the new communications system. Sound communications based on mainly deep buried cable routes were established in the south of the line held by the British Army that required little modification until the Cambrai offensive in November 1917.

With the British Army now well established in the south, attention turned to the north of its line where a summer offensive had long been planned. This manifested itself first at Arras in April and through the summer and early autumn when very slow moving advances were made. This culminated in the Third Battle of Ypres and the capture, at the price of massive numbers of casualties, of the Messines and Passchendaele ridges.

The overall objective of the offensives was to either to break the German line or, failing this, tie up large numbers of the enemy on this front, and to inflict heavy casualties.

The German Army's response was to refine, still further, its system of defense in depth, which it had developed in response to the events of 1916. Following from this, artillery action on both sides exceeded in intensity that used even during the Somme offensive, employing a multiplicity of guns of increasing caliber. This created new problems for the Signal Service. With the German Army established in depth, British attacks still retained some elements of mobile warfare. Signals personnel had not only to provide temporary communications over increasing distances, but were also involved in fighting as infantry in defense of newly established communications points. In this form of attack, artillery had to be constantly repositioned and temporary unburied line communication provided. This resulted in a temporary revival of ground and poled cable for use during the 1917 offensives. However, a return to buried cable and, where applicable, alternative means of communication was required when, on most occasions, the enemy quickly re-grouped and artillery retaliation increased.

The Signal Service had, however, learned much and well from its experience during 1916. For the offensives of 1917 it was fully appreciated that detailed meticulous planning was the key to success, involving a combination of essential factors.

Detailed dress rehearsals preceded all attacks of any significance.[6] Particular emphasis was given to all signals personnel being trained on an organized system and in the use of every means of communication likely to be used in the prospective action. The plan was rehearsed on ground similar to that to be crossed by both infantry and artillery. Forward signals parties, detailed to follow up the attack, rehearsed using full equipment and replicas of landmarks selected for main communications centers. Signals personnel were equipped to clear selected centers of defenders, as an example, pill boxes, before establishing communications. Rehearsals were concealed from enemy observation, especially by aircraft. Artillery was kept closely informed of all plans, particularly details of the main communications routes. Perhaps most importantly of all, the use of limited supplies of cable was planned to best advantage. An important aspect of this was to prevent artillery commanders laying their own ground cable in the absence of a good buried system. Experience had shown this was a dangerous practice. It betrayed battery positions; lines were destroyed by tanks, transport and troops and, in general, seriously diminished the ability to communicate with forward units.

Once detailed preparation work had been completed, the types of attack in 1917 resembled closely those of 1916. They comprised three types: those with limited objectives based on the concept of "bite and hold," those with more far reaching objectives and, finally, slow moving siege warfare. However, the Signal Service now faced a new dilemma.

On the one hand, enemy overhearing had been countered with considerable success by early 1917. Indiscriminate use of the telephone and power buzzer-amplifier had been banned within 3,000 yards of the front line.[7] Emergency use for artillery observation, when all other means of communication failed, was the only exception to this strictly enforced rule. In addition, telephone was replaced by the much more secure Fullerphone[8] though its availability was limited.[9] Only some 10,000 were available to the whole of the BEF before the adoption of effective shortwave radio.[10]

The overall result was that, from an Intelligence point of view, the ideal of almost complete silence on the British front line was achieved. But sustaining an attack was virtually impossible in telephone silence and when other means of communication were either unavailable or could not be used effectively. Some relaxation in the rules had to be accommodated. This was achieved on the basis of Intelligence staff acceptance that, in an attack, the enemy's attention was likely to be distracted from detailed attention to British Army telephone conversation. Enemy listening posts were, in any event, often destroyed by artillery or during an attack. Even when intelligence was gained by the enemy, little time was usually available for this to be passed on and acted upon by the German Staff. Secure Fullerphones, now becoming more readily available though still not in sufficient numbers, could also be used. In addition, providing an element of surprise was achieved in the attack, restrictions could be either lifted or modified, though would be rigorously re-imposed when static warfare resumed.

A further development, already touched upon, which vitally affected the Signal Service during 1917 and thereafter, to its considerably increased effectiveness, was the publication by the General Staff of *Forward Inter-Communication in Battle*, in March.[11] This codified policy, organization and operational practice. It was later consolidated into the more definitive and wide-ranging *Inter-Communication in the Field* in November, which became the Signal Service bible for the remainder of the war.[12] Prepared by the Directorate of Army Signals, in conjunction with the General Staff, it incorporated all current standing instructions. It was also based on the experiences, to date, of signal units at all levels. In addition, it included the policy and practice elements of the series of Circular Memoranda, issued by the Director of Army Signals, up to this point, where they had current application.[13]

For the first time there was a really significant reform in signals policy as the direct result of closer co-operation between the Director of Signals and the General Staff. It was based on a growing realization, by the General Staff, that a fully effective and comprehensive communications system was crucial to the success of all military operations. It was given further impetus by a combined conference for senior Staff and Signal Service representatives in March 1917 and was of fundamental importance to the future operation of the Signal Service for a variety of inter-related reasons. It was the first Staff manual to be devoted entirely to communications throughout the Army. This was an immense advance in signals policy and revolutionary in its effect on Staff and Signal Service relationships. The powers and authority of Signal Service senior officers was greatly enhanced and signals policy was standardized throughout the British Army.

Of equal importance, the Signal Service now had an authoritative document that it could use to enforce all arms co-operation. It provided a standard system based on best practice. However, some flexibility in advocating standardized methods in the varying conditions that applied across the whole of the British Army's front had to be exercised. In practice, it was not possible to legislate for every eventuality. Importantly, however, the Signals Service now exercised control, even where amendments in practice were sanctioned. Corps signals officers now had control of the telephone system as far forward as the cable head, usually close to the front line. They had the authority, through S.S. 148, and later S.S. 191, to insist on standard procedures being followed or varied only under their instructions. The importance of both manuals for signals even farther forward was demonstrated, both in trenches and during attacks. In these circumstances, it was used to best effect when responsible signals officers were delegated to use the manual as an authoritative guide but allowed some discretion in interpretation.

By way of summary and of greatest significance, both manuals demonstrated, beyond doubt, recognition of the Signal Service and hence communications as an indispensable element of command and control. This forms Chapter 11 and is vital to an evaluation of the overall performance of the Signal Service throughout the war.

However, implementation of S.S. 148 inevitably took time and the

Signal Service still faced considerable difficulties as it approached the 1917 offensives. Signal units had to adjust to the changes implicit in the new manual. They had only recently been brought up to strength from inexperienced drafts, made up of either raw recruits or experienced GPO operators or linesmen. These had to acclimatize to the extreme conditions of the Western Front and military discipline. In addition, their training had to be accomplished alongside detailed preparation for the forthcoming offensives. In this, trained and experienced signals NCOs were key and fortunately available, often being overdue for promotion and with indispensable knowledge carried forward from the Somme offensive.

By early summer 1917, however, following the spring offensives at Arras and Vimy, the Signal Service had sustained high numbers of casualties. Fortunately, during the period of more or less static warfare that followed, it was possible for reinforcements to be absorbed and training improved. The Signal Service as a whole gained valuable experience before the opening of the Passchendaele offensive in July. It is this period that is dealt with in the next part of the book. It had far reaching implications for the Signal Service from army and corps through to the front line.

From army signals HQs forward, all signals units were affected by the deadlock on the Western Front that remained the predominant feature of 1917. Changes in signals practice were required, yet again. At Army HQs, signals officers were required to take on greater responsibility for forward signals. This was mainly as the result of the immense growth and changing practice in other arms of the service, for which they had responsibility. It was imperative that scarce signals resources were employed to best advantage. Separate signals units and systems were required to provide facilities for each individual arm, the artillery continuing to be by far the greatest in numbers and most demanding.

For all arms of the service the telephone remained the principal and preferred means of communication supported, when enemy shell fire was light, by DRs. Once again, they re-emerged as a viable means of communication in static conditions, though in relatively small numbers.[14]

Army signal companies now had a vital and increasing role in forecasting the individual requirements of forward signals units. This called for a great deal of experience, flair and imagination. Sound staff work was essential to ensure, particularly, that authorized cable plans, along carefully chosen routes, were strictly adhered to. Close supervision of repairs and the provision of appropriate technical equipment were key issues.

Within corps, the growth of signals systems, and hence their work and responsibility, mirrored those of armies. It was also at corps level that control of artillery signals was grouped with allied means of observation; especially sound ranging and flash spotting. The requirement for artillery communication systems continued to grow rapidly, though unpredictably. Signals personnel had to be available and fully trained to meet sudden concentrations of artillery required for forthcoming offensives or to counter enemy retaliation.

It was, however, from divisions forward that close proximity with the enemy required entirely different communications systems. This area attracted the highest levels of almost constant shelling and ground lines were totally ineffective. The entire telephone cable system had to be buried at ever increasing depths to counter the enhanced caliber of enemy artillery, up to 8 feet deep within 100 yards of the front line. The greatest possible secrecy was required in cable laying to avoid enemy observation and retaliation. Additionally, the system had to be adapted to meet individual and precise circumstances. This is well illustrated by Priestley in relation to the differing requirements for the offensives at Arras and Vimy compared with those at Messines and Passchendaele.[15]

On the one hand at Arras and Vimy, over firm, well-drained terrain, the buried system was laid successfully up to 8 feet deep forward to the front line. It was improved still further, to the extent that it was almost impregnable, by using an extensive system of tunnels, caves and sewers with the assistance of tunneling companies. The result was that many divisions went into action with entirely secure frontline signals, providing them with an unusual, but vitally important, advantage.

On the other hand at Messines and Passchendaele, over low, swampy ground under constant enemy observation, all work for miles behind the front line had to be carried out at night in conditions that were unsuitable for burying cable. Despite the conditions, a reasonable buried cable system was achieved though it had to be completed during intermittent enemy fire when high casualties were sustained. The result was that some reliance had to be placed on inadequate alternative means of communication until the higher ground was captured and buried cable routes could be supplied up to the front line again. This acted as a spur for the more general reintroduction of alternative means of communication.

The Arras-Vimy and Messines-Passchendaele offensives were to provide crucial though costly experience for the Signal Service. The requirement for greater camouflage and protection was clearly apparent. Using detailed careful observation, mainly by aircraft, the enemy targeted buried cable routes. This resulted in high casualties to working parties from the Signal Service, infantry and pioneers involved in the construction and repair of buried cable routes. As a result, in exposed areas, buries were carried out at night only after careful daylight reconnaissance by signals officers. Straight line buries were avoided and cables terminated away from HQ locations. Partially completed cable trenches were camouflaged to avoid daylight observation by enemy aircraft. Additional time and personnel were required to complete this work satisfactorily. Obstacles were created by the Signal Service, causing it unpopularity, to deter troops from establishing regular routes, which inevitably drew enemy fire. Entire systems of dummy trenches were created to misdirect the enemy.

The work was intensive and time consuming. On a typical corps front, prior to an offensive, two months preparation time had to be allowed involving up to 1,000 miles of buried cable. All available divisional labor was required to complete satisfactory communications up to the cable head, adjacent to the front line.

In relation to 1917, the book now deals with two final areas before moving into 1918. The first is a summary of the overall effect on forward signals and the Signal Service of the codification of signals policy, organization and practice in S.S. 148 and S.S. 191.[16] The second, the final battle of the year at Cambrai, requires detailed examination. It provides a useful case study by which to measure the cumulative experiences of the Signal Service and to examine communications, through the chain of command, as they existed at this point in the war. It also had the unique distinction of being the first major engagement when tanks were employed in significant numbers on the battlefield, for which a new communication system had to be devised.

During 1917, in line with the requirements of S.S. 148 and S.S. 191, divisional signals units, the hub of forward signals activity, had increased substantially in numbers. Nonetheless, telephone linesmen and operators, who were the backbone of the communications system, were stretched to the limit. So was the provision of stores and equipment allied to their efforts. Wireless was later to gain considerable credibility as a viable and valued means of communication at Cambrai. However, prior to this, it was employed, mainly as an alternative, when telephones, power buzzer-amplifiers or Fullerphones could not be used by battalion signallers.

To provide a partial solution to the scarcity of resources, in personnel and equipment, the most decisive development for the Signal Service in 1917 was the concentration of communications along one main route. This was provided through the center of each brigade area, with brigade officers connected by telephone or Fullerphone to divisional HQs, using the buried cable system. During offensives, the central communications line was pushed forward and buried into the captured areas. The mandatory telephone restrictions forward of brigade HQs were lifted or, at least, relaxed. Priestley provides a good example of its success.[17] During an advance opposite Arras and Vimy Ridge, one corps completed 1,500 yards in the captured area within 15 hours of zero and a further 1,000 yards by zero+31 hours with very few faults. The route remained open for a further 3 months. But success could not always be achieved to this extent. It depended, almost entirely, on other factors. Principal among these were the supply of labor available, the intensity and weight of the enemy barrage and both the depth and spread of the advance. Nonetheless the advantages of one main brigade route, to include alternative means of communication should the telephone fail, were clear. They were laid down, explicitly, in S.S. 191, as follows[18]:

> The grouping of all Signal Service responsibilities, including HQs, along one main route, provided the most effective and economical use of personnel and resources, with no time or energy wasted in providing cable spurs.[19] It also provided a good base for field service training.

However, there were disadvantages. Where an offensive failed or slowed down the result was the telescoping of lines along the main route. It became hopelessly overcrowded with telephone traffic. In these circumstances, alternative means of communication, which were also concentrated on the central route, provided a partial solution. They included runners, pigeons, visual and wireless, when it could be used from well protected and concealed locations — dug-outs in the south of the British line and pill boxes in the north.

This was the situation particularly at Passchendaele. After heavy rain in August 1917, the shell blasted ground over which the advance was made became entirely impossible for cable laying. This was exacerbated by the fact that, as enemy artillery was re-established, cable was blown to pieces after only partial completion. Similarly pillboxes, occupied by signal units as relay posts, were destroyed by heavy enemy fire. Alternative means to cable had to be employed. Power buzzer-amplifiers were used with some success though in short supply. Wireless, which was now available using shortened, easily erected and less conspicuous aerials, was both much more useful and popular, and pigeons were able to avoid the effects of the bombardment and gas. Where cable was considered essential, as at Pilkem Ridge during Passchendaele,[20] for example, the construction work, which had to be carried out at night, was both dangerous and hurried under intense enemy shell fire, with heavy casualties to working parties. On occasions aircraft were used, with some success, to relay information, though not as prominently as at the Somme. Runners continued to be the last resort of signals officers, although sustaining inevitably high casualties.[21]

Overall, the power buzzer-amplifier was a key and growing means of communication during the 1917 offensives and particularly at Passchendaele. It could function without cable — an overriding advantage. Similarly, as the British Field Set (BFS) became more readily available and trusted by signals personnel, it proved eminently suitable as far forward as battalion HQs. However, its mobility was still restricted by being cumbersome and heavy. A three-man party was needed in operation and even the new shortened aerials remained difficult to hide in sectors where concealment was notoriously difficult.[22] Nevertheless, with the introduction of even lighter loop sets, wireless often proved to be the only reliable means of communication available during the first 24 hours of an offensive.

As the war moved towards the close of 1917, the final battle of the year at Cambrai in November presented additional challenges for the Signal Service. These included the provision of communications for and with tanks, as they entered the battlefield for the first time in large numbers. However, it was able to rely and build on its experiences of 1917 backed by the considerable advantages that S.S. 191 provided in codifying and giving overriding authority to its activities. Consequently, Cambrai presents a valuable and appropriate case study of the cumulative progress and experience of the Signal Service to date, which formed the background to its performance in the decisive developments of 1918.

Cambrai

The Battle of Cambrai, though not an unqualified military success, had a number of features of special interest for the Signal Service. Two were particularly distinctive. The first was the absence of an opening barrage by the British Army's artillery with the objective of cutting enemy wire. The second was that the offensive was to be spearheaded by large numbers of tanks, followed by infantry. It involved, principally, Third Army, III and IV Corps and, at a later stage, V Corps. An understanding of the objectives of the offensive is important in an appreciation of the communication problems that required solutions.

The general concept was outlined, by the Army Commander, at a conference on 26 October 1917.[23] There were three overall objectives. The first was to overcome the enemy holding the line from the Canal de L'Escaut to the Canal du Nord: the second, to secure the possession of the area banded by the Canal de L'Escaut, the River Sensee and the Canal du Nord; the third, to clear the country west of that area of hostile forces. Three stages for the attack were proposed.

The first would involve a surprise infantry attack, assisted by tanks, together with an unregistered artillery bombardment on the German lines of defense. It was envisaged that the Canal de L'Escaut would be bridged at Masnières and Marcoing. The second stage anticipated a cavalry advance to isolate Cambrai, seizure of the Sensee crossings and the capture of Bourlon Wood. The third and final stage would be the clearance of Cambrai itself and the Canal de L'Escaut, River Sensee, Canal du Nord area.

For the Signal Service there were major problems to overcome in preparing a communications system for the forthcoming battle, in the utmost secrecy, for the 9 divisions scheduled to carry out the attack. They are comprehensively covered in the war diaries and reports of some of the major participants and form the background to the case study. Equally, the individual war diary of one participating divisional signals company, though not perhaps performing at its highest level compared with previous achievements, provides a microcosm of experience with communications systems for the majority of all those involved.[24]

The provision of communications for tanks and the protection of all BEF communications systems from damage by the presence of tanks on the battlefield were of primary importance. In addition, the provision of follow-up communications for an advance of unusual speed and depth was needed. In the event, some units achieved advances of as much as 5 miles in only a few hours. Of equal importance was the building of a system of communications to accommodate reserve units and formations moving into the front line immediately before the projected date of the attack. A further requirement was the provision of a system of communications for cavalry units passing through in the planned breakthrough. Finally, sufficient personnel and equipment would have to be available to complete all the systems described, which would involve the laying of 13,000 miles of cable in less than a month before the scheduled attack date of 20 November 1917.

The main solution to accommodate the above was to provide, in line with now well-established practice and in accordance with S.S. 191,[25] one main route forward for each division. The major problem was that, due to secrecy in preparation and the anticipated speed and depth of the advance, buried cable was not a viable option, except for some artillery communications.[26] Therefore, the decision was taken to rely on armored cable — above ground — from the rear areas forward to the front line. In view of the damage anticipated from both personnel and especially tanks, armored cable was laid in supposedly traffic proof ditches 1 foot deep in the bottom of communication trenches. Elsewhere, it was camouflaged along the ground in hedges and ditches. Though the work was carried out with the utmost secrecy, indiscriminate damage still occurred from routine enemy shelling. In addition, tanks proceeding to hiding places in the final hours before the attack caused considerable further damage. This was mainly because they did not use the specially protected line crossing points that had been prepared for them. This was not helped by a general lack of liaison between tank formations and the Signal Service.

The consequences were disastrous. Poled cable was destroyed and ground cable churned into the earth. Communications were, at best, intermittent at a moment when high levels of signals traffic were required.

To ensure secrecy, the communications system had been developed in two parts. They were divided by the boundary created by the limit of generally recognized enemy overhearing, i.e., within 3,000 yards of the front line. At this limit, all forward routes were disconnected and not reestablished until zero day. To the rear, however, communications remained constant. The use of telephone forward of brigade HQs was forbidden in accordance with normal practice. Nonetheless, the forward system had to be tested frequently to ensure its availability at zero hour. This proved extremely difficult in the face of continuous damage from routine enemy artillery fire and the passage of tanks and troops. This was particularly the case under the conditions laid down, in which telephones and power buzzer-amplifiers could not be used. The solution, now fortunately available though not in sufficient numbers, was the Fullerphone. It proved its worth, beyond measure, as it could operate virtually free of enemy overhearing. The overall result, at zero hour, was an at least adequate communications system. This was available to all divisions, cavalry and other formations and units moving into their assault positions, with sound cable backup in the rear areas.

At zero hour on 20 November 1917 the barrage commenced and battalions of tanks followed by infantry divisions began their assault. By 1030 hours the Hindenburg reserve line was overrun and objectives achieved at a depth of up to 5 miles across a wide front into enemy territory. Large numbers of enemy guns were captured, which made the problem of advancing the communications system easier. Briefly cavalry, with a separate line communications system backed up by wireless, prepared to go into action. They were, however, withdrawn when the planned breakthrough did not materialize and were used later, dismounted, as infantry.

Although an adequate communications system had been prepared for the battle, it failed quickly between brigades and divisions during the first 2 to 3 days of the offensive, for which tanks were mainly to blame. Although the poled cable system in these areas was armored, and strongly built with tank proof crossing points, it was continually destroyed, despite gallant attempts by linesmen and cable detachments to repair it. This was because of the uninhibited movement of tanks which ignored the provisions made for them. A tank was capable of destroying 100 yards of cable at a time through careless movement. The position was made even more difficult by having to feed repair supplies through a narrow but deep front.

Under these circumstances, the importance of providing alternative means of communication increased sharply. Well-sited visual stations were required and established for communication with the rear. The open countryside of the Cambrai area was eminently suitable for its use. With the enemy in retreat, without the opportunity to gain intelligence from visual means, two-way communication was also possible. In fact, the main limitation on the use of visual means of communication stemmed from the reluctance of staff officers at all levels to use it.[27]

The same inhibitions usually applied to wireless. It could have been better exploited. Nonetheless, an excellent chain of wireless stations was established and used more than ever before.[28] This was particularly the case between brigades and divisions, when cable routes were broken, though still not to maximum levels of its capacity. It might have been used more freely, and to good effect, if the insistence on the continuing use of cipher and code had been relaxed. This increased the work of wireless stations enormously, despite the fact that, with the enemy in retreat and disarray, the risk of overhearing was much reduced. In the mobile warfare of 1918, the restrictions were relaxed to beneficial effect as will be demonstrated. Power buzzer-amplifier units were used during the initial attack to advantage being unrestricted by cable. However, their limited range was quickly outdistanced by the speed and depth of the advance.[29]

Message carrying agencies were also employed. DRs, mounted orderlies and runners[30] were all used at various stages of the offensive between brigades and divisions. Unfortunately, with roads in bad repair or completely destroyed, they experienced even greater difficulties than usual forward of divisional HQs. In addition, the existing and abandoned enemy line system was available for use and adaptation by the Signal Service when and where it had not been damaged by British Army artillery or tanks. Pigeons were also used during the battle, though in only a very limited way. This was because the enforced secrecy prior to the attack, and the short preparation period, allowed little time for pigeons to be trained to new loft positions.[31]

Following the first two days of the attack, the British Army sought to exploit its initial success by widening the salient occupied by its troops. Nonetheless, increased enemy resistance slowed the pace of its advance. For the Signal Service it was not possible to establish a large-scale buried cable system. All efforts centered on consolidation of the existing poled and ground system, coupled with improvements to the alternative means of communication used. This activity continued until a full-scale enemy counter-attack on 30 November, preceded by a heavy bombardment, damaged British Army communications systems.

The Signal Service was badly affected, particularly in the south of the line, when the British Army retreated in the face of the enemy counterattack. Signals in retreat was not an eventuality anticipated or catered for in S.S. 191! But a communications system had to be improvised as forward and rear systems were destroyed. An exception to this general pattern of destruction saved the overall collapse of the British Army's communication system in the south of the line. This is well illustrated by Priestley.[32] One reserve armored cable route to a division at Gouzeaucourt remained undamaged throughout operations and became the main line of communication for three divisions. Using this line, the extreme urgency of the situation was conveyed down it, resulting in a successful counterattack by the Guards Division — another striking example of the importance of communications to the final outcome in battle.

During the German counterattack, yet again, a large number of Signal Service personnel were drawn into the fighting line as infantry where they demonstrated sterling fighting qualities. Again Priestley provides a striking example.[33] This involved an incident in which a forward wireless station serving a battalion HQ was surrounded by the enemy. Of three operators manning the wireless station, one remained in the dugout to destroy appa-

Typical military wireless installation, Signal Service, location unknown. (IWM No.Q-27049)

ratus while the remaining two manned adjoining trenches with rifles. One was killed and the other taken prisoner. Having destroyed the wireless equipment, the third operator joined the infantry in fighting a rearguard action for the next 24 hours before rejoining his signal company. Fortunately this type of incident was rare as signals personnel were urgently required to carry out their vital duties. These, in any event, called for high levels of courage in the laying and maintenance of lines or delivery of messages under heavy enemy shell fire.

The relatively short Battle of Cambrai provided invaluable experience for the Signal Service. The procedural changes that followed formed the blueprint for signals units in the advance that was to take place on a much grander scale in 1918. The Cambrai offensive had, above all, illustrated the crucial importance of secrecy and thoroughness of preparation. It had provided the Signal Service with an opportunity to study problems on a relatively small scale. It proved of vital importance for future decision making, particularly in mobile warfare, relating to both advance and retreat.

As importantly, the battle also provided the first real test for tank communications. These had been attempted between infantry and tank formation HQs and individual tanks and infantry-artillery units during the attack. The Signal Service had responsibility for providing and maintaining these overall communications. With the rapid expansion in the use of tanks and the formation of a Tank Corps, new signals establishments and systems were urgently required. The essence of successful tank deployment lay in sudden offensives and concentrations. It was difficult to allocate its signals responsibilities that often had to be decided on an ad hoc basis. This required the closest supervision and an Assistant Director, Signals was appointed to the Tank Corps to ensure this requirement was met.

The experience at Cambrai had shown a distinct lack of effective liaison between tanks and the Signal Service resulting in the destruction of an otherwise effective communications system.[34] As it could be predicted that tanks would, undoubtedly, feature prominently in future operations, the existing difficulties could be overcome only by mutual agreement and improved liaison. Improved methods of line laying were required together with better information on safe tank crossing and careful adherence to them. In addition, better signals systems for use within tanks were needed. When first used at the Somme in small numbers, communication systems were extremely primitive using visual means, mainly colored discs, lamps and pigeons. By June 1917, however, new practices were tried using continuous wave wireless sets. These proved, later, to be the only really effective means of communication for tanks. This will be clearly demonstrated later during the mobile warfare in the autumn of 1918. Importantly, by that time, difficulties with wireless aerials had been overcome. This had been a continuing problem. When used with tanks, they were susceptible to damage from artillery fire and the condition of the ground over which they fought. With the introduction of much shorter and less vulnerable aerials, these problems were solved.[35]

The close of the Cambrai offensive, and a resumption of static warfare, coincided with a massive increase in both long-range artillery fire and bombing by the enemy. These had a profound effect in areas to the rear of divisional HQs which had been relatively untouched hitherto. The reaction was a rearward extension of buried cable resulting in heavy casualties to signals personnel as they laid or repaired it. This required immediate action. Protection for systems, personnel, equipment and signals offices had to be improved. The solutions were the diversion of cable routes around the locations of heaviest shelling and bombing, and the provision of duplicate communications systems. Additional requirements were heavily protected dugouts for the storage of signals equipment and safer locations for the increasing numbers of maintenance personnel.

The year 1917 closed with Signal Service strength at around 38,000 officers and men but with immensely enhanced effectiveness based on its experiences during this year.[36] Consequently, it entered the short period of static warfare, which preceded the great German spring offensive of 1918, better equipped to deal with the unprecedented challenges and demands that the final year of the war would place upon it.

CHAPTER 8

A Counterfactual — Passchendaele and Cambrai with Wireless Telephony

This counterfactual assumes that the radiotelephone would have been introduced on the Somme. Under battlefield conditions a number of weaknesses of the radiotelephone itself would have been identified. These could have included mutual interference, power supply, range, transportability, ease of use and ruggedness. In addition details of its operational use would have had to be worked out, including assignment of radios in the chain of command, selection of frequencies to be used, interfacing with infantry, tanks, artillery and aircraft, training of operators, development of communications discipline to minimize interception and organization of a supply chain for radios. The weaknesses of the design would have been addressed by the engineers who had built the units. Mutual interference would have been mitigated by careful attention to circuit design. Problems with the battery-based power supply would have been overcome by making the radio more efficient. Range would have been increased by using a more powerful radio and a better antenna. Transportability would have been improved by reducing weight. Ease of use would have been enhanced by minimizing any required adjustments. Ruggedness would have been increased by sturdier construction and ensuring that the case was well sealed. Successful design requires balancing sometimes conflicting objectives to achieve the best compromise. The development process is an ongoing activity to accomplish this, but field requirements often require putting a design into production for immediate use at some point and postponing further improvements for a later model. Modern terminology speaks of first, second and third generation designs. The first generation designs would have appeared on the Somme. Enough time had passed for second generation equipment to be available in Flanders.

Operational experience on the Somme would have led to placing the radios where they could have done the most good, certainly at battalion, regiment, brigade, division and corps, possibly at company or below. Assignment of frequencies is handled in a modern army by the development of a frequency plan that minimizes interference but allows the reuse of frequencies. Certainly a rudimentary frequency plan would have naturally been developed by the BEF once the radios had been deployed. Rules and conventions for the communications among infantry, tanks, artillery and aircraft would have been worked out. An operational training establishment for radio operators was in fact created in 1918, so it certainly could have been in 1916. Communications discipline is essential to prevent the enemy from exploiting intercepted signals. Such discipline was imposed for telephone communications early in the war. It would have been a straightforward matter to extend it to radiotelephones. (More on this in chapter 12.) The rudiments of a supply chain for radios would have been established for the Somme. By 1917 it would have been fully operational.

Passchendaele

General Sir Hubert Plumer's 7 July 1917 attack on the Messines Ridge had been enormously successful. Assisted by the detonation of nine mines packed with 1,000,000 pounds of explosives and an artillery bombardment lasting three weeks and consisting of 3½ million shells, his Second Army finally took the ridge which had dominated the Ypres position from the east since 1914.[1] Buoyed by this result General Sir Douglas Haig planned an offensive in Flanders to clear the Passchendaele Ridge, secure the rail center of Roulers and then, in conjunction with an amphibious assault by the Royal Navy, capture the Channel coast ports of Ostend and Zeebrugge.[2] His plans met with a great deal of skepticism in London. Lloyd George, the British prime minister, was suspicious of any effort that promised little gain for high casualties. The attacks in 1915 and 1916 had produced over 250,000 dead for paltry territorial gains. His inclinations were to seek operations away from the Western Front, say in Italy or the Middle East, which would have a higher payoff.[3] He was also inclined to wait for the Americans. Haig, on the other hand, argued that pressure must be kept on the Germans. He pointed out that if the Germans were not engaged they would be able to exploit the French Army, weakened by the mutinies that followed the ill-fated Nivelle offensive.

Haig won the day, primarily because no other operation seemed promising to British decision-makers.[4] Preparations were made for the attack to go in on 31 July 1917, including the extensive buried cable system described in the preceding chapter. The 4 million shell preliminary bombardment began on 15 July. The four corps of General Sir Hubert Gough's Fifth Army would lead the attack. The key role in the attack, clearing the Gheluvelt Plateau, was assigned to the II Corps, commanded by Lieut. Gen. Claude Jacob.[5]

The position they were attacking was perhaps the most formidable fortress on the Western Front. The Germans had had over two years to fortify it and to incorporate all of the lessons learned in two years of defensive fighting. The Fifth Army's opponent was the German Fourth Army, whose chief of staff was Germany's top defensive expert, Col. von Lossberg. He had organized a system of self supporting concrete pillboxes, some concealed in derelict buildings, which would have to be reduced one by one in the face of intense machine gun and shell fire.[6] Even if the attackers succeeded in penetrating this wide defensive belt they would be subjected to severe counterattacks from divisions stationed in well protected bunkers behind the front line.

The II Corps attack did not go well. By late morning communication between the infantry and the artillery was lost. Cables were cut and runners couldn't get through or if they did the information was stale. Each of the pillboxes had to be destroyed in turn, a task made much more difficult by the supporting fire from other intact pillboxes. With communications lost the infantry could not call upon the artillery to concentrate its fire on each successive pillbox. In one case a single pillbox destroyed 17 tanks whose crews were machine gunned when they tried to escape.[7]

In midafternoon the Germans unleashed their counterattack divisions, supported by artillery which had survived British counterbattery fire in protected positions. If this weren't enough it started to rain, a torrential downpour that lasted for three days and turned the battlefield into a muddy swamp. On 4 August, this attack was shut down. Despite this setback and continuing bad weather, Haig continued the Flanders offensive, attacking Langemarck on 16 August, and launching three fruitless assaults on the Gheluvelt Plateau.[8] On 24 August, he relieved Gough and put Plumer in charge. Plumer decided there needed to be a pause before the next phase of the battle was initiated. The last attack before the pause took place on 27 August, just north of the remains of the village of Gheluvelt.

Plumer designed a series of "bite and hold" attacks beginning on 20 September.[9] After three weeks of bombardment four divisions attacked up the Menin Road east of Ypres. The rolling barrage in front of them saturated the enemy's defenses to a depth of 1500 yards, the limit of the planned advance. Similar attacks on 26 September and 4 October finally succeeded in taking the Gheluvelt Plateau. On the last of these attacks, the Germans suffered severe casualties because they had placed their counterattack divisions too far forward.[10] They changed this deployment in later battles.

Most historians of this campaign agree that this would have been a good time to shut down this campaign,[11] but Haig persisted. On 12 October he committed the ANZAC Corps to an assault on the village of Passchendaele, located on the highest point of ground east of Ypres. The artillery was unable to cut the wire because the shells buried themselves in the mud without exploding and the assault failed, with heavy casualties, because of machine gun fire to the corps' front and flank. Starting on 26 October, Haig committed the Canadian Corps, whose four attacks finally captured the remains of Passchendaele village on 4 November and consolidated the line on 10 November. At this point the Flanders offensive was stopped. The offensive had cost the British Army 70,000 dead and 170,000 wounded.[12]

The counterfactual for this highly controversial offensive emphasizes the actions on the first day because the new tactics facilitated by radio communication would have been employed again and again throughout its course.

In 1917 Flanders the British Army is equipped with second-generation radios, probably at company level, maybe lower. Because at this time the radios are trusted to function under battlefield conditions there is far less need to construct an extensive buried cable system, but prudent planners would have insisted on a minimal cable system for backup communications. A much reduced buried cable system would have been constructed at the cost of far fewer casualties under these extreme conditions. The labor needed to construct a minimal cable system would have been considerably less and could have been allocated to other tasks, avoiding the casualties sustained in cable laying and maintenance. Another benefit is that the planning for the assault would not be tied to the cable system. Reinforcements could have been allocated where the need was greatest, not where the cable system provided communications. The radios allow communications to all units not only prior to the assault but during it. Radios allow commanders to adapt to conditions dynamically and to be in control of the battle after the troops have gone over the top. The radios allow adjacent units to cooperate with each other, report up the chain of command, receive orders and call in artillery.

In the case of the Flanders assault, on 31 August, once the troops have gone over the top the formidable defenses are immediately apparent. Most of the well protected pillboxes have survived the moving barrage and their interlocking fields of fire prevent forward moment. Using their radios the attacking infantry and tanks report the intact defenses to higher headquarters. Higher headquarters notifies artillery to halt the barrage and bring it back to engage targets identified by the infantry. The infantry and tanks pull back and direct the artillery to fire on each pillbox until it is demolished. The process continues, the infantry moving forward as each defensive obstacle is destroyed. Higher headquarters is informed of the progress of the attack and can direct reinforcements were they will do the most good or halt the attack on the part of the defensive belt that temporarily appears too strong. The attack moves inexorably forward.

Alarmed at the attack's progress the Germans elect to commit their counterattack divisions. They are ordered out of their protected bunkers and sent forward. This new movement is quickly noticed, perhaps by aircraft, and headquarters is informed. The British infantry and tanks are notified and halt to dig in as best they can to await the attack. The British artillery is told to cease engaging pillboxes and to be prepared to engage the counterattack divisions. The counterattack divisions are caught in the open and suffer devastating casualties. The counterattack fails and the British resume their methodical advance. Then it starts to rain. Having enjoyed considerable success so far, the British are undeterred. They continue to move forward until they have managed to overrun the Gheluvelt Plateau, if not on 31 July, then a few days thereafter.

What happens after this is problematical. Since Gough has taken the Plateau, there is no need to relieve him and the tactics used on 31 July appear to be successful. Energized by this victory on the heels of Messines, it is likely that Haig continues the offensive despite the rain. He continues the assault on Passchendaele Ridge. He does so with far better communications. While the enemy artillery makes cable laying impossible, radios provide continuous communications. There is no need to use power buzzers, pigeons or runners. Wireless telegraphy is not used, being far less useful than wireless voice communications. Further cable laying on the Pilkem Ridge is not needed and does not incur heavy casualties.

But, while the radiotelephone has facilitated a major victory, it cannot change the weather. The battlefield becomes increasingly sodden, tanks can't move, artillery shells don't explode in the mud, heavy guns sink below their wheels and infantry drown in shell holes.

If, by using his improved communications, Haig clears the Gheluvelt Plateau and Passchendaele Ridge earlier than he actually did, perhaps he even reaches the rail junction of Roulers, triggering the amphibious attack by the navy and clearing the Flemish Coast. But the above battlefield conditions argue strongly against this optimistic outcome. Even though the British Army is fighting much more efficiently, movement on the battlefield probably has slowed to a crawl. Inability to move artillery and tanks forward to support the infantry properly nullifies the benefits of a combined arms attack. Eventually Haig will be forced to bring the offensive to an end, well short of its ambitious objective, just as he actually did in 1917.

Cambrai

The concept and execution of the 20 November 1917 Cambrai attack was presented in chapter 7. Although the attack was initially successful and considerable ground was gained, the German counterattack regained the lost ground and the engagement ended in a draw.[13] The counterfactual assumes that the second-generation radios available in Flanders in August 1917 would also have been available for this attack. These radios would automatically have provided communications for tanks and would have provided BEF with communications which were invulnerable to damage by tank tracks. The radios would also have provided the communications needed for an advance of unusual speed and depth. The 3 to 5 mile ranges needed for communications in this situation would have presented no difficulties for the radios. The same radios would have met the needs of the reserve units and other formations moving into the frontlines prior to the attack, perhaps supplemented by minimal buried cable. The radios would also have supported cavalry units, being easily transportable by horses or horse-drawn wagons. The labor needed to supply radio communications would have been far less than that needed to lay 13,000 miles of armored cable.

As described in the preceding chapter the armored cable chosen to supply communications failed disastrously when tanks rolled over it. Poor liaison between the tank formations and the Signal Service prevented the tanks from keeping to their prescribed routes and avoiding the cables. As a result communications were lost when most needed. None of this would have happened if the second-generation radios already used in Flanders had been the primary means of communication not only for the tanks but also for the infantry and the artillery supporting the attack. The success of the limited wireless telegraphy sets actually available to the attack demonstrate what could have been accomplished if the much more capable wireless telephone had been used. The need for visual communications, dispatch riders, runners and pigeons would have disappeared.

The German counterattack began on 30 November.[14] It fell upon a British Army which had virtually lost what little communications it had from the bombardment that preceded the attack. This would not have been true if it had relied on radios. The defense could have been coordinated and managed by the commanders; artillery would have been brought to bear on the counterattack spearheads; infantry units holding their ground would have been reinforced; tanks would have been concentrated and sent where they could have done the most good. The counterattack could have been stalled or stopped.

As previously described, a single undamaged armored cable provided communications for three divisions. Once the urgency of the situation had been conveyed down it, a counterattack by the Guards Division successfully blunted part of the German attack.[15] Had more communications survived through the use of radios, other counterattacks up and down the line could have been organized and the German attack halted.

This is not to argue that the second-generation radios would have facilitated a breakthrough of the German line at Cambrai. Tanks by themselves did not change the dynamic of warfare in 1917. A breakthrough was not possible on the Western Front and the cavalry would not have been unleashed. In addition, other factors, such as the limited range of the tanks, their tendency to break down and their vulnerability to direct fire from field guns prevented them from leading a 1940s type of breakthrough. Improved tanks, careful training in radio coordinated tank tactics and radio communication with aircraft lay in the future. They were the key to the blitzkrieg, as envisioned by Guderian in the 1920s. (It is noteworthy that Guderian was himself a communication specialist.)

It is fair, however, to state that the Cambrai battle would have had a much more favorable outcome for the British if the Army had been equipped with second-generation radiotelephones. The initial assault would have been at least as successful as it was if the communications had been better. The German counterattack, on the other hand, would have challenged a British force which had not lost its communications and was able to coordinate a successful defense relying on mutually supporting tanks and infantry and well directed artillery. It's not unreasonable to say that little of the ground gained in the first few days of the Cambrai offensive would have been lost to the German counterattack.

CHAPTER 9

Operational Signals in 1918

Retreat — The German
Offensive of March 1918

The opening of 1918 found the British Army holding the line reflecting its territorial gains of 1917. It awaited an anticipated German attack, which appeared the inevitable and logical outcome of the collapse of Russia, and the consequent transfer of large numbers of German divisions from the Eastern to the Western Front.

As a result, the British Army could not contemplate an offensive of its own, on any significant scale, while a German attack was imminent. Consequently, the first three months of 1918 were used to consolidate the defensive system on its entire front, which now included a further 28 miles taken over recently from the French.

Overall, the position of the British Army was far from satisfactory. It had sustained heavy losses of personnel during 1917 and now had to maintain its position on an extended front. The southern portion was the most precarious with divisions widely spread. The current difficulties impacted as severely on the Signal Service as on any other branch of the Army. Paradoxically, the recent successes of the 1917 battles had carried formations well forward of the safe buried cable systems, particularly to the west of the Somme area. Consequently, in the event of a retreat, following the anticipated German offensive, the British Army would have to traverse the shell-blasted battlefields of 1916 and 1917. This would create huge difficulties for the Signal Service that would have to provide and maintain communications under virtually impossible conditions. The area would be subject, also, to intense enemy artillery fire.

Consequently, the immediate task in this area, requiring huge effort, was to improve the communications network. To do so, the Signal Service had to compete with other branches of the Army requiring the scarce personnel resources available to provide working parties. The improvement and building of new defenses was, for example, another very pressing requirement. The Signal Service was restricted, still further, by an acute shortage of cable. This was required in its efforts to improve communications. In fact, in buried form, this had reached only brigade HQs, in the majority of cases, by the date of the German offensive on 21 March 1918. In many instances, ahead of brigade HQs, cable was either poled or laid over ground. Even between brigade and divisional HQs, which previously had reliable buried cable routes, systems now comprised a mixture of less satisfactory substitutes.

Based on previous experience the Signal Service could now predict accurately that when the inevitable attack came communications would be badly disrupted. In the event, because of the intensity of the German barrage, the devastating effect on communications was infinitely worse than expected. It was abundantly clear that heavier reliance than hitherto would have to be placed on alternative means of communication.

Effectively, this involved visual systems, runners and wireless chains in all divisional sectors, subject to the limitation imposed by numbers of trained personnel and equipment. The buried cable system remained far from complete and the overall situation was made more difficult by atrocious weather.

The result was that, in the areas farthest forward, a reasonably thorough communications system comprising visual means, runners, wireless and limited telephone was established. Behind this, in supporting defense lines however, an inadequate communications system existed in the very area where the British Army, if hard pressed in retreat, would need to make its stand. The overall consequence was that an incomplete and inadequate defensive communications system, for the predicted attack, was available to the British Army when the German Army opened its bombardment on 21 March 1918.

On the British Army's front from Arras to its southern limits on the Oise, the enemy artillery fire was of an unprecedented ferocity, including gas shells.[1] An area of up to 15,000 yards behind the British Army's front line was shelled. HQs, artillery batteries and strong points, previously registered by the enemy, were targeted, decimating the precarious signals arrangements. Many forward unprotected cable routes and wireless chains were completely destroyed. The alternative visual means of communication available were entirely ineffective in the fog and mist, made worse by the bombardment. Owing to the incompleteness of the communications system, many infantry units were completely surrounded and unable to call for assistance. In the face of the enemy onslaught, the British Third and Fifth armies were pushed back to their final defensive positions in front of Amiens and behind the Somme area.[2]

For the Signal Service the retreat, in the face of the German Army's attack, had two distinct phases. Signals practice and organization reflected this. Phase I involved communications during the initial fighting by the British Army from prepared positions. Phase II was the hurried retreat by the Army, with many pauses and rearguard actions, before the final defensive positions were taken up. Both created huge difficulties for the Signal Service and are dealt with in the following section of the book by particular reference to Priestley.[3]

Phase I was influenced by a number of important considerations. Signals practice differed markedly on the front to the south of Arras compared with that in front of Arras and to the north. The British line in front of Arras was subjected to heavy bombardment but not attacked immediately. Only when the German Army had successfully attacked and consolidated its position farther south were divisions switched to the north. Communications in and around Arras were, in any case, less difficult overall. The area had not been so badly affected by the British Army's advances of the summer and autumn of 1917, and not at all by the German retreat of March 1917. It was served by a relatively secure communications system, including buried cable routes. During the March 1918 attack, Arras became the focal point. However, as the attack faltered and eventually failed, the position returned, in almost every way, to providing communications for static warfare conditions, where Signal Service experience in 1917 paid dividends.

To the south of Arras, communications were infinitely more difficult. The opening of the German offensive resulted in the almost complete destruction of divisional and brigade communications systems. There was also some disruption at corps level. As the German attack developed, cable systems, personnel and equipment were captured, with little opportunity to disable communications to prevent use by the enemy. The fallback provided by alternative means of communication, though limited, was still of great value. While visual means remained impossible because of dense fog,[4] power buzzer-amplifiers and wireless became the mainstay of the communications system. Indeed, until late evening on 21 March 1918, many units, even though surrounded by the enemy, had been able to maintain vital contact by wireless. As a consequence, valuable situation reports were passed to superior commanders. As important, the boost to morale within units from the knowledge that they were not completely isolated encouraged stubborn resistance, which helped to stem the German advance.

The incalculable value of the flexibility which wireless provided was demonstrated later, on a much grander scale, in the mobile warfare of the final days of the war. Wireless also proved its value to the rear where, eventually, it became the only reliable method of communication with the destruction of cable routes and the ineffectiveness of other means, in the early hours of the offensive. Visual means of communication were used briefly, later, on 21 March as the fog of battle partially cleared, though many forward stations had been destroyed by enemy shelling. The best results were achieved using Lucas lamps. Runners were little used because the battle conditions made their employment virtually impossible. However, DRs continued to operate heroically between brigade and divisional HQs under extreme conditions, recalling the fine traditions that they had established in 1914. The Pigeon Service had been completely disorganized by the severity of the German attack. As the British Army retreat accelerated in depth, birds became entirely disoriented. Lofts had to be moved or were destroyed by enemy fire or fell into enemy hands.

The aftermath of Phase I was that, in places, the depth of the retreat was up to 25 miles. The conditions under which divisions had survived the initial enemy attack were varied. As examples, one division established 5 HQs within 5 miles over 6 days while another had 14 HQs within 16 miles over 3 days! In every case signals organization was highly fragmented and depended almost entirely on the speed and depth of the retreat.

The two main characteristics of Phase I had been insufficient preparation by the British Army and overwhelming artillery fire, coupled with intensive fighting from well prepared positions by the German Army. In these circumstances, the Signal Service was not able to provide anything more than a fragmented and skeleton communications system. This was achieved only as the result of the heroic efforts of all who came under its command.

Phase II, however, posed different challenges for both the General Staff and the Signal Service. Its main characteristic was a rapid retreat under comparatively light enemy artillery fire with occasional pauses for rearguard actions of fierce intensity. The overall effect of the retreat was to reduce morale among all ranks. This was exacerbated by a general lack of coordination between artillery and infantry, because of poor or nonexistent communications.

The difficulties for the Signal Service were immense. The number of times that HQs, from battalion rearwards, moved locations provided serious problems for the Signal Service. It was not able to provide anything approaching an effective communications system. While some movement was inevitable in a hurried retreat it could certainly have been reduced by more coordinated and detailed planning by staff officers, from corps level forward. The result was that, at corps level, HQs often moved twice in one day. From division forward, moves were even more frequent which, in many cases, could have been avoided. There was also some confusion as to the general line of the retreat. As a result, the main communications route was often exposed to damaging enemy fire from the flank, which its location had been designed to avoid. The provision of lateral communications from the main route also posed an additional difficulty in a hurried and unplanned retreat. In fact, lateral intelligence was often more important than that from front to rear, but was rarely available.

There is no doubt, however, that had the Signal Service been provided with clearer instructions, it could have improvised a more effective lateral communications system. The congestion on roads, caused by retreating transport and personnel and advancing transport with supplies caused further, almost insurmountable, obstacles. The movement of signals equipment over the devastated countryside of the Somme area generally, over which much of the retreat took place, made cross-country journeys virtually impossible. An example from Priestley illustrates an almost incredible paradox. An enemy plane bombed a road and cleared it of traffic, allowing cable detachments to progress forward; this was regarded by its commander as an *unmixed blessing* [emphasis added by authors].[5] Finally, shortages of supplies and equipment created huge problems for the Signal Service, particularly as the armies fell behind the positions that they had occupied in previous battles. Cable dumps were few and far between and the greatest economy in the use of cable was necessary. Certainly, line communication during this period was never attempted forward of battalion and only by about half the formations forward of brigade.

The principal lesson learned by the Signal Service during the German offensive was that the rules established in S.S. 191[6] were equally valid in both retreat and advance. On this occasion they determined that the general direction of the retreat should be controlled by the highest formation actively involved in it. The movement of HQ locations should be decided upon as early as possible and advised to all superior, subordinate and lateral formations as quickly as possible. Additionally, divisions, brigades and battalions should be located, as far as possible, on one main corps communications route or, at worst, one main divisional route. It was clear that effective liaison between infantry and artillery HQs was critical and of prime importance. They had to be within easy reach by physical contact to ensure that communications remained unbroken.

For a full appreciation of the effects of a retreat on communications generally, it is important to understand the ways in which it affected individual methods. First in importance was the cable system. This had to be substantially modified to accommodate the semi-mobile circumstances of the retreat. The degree of success achieved in supplying line communication was heavily influenced by the extent to which existing routes could be utilized, and the availability of supplies. In the event, by far the greatest proportion of the main line system was made up of improvised circuits or ground cable. Within 10 miles of the front, much of the permanent line system had been destroyed. Beyond this distance less damage had been done. The enemy had not been able to move guns forward quickly enough to exploit the situation. Major problems were caused where corps records of line systems were destroyed, lost or incomplete. This substantially increased the difficulties for corps commanders. Their responsibilities, which could include providing line communications for up to 13 infantry divisions, 7 artillery divisions and 5 brigade artillery formations, were immense. The circumstances in which personnel were hard pressed in retreat and supplies critically short made this virtually impossible.

Cable communication remained, by far, the preferred method between divisions and brigades. However, a combination of quick and unexpected moves of HQs, together with poor staff work, resulted in long interruptions to line communication. When combined with a critically short supply of cable and, on occasions, its reckless use, the difficulties of providing anything approaching an adequate system were insurmountable. Experience illustrated that it was certainly not advisable to construct or reconstruct cable routes if a further move was expected within 24 hours. Damage to line communication from the passage of tanks could be catastrophic. Other mechanized and human traffic also caused significant disruption. The situation was aggravated still further by an almost total lack of liaison between all forms of traffic and the Signals Service. Consequently, specially constructed crossing points, particularly for tanks, were often ignored or their whereabouts inadequately communicated. Telephone, nonetheless, predominated as the preferred method of communication, front to rear. This demonstrated the habitual reliance on the telephone by staff officers that had developed, replacing their original deep mistrust of this method. The overall lesson which emerged was that, for an effective line system in retreat, the requirement was for a grid of ground cable laid by corps signal units along a carefully thought out route. This could then be taken over by divisions, falling back in an orderly manner, by pre-arranged stages to agreed HQ locations. Telephone conversation had to be reduced to a minimum, using concise and carefully worded messages. In the event, a skeleton system, at least, was provided despite shelling and traffic.

An example of the success of this policy is well illustrated by Priestley.[7] In one division, signals contact was maintained for 3 days by ground cable to each battalion in the line. Five minutes before retreat was considered inevitable, orders were given to all battalion commanders, by telephone, to disconnect the line and remove signals equipment. The division then retreated using, temporarily, DRs and runners for essential communication. On arrival in new positions, the line system was re-established and eventually replaced by buried cable as the situation became more static.

In the overall performance of those involved in providing cable communications during this period, Priestley considers that no department of the Signal Service did better work in those critical days than the cable sections.[8] None justified to a greater extent the training in mobile warfare that had been carried out.

Despite the courageous efforts of the cable sections, however, the line system was, at best, intermittent in performance. In these circumstances, wireless communication proved an even more valuable backup than ever before. Nonetheless, its performance was subject to some difficulties and limitations. Its usefulness was limited by two predominant factors. The first was jamming from both British Army and enemy wireless sets; the second was the necessity of using cipher and code during transmission. Enemy jamming could not be controlled, particularly as wireless appeared to be a prominent feature in the enemy's entire system for forward work. British Army accidental jamming could be partially alleviated by stricter internal controls. Cipher and code were, by definition, restrictive but where wireless worked well, despite these limitations, it proved of the greatest value. In any event, cipher and code was entirely disregarded in anything approaching mobile warfare. Where it was pedantically insisted upon, the effectiveness of wireless was much reduced. An added difficulty was the lack of familiarity with wireless systems. Their effective use required improvements in procedure and additional training for signals personnel. On occasions this was made difficult, yet again, when signallers were being misused as infantry.

Overall, however, wireless was recognized for the first time as an absolutely essential means of communication, illustrated by Priestley,[9] and confirmed in Rawlinson's papers.[10]

> Soon after midnight on the first day of the offensive, 5th Army in retreat lost communication by wire but re-established it by wireless and on one occasion, at least, a German concentration was broken up by interception of their orders by a British Army wireless station in their area and artillery alerted.

In summary, wireless had justified its use to the full. It had emerged from the retreat with an entirely different perception by the General Staff who would in future consider it essential in mobile warfare.

It is necessary, finally, to consider the other means of communication used during the retreat. Visual was used briefly during the first two days of the German offensive. Indeed, in forward battalion HQs, together with DRs and runners, it was the only means available. It was also used for communication to the rear to brigades. In the confusion of retreat it was particularly useful where it could be improvised to provide ad hoc communications alongside wireless. Lucas lamps, flags and bayonet shutters were all used to good effect. Priestley provides a useful illustration.[11] At one stage in one division, visual was the only means of communication available between brigade and division for the first 3 days of the offensive dealing with 50 messages per day. Visual was, nonetheless an exceptional means of communication rather than the rule, implying the failure of other means of communication and, certainly, the line system. Once again, DRs emerged as an important means of communication during the retreat where, under heavy fire, they located units using considerable initiative. They also completed valuable reconnaissance work, with little rest. Pigeons were very little used.

There were two major lessons learned from the retreat that were to prove of vital importance in the final stages of the war. The first was the value of one main chain of communication forward. This made optimum use of limited signals personnel and equipment and enabled the route to be planned in advance of the retreat. The subsequent transition to retreat in mobile warfare could then be carried out using the best signal system available. To achieve maximum success, the one main line concept needed to be carried through to brigade, division and corps. The axiom of the day was *one formation, one signal route* [author's emphasis]. The second lesson learned was the importance of conserving stores and equipment in the retreat. Even then, some losses were inevitable as they were destroyed, to prevent use by the enemy, by the last unit passing through. Still more were destroyed by both British Army and enemy artillery fire.

On 5 April 1918 the German offensive on the Somme front ended. Troops on both sides were exhausted, and the scene of the action moved north again.

On 9 April there was an intense bombardment along the front from Lens to Armentières followed by an enemy attack, using 42 divisions. Advances of up to 10 miles were achieved. However, it was not able to consolidate the position and the offensive came to a close.

For the Signal Service all units were in need of urgent rest to enable a complete refit to take place. Partially trained reinforcements also had to be absorbed as well as many signals personnel who had again been used as infantry during the recent conflict.[12] Indeed, they had been used in the firing line to an unparalleled extent despite general acceptance that the technical value of a signaller was his greatest asset. Signalers did not have rifle or bayonet training and their use as infantry was seldom justified.

During the retreat, however, the policy of concentrating on training for mobile warfare was justified. This was made clear by the results achieved by the Signal Service in adapting a rigid system to the mobile conditions of a retreat. It was a triumph for forward signals policy and organization and a tribute to the devotion to duty of its personnel to which the official dispatch pays tribute.[13]

> During the long periods of active fighting the strain placed upon the Signal Service was immense. The frequent changes of headquarters and the shifting of the line entailed constant labor, frequently attended by great danger, in the maintenance of communications; while the exigencies of the battle on more than one occasion brought the personnel of signal units into the firing line. The Signal Service met the calls made upon it in a manner wholly admirable, and the efficient performance of its duties were of incalculable value.

Summer 1918

The retreat finally ended on both the northern and southern fronts, held by the British, on 24 April 1918. The Army had lost most of its gains, particularly in the Somme area, of 1916. However, while the German Army had inflicted huge reverses on the Allies generally, it had not achieved either of its primary objectives. The capture of Arras and a drive through to the sea in the north or the capture of Amiens and the dissection of the British and French armies to the south had not been accomplished.

The British Army was exhausted, though it retained a surprisingly strong morale. For the Signal Service a period of re-grouping was essential. Some re-organization was required urgently before it would be sufficiently prepared for any forthcoming offensive, particularly on the scale that transpired in the autumn of 1918. The way in which this took place forms the basis of this section of the book.

In many respects, the ways in which the Signal Service developed during this period of the war were very similar to those that prevailed during previous periods of, mainly, static warfare. There were, however, a number of fundamental changes that needed to be made, based on the hard lessons learned during the earlier retreat. The new order was for signal systems to be established for defense in depth. As a result, communications to the rear, which were now more vulnerable to enemy artillery fire and required greater flexibility in any prospective war of movement, were carefully planned to meet these contingencies. In addition, forward signals personnel needed to be better informed of all routes to the rear. It was of particular importance that they were entirely clear on their fallback arrangements and positions in the event of a withdrawal.

A further requirement was for buried cable to be extended farther to the rear, well behind divisional HQs. Based on the experience of the recent retreat, this had been conclusively demonstrated. Poled or ground lines, anywhere forward of corps HQs, could not survive the fierce bombardment that could be expected to precede or accompany any major offensive by the enemy. As the new defensive communications system developed, and the threats from enemy shelling increased, the buried cable system was extended, gradually, as far back as GHQ. The overall objective of the new signal system was to provide buried cable from behind the forward trenches and all important observation posts, through to the rear. This would ensure that future defensive operations were not jeopardized by the lack of adequate communications.

At this early stage, following the retreat, materials to provide buried cable facilities were in short supply. Paradoxically, the necessity of having to manage with a skeleton system during the recent retreat had accustomed those involved to reducing telephone conversation to the minimum, when it was available at all. A salutary lesson was provided for the later, increasingly mobile, phase of the war.

The exceptions to the general rule of adapting well to scarce signals resources were the officers from divisions, brigades and battalions who had not been actively involved during the German spring offensive. They experienced considerable difficulty in accepting reduced facilities. However, it was essential for them to do so, having regard to the way in which the war developed in the autumn of 1918.

So far as the new buried lines were concerned — now the backbone of the communications system — many of the demands made on those involved were similar to those of the static warfare of 1917. A new and critical requirement was for much greater camouflage to avoid the enemy's much enhanced observation capability. This required the use of large parties of infantry to work alongside signals personnel. Barely adequate numbers of troops in the line and in reserve could be spared. Those in rest had to be employed. The work was intensely unpopular. Troops in rest often had long and difficult marches across devastated areas to the site of their work. Furthermore, their allotted tasks could take long periods to complete. Worst of all, they worked in, almost always, unpleasant and dangerous conditions, which their rest periods had been intended to alleviate.

In these circumstances it is not surprising that they had neither interest in nor enthusiasm for the work. Nonetheless, it was vital and had to be completed supremely well, if the communications system was to work effectively.

The Signal Service officers involved who, individually, had some empathy with the infantry's lack of enthusiasm, had to achieve their objectives. This was especially difficult if the troops involved were exhausted even before the work began. They would not be capable of completing their work effectively, particularly as it had, mostly, to be carried out at night to avoid enemy detection, before its obvious presence attracted enemy artillery fire. Efficient and innovative signals officers devised methods of dealing with this potentially impossible situation. Specific and realistic targets were set for infantry working parties with the guarantee of release and return to rest on completion of their allotted task. The result was usually intense and self supervised work. Emphasis was also placed on the importance of the work by emphasizing its future benefit to infantry. For example, its use in providing artillery support. However, the men involved were much more likely to draw inspiration from its value in ensuring better provision of rations and reliefs! The task, therefore, became a necessary evil rather than a mere imposition.

The overall result, in the best circumstances, was intelligent co-operation between the infantry and the Signal Service. Two examples illustrate the differences between the attitudes — and, no doubt, the results achieved — of those merely operating under military discipline compared with those who could envisage the way in which their work would be of real value.

The first relates to the comments of a disgruntled infantryman within the hearing of Royal Engineers (REs) signals personnel: "If I were digging graves for REs mate, I'd be happy!" The second, by comparison, from a Sherwood Forester digging in unpleasant wet conditions under enemy artillery fire on Mount Kemmel, at least reflects philosophical acceptance: "Well Bill, in six days God made the earth. On the seventh day he made the bloody Notts and Derbys to dig the whole bloody lot up again!"[14]

In this way, buried lines again formed the mainstay of the communications network, though in a more skeletal form than they had been during previous static warfare periods. They were able to accommodate the majority of signals traffic during the preparation for the British Army's decisive autumn offensive. The buried cable system remained crucial to maintaining communications during periods of static warfare. However, because of its limited availability, alternative means, principally wireless and visual, were developed though both were handicapped by the loss of essential equipment during the spring retreat. The result was that a chain of visual and wireless stations that had been a developing feature of static warfare during 1917 appeared again, though on a reduced scale. As with the telephone system, shortages of equipment dictated a more innovative approach by the Signal Service. This applied equally to the sitting of visual stations and the extraction of maximum benefit from wireless by optimizing its range. It was made more difficult, but even more essential, by the British Army's adoption of a policy of greater defense in depth with a proliferation of communications front to rear.

In the main, the means of communication available to the Signal Service remained unchanged. The most important exception was wireless, which continued its now vital development, given considerable impetus by the Director of Army Signals.[15] Wireless, for example, because of its greater flexibility was beginning to replace the more cumbersome and restricted power buzzer-amplifier sets. This was particularly the case between Observation Posts (OPs) and battery HQs and between battery HQs and brigade HQs. It was a great advantage to forward artillery units to have a system of wireless communication that was common to both artillery and infantry. However, the major restriction on the use of wireless, which continued through to the conclusion of the war, was shortage of sets. This prevented its full exploitation when, the book goes on to argue, it could have been the ideal method of communication at this time and, indeed, at a much earlier stage in the war.

Both wireless and visual had fully demonstrated their usefulness as alternative means of communication during the spring retreat. Incredibly, the lack of flexibility by staff officers to make use of them at that time dictated now, instead, the imposition of *silent days* [authors' emphasis] when the use of telephone was forbidden. Alternative means *had* to be used. The tendency to store up messages, until the ban was lifted, resulted in congestion on the telephone system later. However, the overall effect was good in proving to officers at all levels that telephone, though speedy and convenient, was not essential. The vitally important sequel was that, in the autumn advance when alternative means of communication to cable had to be relied upon almost entirely, the British Army had received at least some preparation and training.

Against this background, it is appropriate to summarize the main signals organizational developments that characterized this short period of static warfare in 1918. Their important and immediate impact on the British Army's state of readiness, in terms of signal communications, for the forthcoming autumn offensive was of the greatest value.

Staff officers had become accustomed to dealing with communications in relatively static conditions over a period of more than 3 years. Consequently, the slender system now available was familiar to them and at least adequate for their requirements. In any event, any shortcomings were entirely clear to the Signal Service, which was able, on most occasions, to overcome these. This was made much easier by the now excellent relationships and cooperation that existed throughout the Army between the Signal Service and its principal users. It must be regarded as a real tribute to the hard and dedicated work of the Signal Service.

Nonetheless, divisional signal companies now had actual or tacit responsibility for the provision of forward communications right up to and including the front line. They were well below minimum requirements, in relation to both numbers and expertise, to fulfill their now massive commitment. It demanded an adequate communications systems to cover both the existing period of static warfare and to prepare for the now inevitable offensive to follow. This was the case even though battalions had lost, either as casualties or prisoners, some of their best and most experienced signallers during the recent retreat.

But specialized means of communication, with the relative complexity of wireless, the demand for which was increasing massively, required full time training for operators. It could be completed properly only during rest periods and for limited numbers of signallers. In addition, wireless stations were now needed as far forward as battalion HQs. This required a forward extension of technical qualifications towards the front line, which was eventually achieved as a result of the continuing trend for the Signal Service to take over more and more responsibility from infantry battalions in the training and control of their signals personnel. The result was a move towards specialization, well illustrated by Priestley.[16] Specialization completely reversed the 1917 tendency towards multiply qualified forward signals personnel. The massive increase in the scale of the war dictated that it became essential in all but the most forward of situations. It was impossible for signallers to be proficient in all techniques to the required levels that the new situation demanded.

The recent high casualty levels aggravated the situation still further as training times had to be reduced substantially for the scarce numbers of reinforcements. It could be completed only by limiting and concentrating the scope of the training. As a result, in the period following the German offensive, and for the remainder of the war, forward signalers were all trained in visual means of communication as a basic requirement. Thereafter, specialization according to their basic inherent skills and aptitude was the guiding principle. The least able were trained as pioneers. Large numbers became linesmen, for which ex–General Post Office (GPO) workers were ideally suited. Only a select few were selected as dispatch riders (DRs). The very best were chosen as wireless operators, which required intensive full time training. Experience showed that good results were achieved by providing recruits or reinforcements with training that matched their capabilities with the time available to complete it.

At a higher level there were two further important developments for the Signal Service during this period. The first was the creation of a Signal Service Department under the Director of Staff Duties at the War Office. It provided representation for, and great assistance to, the Director of Army Signals in the coordination of signal facilities. This applied to signals personnel, equipment and training across the whole of the BEF. The second was the involvement of the Signal Service in the training of newly arrived U.S. Army recruits. The opportunity was taken to use technical skills from civilian life to good advantage, after adjustment to specialized British equipment. The result was that U.S. troops selected for signals duties were well trained, based on the acknowledged achievements and experience of the British Army Signal Service.

The Signal Service, in line with the whole of the British Army, was now poised for the final offensive that eventually ended the war. All possible measures had been taken to counteract the effects of constant bombardment and raids by the enemy. Careful thought was given to the choice of cable routes and their protection. Together with effective maintenance, it minimized the damage sustained and consequent breakdowns in communications. This was achieved in the face of the enemy's growing anticipation of an Allied offensive that resulted in increased artillery fire at irregular intervals. The situation was further complicated by the inclusion of gas in the enemy bombardment, which required a constant state of readiness and added considerably to the difficulties of the Signal Service. Priestley provides a typical example of the situation in the area dominated by Mount Kemmel that was captured from the French by the enemy in May 1918.[17] Enemy observation was perfect so that daytime work was impossible. All burying and maintenance of cable routes had to be completed at night. Even so, lines were constantly shelled and received direct hits from 5.6- and 8-inch shells, so that repairs and maintenance were a constant factor.

Up to this point in the war, massive Signal Service effort was directed towards building a complete and wholly reliable communications system. However, the situation changed fundamentally from July 1918 onwards. Thereafter, the BEF, in cooperation with the French, gradually pushed the German Army back from its gains of previous months and a new offensive phase opened on 8 August. It continued until the Armistice on 11 November 1918. This phase posed entirely new and distinct challenges for the Signal Service, consideration of which forms the final section of this part of the book.

The Final Advance to Victory

The enemy's limited offensive faltered and then ground to a halt in the area surrounding Reims. Thereafter, the German Army was gradually pushed back from the final position it had established by June 1918.

The first and immediate problem for the Signal Service was to adapt the British Army XXII Corps communication system to that of the French

Army, to which this corps had been added. The French system was much more restricted in scope. It relied, almost entirely, on telephone from the front line to the rear, with occasional use of wireless as an alternative. The French Army made little use of lateral line communication that was fundamental to the relative success of the British system. As a result, lateral communication with French forces was established by the Signal Service using mainly telephone. An immediate difficulty was that of language which created problems for operators. These were overcome, to a degree, by the use of interpreters, although they were in short supply in both the British and French armies. In the event, while sufficient interpreters could be found to assist at corps level, from divisions forward the shortage of supply caused serious delays in communication.

A further immediate and urgent problem was the provision of sufficient cable to augment the French routes. This had been hurriedly constructed over rough country. Small amounts could be brought up fairly rapidly by rail, but much more was needed quickly. The ways in which this problem was gradually resolved will be illustrated later in this section of the book.

For the moment, with the German Army in retreat, it was reasonably possible to maintain a reliable line system as far forward as battalion and battery HQs. This was, however, very basic owing to the shortage of cable. The most usual system was a central brigade route to which battalions were added as spurs. Every effort was made to achieve effectiveness from the limited cable available, but absolute priority was given to communications between batteries and observation posts (OPs) that had a crucial role to play at this stage.

Despite strict cable economy, however, the British Army had virtually exhausted its limited supplies. It had to rely on small amounts borrowed from the French until the supply arrangements improved. A major lesson learned, at this late stage of the war, was that the supply of cable required the same priority as, for example, ammunition.

On 8 August 1918 the British Army began its new offensive. It was to be an intense period of activity for the Signal Service, from this date forward until the Armistice, which will form a final study in this section of the book.

During the final offensive, there were two distinct phases for the Signal Service with different problems in providing adequate communications. The first phase was that which preceded the forcing of the Hindenburg Line and its reserve positions at the end of September 1918. During this phase, in some cases, the enemy's position was established in a series of strongly built defensive areas; in others it relied on the protection provided by defensive systems built around machine guns and artillery, established in woods and villages. It could be dislodged only by a series of actions similar, in some ways, to those of the battles of 1917 but with a strong emphasis on the absolute necessity to preserve manpower. In the relatively short and infrequent interval between actions, the Signal Service had to provide communications suitable for semi-static warfare conditions in the face of a slow and methodical retreat by the German Army.

In the second phase, after the Hindenburg Line had been broken, the enemy's retreat was much more hurried, punctuated by pauses on stronger natural defensive lines such as canals and rivers. The British Army's advance was much more sustained and as it accelerated the enemy's retreat was more disorganized — to quote Priestley, "more of a rout than a calculated retirement."[18]

In the new mobile warfare, the major problem for the Signal Service was to provide adequate communications for the rapidly advancing British forces in the face of declining German resistance. The main difficulty was to adapt a massive and complex organization, which had been established at these levels during predominantly static and often defensive warfare, to the requirements of an almost fully mobile British Army.

Recognition of the serious problems involved and their solution is covered by an Official Dispatch, dated 7 January 1919.[19]

> The constant movement of the line and the shifting of headquarters has again imposed an enormous strain upon all ranks of the Signal Service. The depth of the advance, and the fact that during the latter part of it the whole of the British armies were simultaneously involved, made the maintenance of signal communication most difficult. The fact that in such circumstances the needs of the armies were met reflects the highest credit upon the zeal and efficiency of all ranks.

In some aspects the second phase of the offensive, after the end of September, had similarities with the more restricted advances made in 1917 but on a much greater scale. The lessons learned from the previous period could be incorporated, with some confidence, into the later and successful communications system, which had to take these into account. Fundamentally, and for the first time during the whole of the war apart from the early days of 1914, the area of forward movement by the British Army involved its entire fighting force as far back as GHQ. With the whole front affected, serious difficulties were inevitable in switching both personnel and equipment from other parts of the line to make up for local signals deficiencies.

However, the Signal Service had benefitted considerably from hard lessons derived from 1917 and early 1918. This enabled it to provide an adequate communications system, despite the scale and speed of the current offensive. Simplicity in construction and maintenance, the speed with which it was completed and its economy in the use of personnel and equipment were the distinguishing features of the system. In addition, the speed of the offensive required an advance GHQ to be established. This again called for an increase in the Signal Service workload that was felt, progressively, towards the front line. In general, a 24-hour period usually proved sufficient for the Signal Service to provide the minimum communications required by HQs at all levels. It was, however, strictly limited to what was absolutely necessary, with some limitations on the facilities available to subordinate units and commanders.

Fundamental to the success of providing adequate communications during this period was Signal Service recognition of the need to provide for as many different means of communication to be available as possible. They were essential for a now widely dispersed Army. The absolute keys to success were flexibility and speed of action. Delivering communication systems that met these requirements was immensely difficult in areas where the Army was advancing over devastated terrain. Both Signal Service construction companies and DRs were severely hindered by badly damaged roads and bridges. Lateral communications had to be neglected and priority given to main communication routes. With each pause in the British Army's advance, the telescoping of the armies, during temporary halts, created huge increases in traffic on communication systems. These were far greater than those experienced in similar situations in 1917. In one army alone, for example, 20,000 telephone calls were made during a 24 hour period.[20]

Despite pauses in the offensive however, the predominant feature was mobility from corps HQs forward. All divisional forward signals policy was controlled from corps during this final period of the war, in which its HQ might move forward as much as 20 miles at very short notice.

The fundamental requirement remained. Effective communications along one central main route in each corps through to the front line, had to be provided. It had to extend at least as far forward as battalion HQs. During mobile warfare, this was extremely challenging. One of the greatest difficulties was to persuade staff officers not to expect the level of communication facilities, particularly telephone, which had been available previously. This was certainly the case where those concerned had not been involved and gained recent experience of mobile warfare at, for example, Cambrai. In more general terms, it was difficult to effect a switch in operational thinking from the previously slow semi-mobile or static conditions.

However, as moves of HQs became more frequent, the Signal Service adjusted to the speed of the advance. It was able to provide the minimum required signal communications, now recognized as an absolutely key factor to success in mobile warfare. This method of operation was also entirely in line with the principles laid down in S.S. 191, with very little modification.[21] In summary, this endorsed the need for as many means of communication as possible with visual, runners and mounted orderlies being as important as the line system, in brigades and battalions. All means needed to be established rapidly, as near as possible to the leading troops, and their locations advised accurately to all concerned — delightfully simple in concept but highly complex in practice!

Among and underpinning changes in attitudes throughout the Army as a whole, the most significant for the Signal Service was the realization and acceptance by the General Staff that its policies and those of the Signal Service were entirely inter-dependent. Close co-operation between the two was vital. For the Signal Service, this was beyond doubt the most significant development, during the whole of the war to date, to enable it to fulfill its role effectively. The General Staff had now realized that a well-considered signals policy required careful forethought. This eliminated uncertainty in direction and any consequent duplication of communication routes. The immediate result was that, with limited personnel available for all signals duties across the whole of the British Army, scarce resources were not wasted in constructing unwanted routes. Changes to planned routes were now made only when absolutely essential, owing to unpredictable circumstances. It had already been amply demonstrated during the March retreat that when there was good Staff work at senior levels throughout the Army, and efficient control exercised, then adequate communications could be virtually guaranteed. In the absence of either of these key factors, chaos was the almost inevitable result. This lesson had been thoroughly learned and now put into practice.

The final key to success in maintaining sound communications in mobile warfare, as previously emphasized, was the establishment of main corps signals routes comprising all appropriate means. In relation to cable, spurs to divisions and, in turn, divisions to brigades and on to battalions were required. The overall result was to provide valuable savings in personnel, cable and maintenance. It was also relatively safer in construction than under previous and less satisfactory policies. Nonetheless, in establishing main routes, the work involved fell mainly on divisional signals personnel. It was not only highly dangerous but also particularly demanding. All types of cable had to be laid using natural features, for example, hedges, in constantly bombed and shelled areas. The work was carried out with gallantry and distinction to which the high number of awards to Signal Service personnel at this time pays tribute.[22] Moreover, their presence on the battlefield in such constantly hostile conditions earned enormous respect from the infantry whom they worked alongside. The speed of the advance also caused unique problems. Corps and divisional HQs were often 10 to 20 miles apart, using a mixture of somewhat ad hoc cable facilities that made speech over the telephone almost unintelligible over such long distances. The requirement in a rapid advance was for a greater number of lines to be completed over shorter distances as quickly as possible, completed by the most competent men from the construction companies. Although before the offensive carefully camouflaged permanent cable routes had been installed, this had involved the laying of, for example, 53,000 yards of poled line in a 16 day period by one corps alone.[23]

Shortages of cable required routes to take the shortest possible line over devastated countryside, which seriously aggravated the difficulty of the work involved. Congested roads over which signals stores were carried, and the difficulties caused by deliberate flooding of the battle area by the enemy, added to the general confusion. This was in addition to damage caused by mines placed at crossroads and other busy routes. The Signal Service was helped, however, by the enemy confining damage from artillery fire to main roads only, which were targeted by map reference. Routes avoiding these were generally safe. Finally, as the advance proceeded, attempts were made to use lines abandoned by the enemy, but these were of only limited use as they were in a very mixed state of repair.

Overall, good organization was the key to establishing the main forward routes. Rapid reconnaissance was carried out by signals officers on motorcycles, who were assisted by fine weather. Airplanes were also used to good effect. They were able to report back on the current communication requirements, not only in the areas held by the British Army's forward troops but also, for future reference, those of the enemy's rear guard. The information that they provided was found correct in almost every detail.

The main corps communication route, now established in the prevailing circumstances as the *sine qua non* of forward signals, was more and more reinforced by a chain of wireless stations. Paradoxically, they were used mostly when corps were not advancing. The main wireless directing station was located at corps HQ, with advanced stations at advanced corps HQs that controlled all forward stations. In fact, the Canadian Corps, for example, relied entirely on wireless as an auxiliary system for surplus traffic that could not be transmitted down the main route. As an important ancillary benefit, the use of wireless in mobile warfare helped to consolidate relationships and improve liaison between divisional artillery and infantry signals.

Another new and developing role for wireless was its use by heavy artillery batteries, which could have been even greater if more sets had been available. This had the effect of completing an effective chain of communication involving all units in an advance, including the various support functions.

As a vital factor in the completion of effective forward communications, it was essential for corps signal units to anticipate the direction and speed of the communications route. This was needed well in advance so that it was at the disposal of staff officers and commanders immediately when it was required. Against this background, it is important to understand that the entire question of providing adequate forward signals for mobile warfare posed two problems with distinct solutions. Firstly, each advance, whether for short or longer periods, required a specific signals policy from corps level forward to the front line, to accommodate differing conditions. Secondly, each advance was followed by a period of intensive action similar to those that had been the predominant feature of 1917. On both 8 August and 29 September 1918 it was on a scale previously unsurpassed and considered later in the book.

The major difference between the actions mentioned above and those of 1917 was the relative strength of artillery used by both sides. It was in the approximate ratio of 10:1 in favor of the BEF. Apart from other considerations this was, in itself, a great morale booster not least for the Signal Service as well as the infantry and artillery involved. From the point of view of the Signal Service, it was a crucial factor in the survival of the ground and poled cable network which was the mainstay of the communications system as the advance progressed from 8 August 1918 onward, which is considered now.

On 8 August and later, in greater strength, in the same month, the

British Army attacked on the majority of its front from well-prepared defensive positions. This included an efficient and relatively safe buried cable system. However, the success and consequent speed of the attack rapidly carried corps and divisions away from the buried cable system. In fact, this effectively marked the end of buried cable for the remainder of the war.[24]

Thereafter, halts in the British Army's advance were of short duration. There was, therefore, insufficient time available to bury cable that, in any case, did not justify the use of valuable and scarce signals personnel.

However, although buried cable as an element of the forward signal system had disappeared, line remained the principal means of communication. The main threats to the line system, now above ground, came from the British Army's own forces in the form of tanks, other means of transport and the rapid and often careless movement of its own troops forward. Despite the rapidly changing circumstances, however, the single divisional route had now become, through force of circumstances, the strongly preferred option for the Signal Service for forward communications.

The main route was carried forward avoiding major roads and valleys. It was in these areas that the enemy was most likely to concentrate his artillery fire on suspected communications centers. Previous experience illustrated, beyond doubt, that the advance could not be properly coordinated without a fully operational command telephone system as far forward as battalion HQs. An effective liaison between artillery and infantry units was also of vital importance. While, in the circumstances, this demand could not be fully met, a reasonably high level of telephone communication was provided from corps HQs forward. Initially during the advance, with limited resources of both personnel and equipment and consequent congestion of telephone traffic, some operational efficiency was inevitably lost.

With, of necessity, the return to a slender but nonetheless effective system of signal communication essential for mobile warfare, operational control was re-established in the battles that followed. In this, two factors were of particular importance. The first was to establish a reserve unit of both personnel and equipment at divisional HQs. This could move forward immediately after an attack was successful along a route where preferred signals locations had been chosen, well in advance, through good reconnaissance. The second, as the advance proceeded, was for the communications route to be carried forward with divisional HQs; corps usually took over the existing divisional HQ system. It was important, in these circumstances, for the separate artillery signal system to be able to link into the main communications route, as it advanced. This required careful planning. It often required the pooling of infantry and artillery signals personnel and equipment to optimize their use in establishing the most effective forward communications system possible.

The way in which the main line was established varied, almost entirely, with the circumstances in which the advance was made. At this stage, the effect of the enemy's artillery was a negligible factor in choosing the site of the main communications route. The choice was influenced, much more, by the type of countryside to be crossed during the advance. If the countryside was predominantly open in character, then the route was established as poled or ground cable in ditches or by using existing German open cable trenches. In less open country, hedges were used. Where tanks were likely to operate, attempts were made, through never with complete success, to locate cable high enough to avoid damage by their passage.

There were three basic types of countryside to be crossed during the advance. The first was the devastated area of the Somme. This confined essential signals traffic, particularly cumbersome cable wagons, to already overcrowded roads, comparable to the circumstances of the spring retreat. The second was the more open countryside typified by the Cambrai area. While exposing cable to a wide variety of problems from the passage of personnel and equipment, it did allow cable wagons to move forward more easily. The third was the area of hedged countryside beyond the Sambre–Oise canal, where natural features could be used to install and protect cable.

While cable remained the backbone of the communications system in the advance, some damage was inevitable. Enemy shelling, though now negligible, still caused some line breakages. In addition, kite balloons passing along crowded roads inevitably caused lethal damage when their trailing wire hawsers demolished poled lines. Protective measures were virtually impossible, particularly as the personnel responsible had little regard for the damage in the face of their own more overriding problems. Tanks were also major offenders, particularly in mobile conditions, where effective liaison between them and the Signal Service was much more difficult.

Cavalry, as at Cambrai but now on a much larger scale, interfered with cable routes. Equally, divisional infantry transport, particularly in the open Cambrai area, used cable as a guideline for its forward progress, often ploughing up the line in the process. Perhaps most serious of all, infantry units caused serious disruption to communications by often willful cutting or complete destruction of routes with which they had no personal involvement. These were regular and often bizarre occurrences.[25]

Along the main route, from brigade HQs forward, the communication system was much more basic. It comprised light line laid by brigade signal sections to battalion HQs with visual signals and runners the sole available means farther forward. Although the line system was very basic, the installation work involved was extremely arduous, requiring large numbers of scarce personnel to complete.

The real key to ultimate success in providing reliable communications forward from brigade to battalion HQs was an adequate supply of cable. Fortunately, this had generally been well planned in advance to include the use of abandoned German lines where available. The overall consequence was that most divisions, during the final advance in September and October, had adequate supplies of cable but less than adequate numbers of personnel available for its installation and maintenance. As the result of the Herculean efforts of the Signal Service an at least adequate system was, nonetheless, provided.

However, despite every effort to maintain cable communications intact up to battalion HQs, when this inevitably failed the only real alternative — wireless — was of vital importance. Its operational use was now a major factor in corps and divisional communications, with additional forward stations allowing expansion of wireless communications along the whole of the main signals chain. With its increased and judicious use, wireless was now almost always available. This would be as an ancillary to line communication or as a complete alternative when the line, inevitably, lagged behind the rapid general advance.

Forward of brigade and battalion HQs the available sets could operate at distances of up to 4,000 yards and were of great value between battalion and company HQs and batteries and OPs. Nonetheless, a few divisions persisted with the use of visual signals and runners for forward communications, though on a much reduced basis. However, the days of the power buzzer-amplifier, as a poor substitute for wireless, were numbered if not completely past.

The consequence was that wireless now became an integral part of the divisional communications and up to 80 messages per day were being transmitted along a typical divisional chain. The extent of its use was very much influenced by the requirements for cipher and code. The almost universal rule during the mobile advance was for transmission to be in the clear. Where this rule was not applied, wireless traffic dropped significantly and the more secure and scarce Fullerphones were overloaded in consequence. It was now clearly demonstrated that one of the major obstacles to much greater use of wireless in the past had been the insistence on using cipher and code in all circumstances. This is a vital issue requiring operational consideration.

The insistence of the General Staff on the use of cipher and code related entirely to its fear of enemy overhearing. In fact, a balanced judgment had to be made, in circumstances of mobile warfare, compared with the previously more static conditions, where it had presented genuine problems and dangers. Transmission in the clear had distinct advantages of speed and greater acceptability while code and cipher prevented many of the dangers of useful interception by the enemy. Experience suggested strongly that regulation should have been delegated to the Signal Service. Those actively involved in wireless particularly could, with modest increases in personnel, make more effective, situation by situation, on the spot decisions.

The ranges over which the variety of wireless sets available could operate presented problems. Certainly, more powerful sets were required by corps and divisional HQs. They often had to operate with sets at the maximum limit of their range and, hence, efficiency. The growing number of continuous wave wireless sets becoming available provided the solution. They were also used with artillery for flash spotting of enemy fire that allowed retaliation with very good results. Indeed, many targets spotted in this way would not have been hit without the benefit of wireless. Experience demonstrated that the greater availability of wireless in the British Army was a significant factor in improving the accuracy of its artillery compared with that of the enemy, with less wireless facilities. However, the sets available to the artillery were heavy and cumbersome and liable to sustain considerable damage when transported over rough roads on unsprung vehicles.

Overall, wireless often provided the only reliable situation reports available to the General Staff.

During the summer of 1918, the enemy engaged in increased long distance bombing. The RFC used wireless during operations to combat this by providing sufficient warning of the approach of hostile aircraft for evasive action to be taken. Wireless also proved invaluable when used at rail junctions to handle and control traffic.

In assessing wireless generally, at this stage of the war, there is no doubt that it was being used more effectively. It was also being constantly improved and was certainly vindicated, in its more general application, during the last few months of the war. Jamming by the enemy could still be a serious problem forward of division. However, in the main, it had emerged as the most effective and flexible means of communication for mobile warfare.

Before finally completing the operational section of the book it is necessary to look, briefly, at the way in which other means of communication available performed at this late stage in the war. Pigeons and messenger dogs were still used very occasionally but in much reduced numbers. Signal rockets had been abandoned as a viable means of communication. DRs and mounted orderlies were still used in significant numbers though the early fogs of the autumn of 1918 made their task difficult and often impossible. Runners were as reliable, though as vulnerable as ever, for forward communications. Good results continued to be achieved by aircraft in signaling messages using, mainly, message-dropping zones that formed part of the divisional signals establishment. Visual, still the mainstay, with runners, of forward communications, continued to be much hampered by the mist and smoke of the advance. Its effectiveness was often reduced to such a degree, particularly in the early morning, that the entire Army had to guess its way forward gaining some directional indicator mainly from the trajectory of its own artillery! Nevertheless, if telephone lines and wireless were both out of action, visual means of communication were still valuable and, indeed, essential forward of battalion HQs. Lucas lamps were, by far, the most extensively used and effective form of visual communication.

By 11 November 1918 the Signal Service had adapted completely to the recent mobile warfare. Divisional and brigade signal units, which effectively controlled all forward signals, were operating at high pressure but with equally high morale, reflecting their performance over the past few months. The Signal Service had been successful in keeping the divisional communications system well ahead of the demands made by its brigades. When the advance to victory finally ended, the Signal Service was able, with the minimum of difficulty, to provide a telephone system capable of serving the entire British Army from the General Staff through to the front line. Of greatest value and significance, it now had available a much more comprehensive wireless network as an alternative.

CHAPTER 10

A Counterfactual — The German Spring Offensive and Hundred Days with Wireless Telephony

In 1918, in the counterfactual world, the British would have been two years beyond the prototype radiotelephone sets used at the Somme and would have reliable rugged second or third generation military radiotelephones capable of two-way communications. They would also have a trained cadre of communicators distributed throughout the BEF down to battalion and even company level. Having seen the benefit of reliable communications, commanders from the highest to the lowest level trust and depend on their communications network. By trial and error commanders have learned how to control operations, continue or discontinue an action and minimize casualties. They have solved technical problems relating to mutual interference between friendly sets by adopting a frequency plan across the Western Front which carefully allocates frequencies to competing users in such a way as to prevent geographically adjacent users from interfering with each other. They have dealt with the interception problem by stern exercise of communications discipline, confining the use of tactical radio to the transmission of information which the enemy cannot rapidly exploit and using more secure means of communication for the transmission of tactical and strategic plans that must be kept secret.

The German Spring Offensive

On 21 March 1918, when Russia was virtually out of the war, freeing up about a million German troops for service on the Western Front, the

Germans launched the Michael offensive, designed to split the British from the French and to back the British up against the English Channel.[1] The battle opened on a 40 mile front between the Sensee Canal and the Oise River. The offensive was primarily directed against the British Third and Fifth armies commanded by Gen. Sir Julian Byng and Gen. Sir Hubert Gough respectively. The offensive was only the third occasion during the war when the German Army attacked, the others being the initial offensive in 1914, and the Verdun offensive in 1916. The Germans had had ample opportunity during the war to observe the allies futilely attempting to accomplish a breakthrough of fixed defenses anchored by machine guns and defended by artillery. They had learned a great deal about what worked and what didn't, about sustaining an offensive over broken ground and about how to design an artillery barrage to facilitate a breakthrough.

By this time in the war front lines were no longer defended by a continuous line of infantry standing shoulder to shoulder in a deep trench. From bitter experience both sides knew that the artillery barrage accompanying the assault would decimate defending troops arranged in such density. Instead the forward zone of the British front was thinly held and consisted of mutually supporting outposts containing a platoon, or, more likely, a section, each of which contained one or more machine guns plus ample ammunition and bombs (grenades). Behind the outposts, but still in the forward zone, were redoubts, which were held in company strength but which were too far apart to provide mutually supporting fire to each other.[2] One to two miles behind the forward zone was the battle zone, containing additional redoubts and multiple batteries of 18 pounders, 4.5 inch howitzers and single anti-tank guns.[3]

The problem the Germans set themselves was how to penetrate not only the forward zone but also the battle zone in one bound, so they could continue the offensive in open, i.e., non-fortified, country. This very difficult problem had not been solved by the Allies. The forward zone defenses were designed to delay an attack long enough for reserves to move into the battle zone defenses which were then sufficiently strengthened to repel any attackers who had penetrated the forward zone. The Germans elected to do two things in order to solve this problem: first, to design an artillery barrage of sufficient intensity and variety to completely blind and neutralize the forward zone defenses and their supporting artillery[4]; second, to train the assault troops in new tactics, called infiltration, whereby the forward zone strongpoints were to be bypassed and the battle zone defenses assaulted as soon as possible before the defender could reinforce them.[5]

Bypassed strong points and redoubts were to be reduced by follow-up infantry units moving more slowly than the assault troops.

The artillery barrage was designed by Col. Georg Bruchmuller, a legendary figure of the First World War.[6] He had designed the artillery barrage used at Riga which was so successful that Ludendorff adopted it for this attack. There were two aspects of this barrage. In order to attack the enemy artillery Bruchmuller recommended the use of gas instead of high explosive. Gas left the ground intact and poisoned the area sufficiently to affect reserve gunners brought forward to replace casualties. Second, Bruchmuller favored the use of a short, intense bombardment of the front lines without pre-registering the guns. At this stage of the war sufficient data had been gathered regarding the influence of different types of ammunition, of meteorological conditions and of gun performance (including tube wear) that it was possible to predict the fall of shell without using trial shots. Trial shots warned the enemy that an attack was imminent, thus sacrificing surprise for a dubious increase in accuracy.

Infiltration tactics were not new. They had been used before in 1917 at Caporetto,[7] and in the German counterattack at Cambrai, where they had proved enormously successful. As discussed in his book *Infantry Attacks* Erwin Rommel and his fellow company commanders literally turned the flank of the entire Italian Second Army by successively attacking apparently secure Italian mountaintop positions from the rear.[8] Their success resulted in the worst defeat suffered by Italian arms since Cannae.[9] The successful demonstration of these tactics led Ludendorff to comb his Army for his most aggressive and resourceful soldiers and organize them into special assault troops called storm troopers. These would lead the Michael attack.

The initial stages of the attack went exactly as planned. The thinly held forward zone was devastated by the artillery barrage. In many cases the defenders could not see the attackers or visually communicate with each other because of a significant ground fog.[10] The survivors of the barrage were either taken prisoner or attempted to reach the redoubts in the forward and battle zones. The troops manning the redoubts were also surprised by the intensity of the artillery bombardment and by the speed of the attack, which left little time to call for reinforcements. Communications to these redoubts, which consisted of cable supported by poles or laid over ground, as described in the previous chapter, were immediately cut by the barrage and the redoubts were isolated. They could not contact brigade or division headquarters and thereby receive artillery support; they could not know the status of other redoubts, could not know if what they were observing was local to them or widespread across the front, and could not know whether to abandon their position or to keep on fighting because relief was on the way. To complicate their plight, the redoubts' ability to fire on their attackers was also limited by the ground fog. In other words the redoubts' defenders were in the worst possible position for troops in battle. Many of the redoubts surrendered, some without much of a fight.[11] Troops in other redoubts attempted to retreat through ground now controlled by the attackers and became casualties or were taken prisoner. Once the redoubts had been bypassed it was easy for the attackers to cut the remaining communications to them and to other strong points.

By the end of the day on March 21 the forward zone had been taken at all points.[12] The attack on the battle zone had mixed success: the Germans were through it for 18,000 yards of front; they had been held at the rear of it on 16,000 yards of front; they had been held within it for 19,000 yards of front; and they had been held at the front of it for 14,000 yards of front.[13] The Germans also captured about 500 guns. Although the Germans had not gained all the objectives planned for the first day of the offensive, the attack was a huge success by the standards of the Western Front. Following the events of the first day, the British Third Army retreated to Amiens and the Fifth Army virtually disintegrated and was unable to reconstitute itself until it had retreated close to 25 miles.

Constructing a counterfactual to these events is straightforward. Much like the blitzkrieg tactics of the Second World War, a direct descendent of infiltration, the purpose of this type of attack is disruption. When defenders are bypassed and their communications are cut off they are necessarily confused about what they are supposed to do. Certainly telling them to hold at all costs is a viable tactic, as was shown by the German Army in Russia in 1941. And it can work. If defenders continue to resist, this tactic can ultimately slow down the attack. The attacker pays a penalty if he leaves large forces in his rear which can interrupt his own communications and logistical support. On the other hand defenders can be told to retreat and to do so in an orderly fashion. If the commander has a good picture of the battlefield he will know what he controls and what the enemy controls. He can therefore assist retreating troops in finding a path to safety and identifying the location of friendly forces.

In 1918, the key to restoring order out of confusion was communications. Once telephone lines were cut the forward troops had no idea what was going on. Not only were the forward troops blind, but divisional and brigade communications were destroyed, as was pointed out in the previous chapter. In the counterfactual, destruction of telephone lines does not lead to loss of communications because the troops and the higher headquarters all have radios. The German attack, while a surprise, was made against understrength but veteran units.[14] Men who had survived on the Western Front until this time were well aware of the stakes involved, knew how to take care of themselves, and realized that strength lay in mutual support among their fellows and support from their artillery. All they needed was to be told what to do. It's fair to assume that if they had survived in a particular redoubt their radio would have. They had had radios for two years and knew how vital they were to their success, so they would have protected them.

Given that troops in the redoubts that survived the artillery barrage would have retained their radios and maintained communication with brigade and division headquarters it is highly likely that some kind of organized defense could have been created. When the redoubts reported in their commanders would have had a clear picture of where defenses existed and where the holes were. At this point rational decisions could have been made regarding which positions to continue to hold and which positions to abandon. The previous chapter mentions that in reality some units were able to maintain contact using the limited number of wireless telegraph sets available and resisted stubbornly knowing that they were not completely isolated. This reinforces the point that if radiotelephones had been distributed throughout the Army, stubborn defense would have been the rule rather than the exception. In addition safe withdrawal paths could have been identified for retreating troops, who, in constant contact with their commanders, could have been told where and when to move or stop and join an organized defensive line. As pointed out in the previous chapter, when the actual retreat began, little or no fixed communications were available at locations where the Army chose to stand. This would not have happened if they had radios and were bringing their communications with them. Maintenance of communications, in other words, would have facilitated either the continuing defense of a redoubt or an orderly retreat instead of the virtual rout that followed the rupture of the Fifth Army's forward defenses.

The previous chapter pointed out the immense difficulties encountered by the Signal Service in providing communications for a retreating army. The main communications route was vulnerable to flanking fire, lateral communications were hard to provide, pre-positioned cable supplies were nonexistent and cable detachments could not move forward because of congestion on the roads. Had radios been distributed to all commands, these difficulties would not have existed. The installation of fixed communications could have waited until the front was stabilized. Other means of communication such as visual, DRs and runners would not have been necessary.

In the introduction to this book it was pointed out that a continuous wave transmitter can support both the radiotelephone and the wireless telegraph. It has another characteristic, discussed at length in chapter 12. It is highly resistant to jamming, being able to penetrate broadband jamming such as that from a spark transmitter and to counter a narrowband jammer by changing frequencies. In the 1918 retreat the British Army's radiotelephones would not have suffered from jamming by their own wireless sets or by the enemy's. As previously mentioned, the CW transmitter that made the radiotelephone possible could have replaced the spark transmitters which supported the Army's wireless telegraph. (The Signal Service actually began to do this in 1918, but the conversion was far from complete.) This means that the Army's communications, both radiotelephone and wireless telegraph, would have been impervious to the jamming mentioned in the previous chapter. The difficulties associated with the use of cipher and code could have been overcome by segregation of telegraph traffic into that which had to be protected and that which for tactical reasons did not. (Further discussion of this issue is presented in chapter 12.)

Is unrealistic to suggest that the Michael attack would not have attained some degree of success. The manpower and matériel superiority possessed by the attackers virtually guaranteed that the Third and Fifth armies would have been forced back. Had intact communications allowed them to retain cohesion, however, they would have exacted a much higher price from the attackers than they did. Instead of achieving what appeared to be an almost decisive victory Ludendorff would have accomplished only one more of a long series of inconclusive battles on the Western Front. This one, however, would have exacted a very high price for little gain. This result would have been accomplished after the very best effort possible employing all the available resources of the German Empire. A realistic assessment might have convinced the German high command that they could accomplish no more and that subsequent attacks in 1918 offered little hope of improving their position. If the best they could do with overwhelming artillery and elite infantry was to advance a few miles against tired British infantry, the question would have been: What could they hope to accomplish with far less superiority against the one million or more Allied soldiers coming from America? It could have been a good time to start negotiations for the end of the war.

The Hundred Days

The Hundred Days is the time between 8 August and 11 November 1918 when the Allies launched the combined series of offensives that defeated Germany in the First World War. On 8 August the British Fourth Army opened the Battle of Amiens with an attack supported by more than 500 tanks.[15] Through careful preparations the British achieved complete surprise. The attack broke through the German lines and tanks attacked German rear positions. By the end of the day a gap 15 miles long had been created in the German line south of the Somme. The Allies took 110 square miles of territory and captured 13,000 prisoners and 330 guns.[16] Total German casualties were estimated at 30,000 while the Allies had suffered about 6500. The collapse in German morale led Ludendorff to call it "the Black Day of the German army."[17] The advance continued for three more days but without the spectacular results of 8 August since the rapid advance outran the supporting artillery and ran short of supplies. During those three days the Allies gained 12 miles but most of that occurred on the first day. Once the Germans added reinforcements the advance slowed. On 10 August the Germans began to pull out of the salient they had occupied since operation Michael in March.

At Foch's urging the Fourth Army resumed the offensive on 21 August. The offensive was very successful and brought British forces to the Hindenburg Line by 31 August.[18] At this point Foch planned a concentric attack on the Hindenburg Line, which commenced on 12 September. The main attack on the Hindenburg Line by the Fourth Army began on 29 September. This attack succeeded in breaching the entire depth of the Hindenburg defenses by 5 October. The Canadian Corps broke through the Hindenburg Line at another location on 8 October. The success of these and attacks by the Americans and the French convinced the German high command that the war had to be ended.[19] The German armies continued to retreat from the Hindenburg Line while armistice negotiations took place and ceased fighting on 11 November.

A counterfactual for this case does not encompass any dramatic change to the outcome, merely that the nature of the defeat would have clearer to the German people than what they were subsequently led to believe.

Starting at the battle of Amiens and at an accelerating pace thereafter static warfare gave way to open warfare. As has been pointed out, communications based on wire deteriorate rapidly when troops are moving. It is very difficult to keep laying adequate wire at the same pace at which the units supported by the communications are moving. Besides the logistical difficulties of transporting heavy spools of wire, the wire must be laid on the ground or on poles and is subject to being torn up by shells, vehicles and marching feet. Burying it is out of the question. In view of these difficulties, wire communication with advancing troops had to be supplemented by a multiplicity of communications methods, such as visual, runners and mounted orderlies, as pointed out in the previous chapter. These methods had the usual disadvantages of sensitivity to weather conditions, lack of timeliness and interruption when the messenger became a casualty. In addition the methods were focused on maintaining the central main routes in each corps through to the front line, or at least to battalion headquarters. Lateral communications had to be neglected. The troops' ability to conduct cooperative operations with other troops, their ability to call on prompt artillery support and their ability to act on reconnaissance was limited. Their commanders' ability to react to favorable circumstances by reinforcing success and to respond to unexpected reverses by halting or redirecting the advance was equally limited. Lack of adequate communications during the British advance significantly slowed the speed of the advance.

When the units are equipped with lightweight radiotelephone sets, it is a different story entirely. First of all there is no pressing need to lay cable, thereby reducing the casualties to signals personnel performing this dangerous work. The previous chapter pointed out the exceptional difficulties created by cable shortages, requiring the use of direct routes encountering terrain obstacles or floods. With radiotelephones providing immediate communications, cable can be emplaced later and more safely when the situation stabilizes. Secondly, and more importantly, the advancing units can react much more quickly to developments in front of them. A tenet of the infiltration tactics the British were following at this point of the war is to keep moving. If a platoon, company or battalion is held up by an obstacle such as a machine-gun post, it needs to call in artillery to destroy it or pass around it and leave its reduction to the following infantry. Coordinating this activity requires communications. Without communications the task is very difficult, perhaps impossible to accomplish. With the radiotelephone the task can be accomplished expeditiously.

As previously pointed out, wireless telegraphy was actually used for corps communications, but only when the corps was not advancing. In the Canadian Corps it was used only as a supplement to the main cable route. Wireless telegraph support to the heavy artillery batteries was welcome but restricted to the limited number of sets available. When cable communications failed, as they often did, due to enemy shelling, or cutting by friendly tanks, horses or balloon hawsers, wireless telegraphy was the only means of communication for corps and divisions. Wireless telegraphy was also useful for communication between artillery batteries and company and battalion headquarters. The actual usefulness of wireless telegraphy in the 1918 advance underscores what might have been accomplished if the radiotelephone and its companion, the CW wireless telegraph, had been more widely distributed throughout the British Army.

Faced with a faltering and demoralized enemy the allies had an opportunity to turn an orderly retreat into a rout. By moving quickly they could have prevented the enemy from halting and constructing prepared defenses. By 1918, in the counterfactual scenario, the Allied units would have had in hand the means to communicate under mobile conditions and to ensure that their advance stayed close on the heels of the retreating German Army. The faster they moved the more rapidly the Germans would have had to move, losing any semblance of cohesion and control. As its Army disintegrated it would have become clearer and clearer to the German populace that Germany had suffered a devastating military defeat and that the Armistice had to be signed to prevent utter chaos in the German nation. Would the Armistice have been signed any sooner? Probably not. The time it took to complete negotiations was the dominant factor. Would the German Army have been readier to acknowledge that it had been beaten and beaten badly? Probably. When an Army leaves the battlefield as a disorganized rabble instead of marching away in formation under its own colors, it is impossible for it to ignore that it has suffered a severe defeat. It would have been harder and harder over time to sustain the myth that the German Army had not been defeated in the field, but had been stabbed in the back.

CHAPTER 11

Command, Control
and Communications

A detailed study of operational signals during the war, in previous chapters, has been an essential prerequisite to making an evaluation of the performance of the Signal Service in providing the third key element of success in modern warfare — effective communications. This chapter draws conclusions based on previous source material.

John Terraine's assertion that the First World War armies lacked voice control — in his words "an audible voice in battle" — a problem, he goes on to say, "that was never solved satisfactorily during the whole of the war"[1] — echoes the generally held view among those involved at the highest level in the conflict. It is fully supported by professional historical evaluation. His further contention that "the First World War was the only war ever fought without voice control" and "that once troops were committed to attack, all control was over" also raises little disagreement in similar circles.

Terraine receives strong support in his views from other distinguished commentators. Van Creveld is unequivocal in his view that "the network of communications that is vital to the functioning of modern warfare was absent from the Great War battlefield,"[2] while Griffith refers to "the formidable difficulty of bridging the wide beaten zone between the general in his chateau and the subaltern in the front line trench."[3]

There is certainly no doubt about the generally held concept of signals at the front line. It is emphatically one in which those controlling the battle, at every level, had at best a blurred and, more often than not, a non-existent picture of events. However, against this background, and in the light of a detailed assessment of operational signals previously presented, this work will argue that the reality of the situation was much more complex and highly fragmented. It was heavily influenced by the specific circumstances of each phase of the conflict. This takes full account of the development and experience of the Signals Service as the war progressed. It also studies the emerging technology, its use as it became available and, crucially, the changing attitudes of Staff officers, at all levels, towards the vital importance of communications as a key factor in the successful prosecution of the war.

This does not dissent from the generally held view of communication during the war. It seeks, much more, to put this view in perspective and, on occasions, to offer an alternative assessment. It is based on what is, almost certainly, the only detailed analysis of communications since Priestley's well-respected but highly impenetrable work, which has required, in this book, considerable historical reappraisal.[4] This does not imply that the book ignores inadequacies in the performance of the Signal Service or the clearly evident and often disastrous shortcomings of communications during the war. It recognizes, however, that by early 1917 the Signal Service with tacit, if not official, responsibility for communications right up to the front line, had received general recognition as a professional organization. It had a detailed command structure, under the Director of Army Signals,[5] providing, in the main, an adequate signals system, despite the extreme difficulties and constraints under which it operated.

It is not in the least surprising, however, that the strongly held historical view that an inadequate signals communication system operated throughout most of the war predominates. On the vitally important occasions on which it failed, the results almost invariably had dire consequences. The book argues, however, that inadequacies in communications, where and when they occurred, were heavily affected by Staff attitudes, particularly up to mid–1917. To this must be added the extreme difficulties that they faced of controlling the conflict on the vast and unprecedented scale on which it was conducted, together with exponential increases in both the numbers and power of the weapons involved, as the war progressed.

An analysis of the relative success of signals communication is best achieved by reference to each phase of the war as detailed and examined previously. The extent of the problems that faced the Signal Service certainly reached their highest level during the Battle of the Somme. Thereafter communications improved gradually during the predominantly static warfare of 1917. Though still far from adequate, they showed surprising resilience during the German spring offensive of March 1918 and reached the highest level of efficiency during the mobile warfare of the final hundred days of the war. From this analysis, a balanced contribution towards the generally held view of communications during the war can be made.

The first and short period of the war through to September 1914, when the British Expeditionary Force (BEF) finally established itself on the Aisne presents, in fact, a microcosm of subsequent communication experience, both of success and failure. It is therefore of considerable significance, despite its brevity.

Bearing in mind that the experience of the South African War was used as the basis on which the signals element of the BEF was established, it is not surprising that it very quickly proved inadequate to the tasks it faced. When these escalated, with great rapidity, the Signal Service was confronted with entirely new and very demanding challenges. At this stage in its development they were entirely unattainable.

Initially, in almost peacetime conditions, and prior to the retreat from Mons, good effective communications were established. The pre-war command structure, under the Director of Army Signals, who had full powers and responsibility from GHQ forward to battalion HQs, proved adequate to the limited tasks demanded of it. However, even at this early stage, there were clear indications of massive difficulties to follow. Looseness in organization and unworkable elements in his chain of command would be made clearly apparent during the imminent and huge increases in the scale and intensity of the conflict. Fundamentally, the Director of Army Signals lacked clearly defined responsibility for both artillery and battalion signals, which was entirely illogical. His task was made even more difficult by his having to assume, perforce, tacit responsibility at this early stage of the war.

The Director of Army Signals had to contend, in addition, with increasing responsibilities with what rapidly proved to be totally inadequate and, consequently, thinly spread resources of both signals personnel and equipment. Both were at varying states of readiness for war, supported by sparse reserves. Crucially, in relation to equipment, it was not generally appropriate for the demands of modern warfare.

Signals training was generally fragmented, resulting in mismatches of supply and demand of personnel, in any given situation. For example, battalion signallers, who had exclusively visual training, were not proficient in line laying for the provision of telegraph and telephone, when these were the clearly appropriate signals requirement. Fortuitously, dispatch riders (DRs) were able, on many occasions, to bridge the gap in communications, though only by showing great courage in the face of unacceptably high casualties. The provision of the appropriate signals medium to suit given requirements was further hampered by General Headquarters' (GHQ) inherent antipathy towards telephone. This was based on their fear — bordering on paranoia — of enemy overhearing on the uncoded telephone line. There is clear evidence, on numerous occasions, that they would prefer to have no conversation or communication whatsoever rather than resort to the use of telephone!

When, therefore, the BEF was forced to retreat to the Marne in conditions of mobile warfare and in the face of artillery fire of unprecedented magnitude, it was impossible to establish an adequate line system. This was caused not only by the speed of the retreat, but also because of the deficiencies in personnel, equipment and training outlined. Communications chaos ensued. There was a serious lack of reliable information on which strategic decisions could be made. The absence or destruction of the communications chain resulted in resources being misemployed and avoidable risks undertaken. This was, very much, a forerunner of things to come and a clear reflection of GHQs inexperience in modern warfare. It was particularly the case in retreat when, for example, even at this early stage in its development, some consideration at least of the limited use of wireless would have been appropriate, even if rejected.

Strategically, for signals communication at this early stage of the war, an appreciation of its importance as a vital aspect of command and control was fundamentally lacking. This resulted from ignorance, suspicion and prejudice in relation to the developing and emerging technology. This was perhaps understandable, though certainly not excusable, in circumstances where previous experience was limited and military thought hidebound by adherence to rigid systems. The seeds of much greater future problems for signals communications were undoubtedly sown at this early stage of the war. Only the extreme pressures of events forced a reappraisal of the role of the Signal Service that later benefitted greatly from its early, if unsatisfactory, experience. This will become apparent as the evaluation progresses.

Despite previous difficulties, the Signal Service entered the long and attritional phase of the war from early 1915 onwards with communications in relatively good order. However, this was based purely on the comparatively small scale required at this early stage of the conflict. It had been made possible by the short pause after the retreat to the Marne when some general regrouping of the BEF took place. Subsequently, with the speed of the advance to the Aisne, the Signal Service was able to exploit the use of enemy cable, establishing good communications with minimal casualties and the provision of a sound link between GHQ and divisional HQs.

Thereafter, however, with its forces redeployed around Ypres-Armentieres, the British Army had to contend with an entirely new set of circumstances. Hereafter, the war was conducted on a massive scale, of unprecedented intensity. The objective of both sides was to secure a decisive breakthrough that was never remotely achieved. At this point, the major Signal Service responsibility was to provide the appropriate means for the Staff to in keep in close touch with developments. This was designed to provide early information on the position, movement, and strength of enemy formations as a key element of command and control.

From the First Battle of Ypres onwards, the requirement was to provide good communication systems in the face of sharp increases in both enemy artillery fire and the number and size of British Army formations. The Signal Service had to expand accordingly. It had, at the same time, to adapt to the new conditions and to adopt an innovative approach to the means of communication best suited to them. By far the most demanding was the requirement of integrating its scarce resources effectively in early moves towards its tacit, though never officially confirmed, responsibility for communications at the front line. This required a complete reappraisal and reorganization of administration, equipment, reinforcements and training, on an expanding scale. Its effective coordination, coupled with the establishment of a Signals *esprit de corps* by the Director of Army Signals, was the key to its success or failure.

In early 1915 there were three major developments of key strategic importance that heavily affected the Signal Service specifically, and the provision of communications generally. The first was the relationship between the Signal Service and the expanding artillery forces. At this point, GHQ held the Signal Service responsible for providing effective communications, even though this was not recognized formally until 1916. The principal and urgent requirement was for a separate command communications system. The second and predominant demand was for increased telephone systems to accommodate GHQ (which had overcome its earlier mistrust of the medium) forward to the front line. This required extensive organizational reform and evolution of the Signal Service that, from this point onwards, led to a seemingly endless expansion and revolution in signals responsibilities.

The third, of less significance at this stage of the conflict, but to have huge implications later, was the development and acceptance of the use of the basic wireless facilities available. At this point, its use was restricted to the interception of enemy messages and for Royal Flying Corps (RFC) spotting reports. The first indications of a lost opportunity are clearly evident. Even at this stage, it could have had an early, and beneficial, impact on the strategic conduct of the war. This was exemplified at the Battle of Loos in September 1915, when it was tested with a degree of success under demanding conditions. At this crossroads in its development it was inhibited by continuing Staff prejudice based mainly, and with some justification, on the fear of enemy overhearing. While an entirely valid, if exaggerated consideration, it was capable of solution, as proved later to be the case. It became a major issue, which, through Signal Service perseverance, was resolved to considerable strategic advantage as the war progressed.

By the close of 1915 the Signal Service was a much more cohesive force with a distinct identity. There were also the first indications of a realization, by the High Command, that an elaborate and effective signals communication system was an indispensable aspect of command and control in modern warfare. This was, potentially, of huge strategic significance. The change of attitude inevitably took time to filter down the chain of command to subsidiary units. However, an Army and Signals conference, held in the autumn of 1915, helped to increase the level of trust and cooperation between the Signal Service and those arms for which it had the greatest communications responsibility, especially artillery.

Thus, as the Signal Service approached 1916, and by far its greatest test so far at the Battle of the Somme, there were some improvements in its overall effectiveness. Its areas of responsibility were better, though by no means fully, defined. It had a more specific and certainly well directed chain of command. Consequently, there were improvements in the continuity of signals policy with better coordination of reliefs, training, reinforcements, equipment and stores.

During the early months of 1916, Signal Service activity was mainly concentrated on the massive preparation required for the forthcoming battle. It would be of a greater scale and intensity than anything approaching its previous experience. With sufficient labor, time and resources this might just have been achievable though, nonetheless, representing a huge challenge. Faced with the reality of deficiencies in all areas, it proved impossible for the Signal Service to meet the requirement, essential to the overall strategy for success in the battle, of providing appropriate and adequate communications. In this respect, providing a communications bridge across no-man's-land was the most essential and yet, at the same time, difficult to achieve.

The overall requirement was for a communications system which was able to link HQs from GHQ through to the front line as the battle progressed and under unpredictable circumstances. At this stage Van Creveld contends that communications took control of the war, an opinion the book supports.[6] What is beyond doubt is that this became a strategic imperative for an Army that had experienced massive growth and faced with a battle of unprecedented proportions. Brigadier-General Charteris,[7] Haig's Chief of Intelligence, describes, in April 1916, the enormous organization an army in the field had become. He also contends that individual departments lacked a general appreciation of the wider strategic issues, among which the proper integration of adequate communications was key.

The more forthright Fuller, not surprisingly, put it more strongly. He was in no doubt that

> when generals became divorced from those under their command, relying more and more on inadequate communications, there was nothing more dreadful to witness than army commanders sitting in telephone boxes talking, talking instead of leading, leading.[8]

Van Creveld also takes a controversial view, to be developed more fully in subsequent chapters of the book. He is in no doubt that the High Command's almost exclusive reliance on line communication severely restricted the scope of its strategic planning and effective control of the 400,000 men, 100,000 horses, 1500 guns and 3 million artillery shells required for the initial battle.[9]

During the early days of the Battle of the Somme, which is exhaustively documented, with the enemy's defenses unexpectedly intact, massive difficulties of an intense and unanticipated nature were immediately apparent for the British Army and the Signal Service alike. The requirement remained for a reliable communications chain across the chaos of no-mans'-land but now in circumstances of almost insurmountable difficulty. The Signal Service was well and properly cited for its professional efforts and courageous devotion to duty but, despite its best efforts, communications must be judged as highly unsatisfactory. The hardest lesson learned, in the toughest of circumstances, was that no communication method was infallible. All were vulnerable. Nevertheless, the Staff expectation remained for full and continuous communication facilities.

Wireless was not, as yet, considered entirely suitable or efficient for the exacting conditions that prevailed. More critically, it was still unacceptable to all but its most ardent supporters. Consequently, it was clearly apparent, as the battle ground to a halt in November 1916, that the British Army's communications strategy required a full and urgent review. This commenced in March and was later completed in November 1917. It was of the most vital significance for the Signal Service.

As the Signal Service approached 1917, the British Army's overall strategy of mobility continued to be applied. This was despite GHQ's anticipation and preparation for a prolonged conflict in which the conservation of resources and their careful apportionment applied fully to the means of communication. The inevitable consequences were shortages of both stores and equipment — particularly telephones, cable and wireless — to meet the Army's growing requirements, the artillery continuing to make the highest demands.

In addition, the Signal Service's tacit responsibility for frontline communications became increasingly demanding. The blurred chain of command resulting from this anomalous situation exerted increasing pressures.

In the face of the very difficult circumstances that challenged the Signal Service in so many areas, the principal initiative emanated from the Director of Army Signals, for which considerable recognition must be given. He initiated the spread of best practice across the whole of the British Army's sector of the Western Front, through the codification of procedures, based on hard won experience in the previous tumultuous years.

For the moment, at the start of 1917, the British Army was reasonably well placed. However, the year as a whole was to prove one of huge development for the Signal Service, amid operations on a massive scale. After elements of semi-mobile warfare on the Army's Southern Front, in the face of a well-planned German withdrawal, the enemy regrouped and showed strong resistance. This continued, more or less unabated, until the Battle of Cambrai in November 1917. But on its Northern Front, in the autumn of the year during the Third Battle of Ypres, the attritional fight for the Passchendaele and Messines ridges was at huge cost. This applied to all areas of the BEF, and certainly not least to communications.

A pervading atmosphere of deadlock affected the whole of the Western Front during 1917. In the face of the heaviest concentration of German artillery of the war so far and with its personnel often engaged in the front line as infantry, the Signal Service nonetheless made significant alterations and additions to its overall strategy. Potential actions were well rehearsed. This enabled the Signal Service to forecast its minimum requirements more accurately. It also exhibited considerable flair and imagination in decision-making that made a major contribution to an improvement in its per-formance. The situation for the entire British Army was further improved by greater success in combating enemy overhearing in which the Signal Service played a full part. The most significant contributory factor was the stipulation that no telephones or power buzzers were to be used within 3,000 yards of the front line. For GHQ, the ideal would have been com-plete silence throughout the whole of the British Army's front line. This was not only unworkable but also highly undesirable and, clearly, had to be relaxed in attacking situations. With the increased use of Fullerphones, an element of surprise could still be maintained.

Before considering the final stages of 1917, principally the Battle of Cambrai in November, it is essential to study perhaps the most important strategic development for the Signal Service in the war, so far. This ran in tandem with the year's momentous events, particularly on the British Army's Northern Front. This was the publication of *Forward Inter-Com-munication in Battle S.S. 148*,[10] published in March and later, in November, *Inter-Communication in the Field S.S. 191*,[11] which included and revised the earlier publication. It became the Signal Service bible for the remainder of the war.

Their main features, which were of the greatest strategic importance, represented a historic reform in signals policy. They represented the direct result of close co-operation between the Director of Army Signals and the General Staff. Co-operation was based on the critical realization, by GHQ, that fully effective and comprehensive communications systems were crucial in all military operations. Above all, they were an indispensable third ele-ment, with command and control, for success in battle.

They were the first Staff manuals devoted entirely to signals through-out the Army, representing a huge development in policy. The major out-comes were that signals policy was standardized. The powers of the Signal Service were enhanced and it had an authoritative document to enforce, if necessary, all arms co-operation. Furthermore, it retained sufficient flex-ibility and discretion, where required, which was particularly important for front line signals.

The practical result was the optimum use of signals personnel and equipment. There was also important and fundamental agreement that, in the majority of situations, the concentration along one main route down the center of each brigade area, at this stage of the war, was by far the most effective and best practice.

The final battle of 1917 — Cambrai — was fought against the background of the recently codified signals policy and practice. It had some unusual features. The absence of an opening barrage and the use of tanks as the spearhead of the attack were the most significant departure from previous strategy. For the Signal Service, this presented a unique challenge. Firstly, its preparations had to be carried out in the greatest secrecy. Secondly, reliable communications had to be provided for large numbers of tanks. They required follow-up communications in anticipation of an advance of greater speed and depth than hitherto. One main brigade communications route remained the key to success. Not unusually, the outcome did not live up to expectations. Tanks destroyed well prepared cable systems. Wireless was not used to advantage where it certainly could have been.

In addition, during the enemy's counterattack, the communications system was badly affected as the British Army retreated. Signal Service personnel were, once again, drawn into the fighting line, as infantry. Nonetheless, lessons were drawn from the battle by the Signal Service and used, to considerable advantage, as the blueprint for its planning for the eventual advance to victory in the late summer of 1918. Thereafter, the Signal Service faced perhaps its most difficult challenge of the war to date in its preparation for the German spring offensive.

During the first three months of 1918, the Signal Service was fully occupied in preparing, along an extended front, for an inevitable German Army offensive. This was the logical outcome of the addition of massive reserves to its ranks, transferred from the Eastern Front. Paradoxically, the British Army's limited successes of 1917 resulted in its forces being well ahead of the safe buried cable route. Furthermore, in the event of any retreat, it would have to traverse the previously devastated battlefield. This would have to be made under, predictably, intense enemy fire. The challenge of maintaining anything approaching a reliable communications system, in the face of such potential difficulties, was immense.

Strategically, for the Army's defense planning, the establishment of a resilient communications system should have been a top priority. In the event, the Signal Service had to compete for scarce manpower to build its system while, at the same time, cable was in desperately short supply.

However, with cable in short supply during preparations, alternative means to the telephone system had to be considered. Among these visual, runners, dispatch riders and, of the greatest strategic significance, wireless were key. Nonetheless, the defensive communications system, prepared for the inevitable onslaught, was far from adequate.

The result on 21 March, particularly from Arras to the South, was that the majority of cable communications were completely destroyed by enemy artillery fire of unprecedented intensity on pre-registered frontline strong points. The outcome was that the British Third and Fifth armies were driven back to Amiens, behind the Somme area.

Thereafter, for the Signal Service there were two distinct phases creating quite different problems: the first, when the British Army was fighting from prepared positions; the second, during its hurried retreat, involving rearguard actions, to final defensive positions.

Signals practice also differed geographically. In the area around Arras, which had not been affected so badly, comparatively, by the events of late 1917, well prepared line systems enabled reasonably good communications to be maintained. However, south of Arras the situation was truly disastrous. Brigade, division and even corps communications were severely or completely disrupted, with the inevitable paralysis of command structures.

Travers cites three typical examples. The first, from an officer of 12th Royal Irish Rifles. He, in describing the bombardment of his regiment with high explosives, trench mortars and gas, records as a seemingly inevitable and even acceptable conclusion that as a result all telephone wires were cut immediately. The second, from an officer of<frsp>2/6th Sherwood Foresters who recalled that all communications were severed immediately at the commencement of the enemy's attack. A third, and perhaps the most revealing, from an officer of 14th Division who recorded: "We had in the divisional area deep cable trenches which were a snare and delusion. They had been photographed from the air by the Germans with the result that they fired at the junctions and everyone was disconnected in a few minutes."[12] J.F.C. Fuller, in characteristic style, sums up succinctly the result of this critical loss of communications over the ensuing early days of the offensive, in his diary of 25 March — again by reference to Travers — in recording: "Who is fighting this battle? No one. GHQ and armies know next to nothing of what is going on."[13] It has to be acknowledged, of course, that the March battles were, in fact, being fought by divisions, brigades and battalions, but the point is, nonetheless, well made.

However, among this chronicle of disasters, wireless began to emerge as the mainstay of communications being, comparatively, far less vulnerable than other means of signaling. It was certainly not wholly adequate, or in

RE fixing telephone wires in a tree near Fricourt, September 1916. (IWM No. Q-4137)

sufficient supply, to provide anything approaching a complete communications chain. However, it did allow vital contact to be at least maintained during the turbulent events of 21 March. This was particularly true where units were completely surrounded. Wireless allowed invaluable situation reports to be sent and requests for help, where this was available. It was also a very important factor in boosting the morale of those surrounded.

RFC men repairing overhead telephone wires at a crossroads on the Mametz-Contalmaison Road, November 1916. (IWM No. Q-4577)

It was also used with some success to the rear, as the retreat quickened, when cable was destroyed and all other means proved ineffective apart from, once again, dispatch riders. They continued to operate with customary heroism though sustaining high casualties. This was the first real indication of the true value and effectiveness of wireless which hereafter was demonstrated, conclusively, as the war progressed. It became, beyond doubt, the most appropriate means of communications during the final and decisive months of the war, in fully mobile conditions.

As Phase I developed into the full-scale retreat of Phase II, the overriding feature was overall lack of command and control. This was as the direct result of poor or non-existent communications, in which the limited use of wireless could make only a marginal, but valuable, contribution. For the Signal Service, the ensuing difficulties were almost insurmountable. Much improved planning by Staff from corps forward would have done much to alleviate the situation. With frequent movements of HQs, at all levels of command, the line of retreat became confused. Lateral communication, a key feature of control in these circumstances, was virtually impossible. In addition, congestion on the roads over the old battlefield caused serious problems for the Signal Service. Infantry and tanks, without proper liaison, caused serious damage to signal facilities in circumstances where shortages of equipment — particularly cable — were a constant feature.

The most important implications for future communications policy to emerge from the March retreat were to have vital application for the remainder of the war, particularly during its final 100 days. The first was the inestimable value of providing communications down one main route, preferably through brigade. This had to be made available along a carefully planned course. HQ locations needed to be advised well in advance and, except in the most extreme circumstances, adhered to. Control must be exercised by the highest formation involved, in accordance with now established signals procedure.

The second was the value of wireless communication. This opened up entirely new parameters for strategic planning. For the moment it had at least added some resilience to a communications system that had all but collapsed in the massive difficulties of the retreat. Perhaps even more importantly, it had extended military thinking towards its use in other circumstances. This was particularly true, during the attack, when the restriction of using cipher and code could be somewhat relaxed, with the enemy under pressure. This must be regarded as a triumph for forward signals policy and organization. It was, above all, a tribute to the great perseverance of the growing numbers within the Signal Service who had championed its cause.

The German offensive finally halted with both sides exhausted. For the Signal Service a period to refit and train reinforcements was urgently required. Fortunately, this was provided for by the relatively short period which preceded the final advance to victory, involving truly mobile warfare.

The Signal Service, from this point forward, adopted an entirely new approach to the way in which its policy was developed. This was the result of a combination of years of hard earned experience and changes of attitude towards the importance of communications at all levels of command. It was based on the simple and straightforward concept of providing a sound communications system for defense in depth but allowed for a rapid switch to the offensive. It involved historic reversal of previous communications policy. Thereafter, innovation, flexibility and the provision of essential command information were considered absolutely key requirements. In this, wireless played a vital, indispensable and increasing role.

Above all, the most important development for future communications policy was the now excellent relationship that existed between the Staff and the Signal Service. Taken together with the Army's ability to operate effectively with much more slender facilities, as the result of recent experience, it was the basis on which communications were built for the forthcoming and final offensive.

With now tacit responsibility for all forward communications, the Signal Service was poised to play a well-coordinated and vital part in the final stages of the war. This opened with the Allied offensive on 8 August. During this, the Signal Service came of age, establishing the provision of excellent communication as a *sine qua non* for success in all future warfare.

Following the BEFs new offensive on 8 August, the Signal Service was called upon to provide communications for two distinct phases of warfare until victory was achieved. The first covered the period preceding the forcing of the Hindenburg Line at the end of September; the second, the period of predominantly mobile warfare which continued until the Armistice.

The first phase involved a series of mobile actions against an organized German Army retreat from strongly built defenses. It was punctuated by short pauses of relatively static warfare that required, from the Signal Service, an extension of its communications strategy of late 1917. The important distinction now, however, was that it was able to build successfully on the lessons learned during the earlier period of warfare. The main requirement for a flexible and sustainable system remained the key strategy.

The second phase, however, presented new challenges. Communications were required for mainly mobile warfare, interspersed with set-piece actions. Facilities were limited to meet essential requirements only. They were based on a system which was simple in concept, easy to maintain and allowed for speed in completion, with economy of personnel and equipment both of which were, in any case, short in supply. The unusual circumstances of an advancing GHQ, with its attendant demanding requirements, were an added pressure. The adjustment from the massive complex organization needed for the extended and relatively static period of the war to the current mobile phase also required an innovative approach. In this, the provision of a variety of means of communication to meet unpredictable circumstances was of fundamental importance. For example, despite the predominantly mobile nature of this period of warfare, the Army was forced to make a series of short, unscheduled halts in its advance. This added new complexities to communications planning.

A developing feature, with the speed of the advance, was that corps HQs with their constant forward movement and relative proximity to the front line were more involved in direct control of the action. Consequently, while one main communications route remained the key requirement, it now ran from corps rather than brigades. Divisions and battalions were located on spurs to the main line, entirely within the spirit, if not the letter, of S.S. 191.[14] A temporary problem of educating Staff officers, mainly those who had not been involved in the Cambrai offensive, to accept reduced facilities, particularly telephone, remained. However, the exigencies of the moment usually forced a solution!

Probably of greatest assistance to the Signal Service, in providing appropriate facilities, was the ever-increasing cooperation between it and the General Staff. The most immediate benefit was that the General Staff now included a more detailed consideration of forthcoming communications requirements in its overall planning process. The result was that limited signals resources were used to best effect and, with good Staff work, at least adequate communications were more or less guaranteed.

However, a problem emerged of communicating over long distances for which there was no precise comparable experience. It was exacerbated by shortages of cable and congested roads. Good reconnaissance of the difficult routes to be crossed assisted the planning process and a very substantial reduction in the intensity of enemy artillery fire helped greatly. The real key to successful communications, in these circumstances, wireless, was finally accepted fully and irrevocably, as by far the most effective communications medium for modern mobile warfare.

Indeed, buried cable was reaching its nemesis as the BEF's advance increased in pace and there was insufficient time to build a follow-up system during temporary short halts. Therefore, while a slender line system remained as the nucleus of the main corps communication route forward, there was a rapid expansion of wireless along the whole of the communications chain. With some relaxation of the insistence on code and cipher, in appropriate circumstances, it was now firmly established as an integral part of all future systems.

With the continuing improvements in wireless sets, both in relation to power, reception and, most significantly, weight, its more extensive use was fully vindicated. During the final stages of the war, it was acknowledged as the most effective and flexible means of communication, particularly though not only, for mobile warfare. A much more detailed analysis in relation to its strategic development throughout the whole of the war is presented in the following chapters.

CHAPTER 12

Intercept, Encryption
and Jamming

As discussed in previous chapters, the interrelated issues of intercept, encryption and jamming had a profound influence on the development of wireless for military use. It is therefore worthwhile to devote some attention to them, to understand why they were important, and to place them in the proper context, to show that, except for jamming, they were not unique to wireless and that they needed to be considered for all means of communication. Intercept refers to the ability of an adversary to obtain information from an opponent's communication system, regardless of the means of transmission. Any information transmitted, whether visually, by pigeon, by courier, or electronically, can be intercepted and used. Encryption refers to the methods employed to protect the information contained in a message in order to prevent the enemy from using it. Jamming is the method employed to break wireless communication between source and recipient. Cutting wires or shooting down pigeons are methods to accomplish the same end for telephone or courier pigeon communication. These issues will be discussed in turn as they relate to the development and use of military wireless.

Intercept

Interception of wireless signals by the enemy, or overhearing as it was called early in the 20th century, had been a major concern since its invention. A wireless signal broadcast by a transmitter could be received by any suitably designed receiver, whether in the hands of the intended recipient or of the enemy. If the signal was in the clear, that is unprotected by encryption, the enemy would therefore know what had been sent and could react to it. As discussed in chapter 1, the British Parliament convened a committee in 1912 to consider the issue and recommend measures to deal with it. The wireless committee reached the unfortunate conclusion that because of overhearing it was better to abandon the use of wireless than rely upon it in wartime.[1] The findings of this committee had a negative and long-lasting influence on the subsequent development of wireless in the British Army. The committee consisted of senior scientists, engineers, civil servants and political figures. The committee's charge had been to consider all aspects of the application of wireless to land warfare, so its conclusions and recommendations should have reflected the positive contributions as well as the negative considerations associated with wireless. At the very least one would have expected the recognition of potential trade-offs. The unique ability of wireless to provide communications to mobile military units could have been balanced against its vulnerability to intercept. On the other hand, if the committee chose to interpret its charge to evaluate whether the vulnerability of wireless to intercept negated its usefulness in military operations, then its conclusion becomes more understandable.

The qualifications of the committee were outstanding. Among other experts the committee had consulted with Colonel George Squier of the United States Army Signal Corps, who had received a Ph.D. in electrical engineering from Johns Hopkins University, one of the first awarded in the United States. Squier was available because he was serving as United States military attache in London. He was an exceptional individual who left his mark not only on the Signal Corps but also on the development of military aviation in the United States, a Signal Corps responsibility at the time. During the war he reached the rank of Major General and became the commander of the Signal Corps. In this position in 1918, he sponsored Howard Armstrong's development of the superheterodyne receiver, originally designed for military purposes but which became the basis of the extraordinary expansion of commercial radio in the United States in the 1920s. Later on, he founded the Muzak Corporation, today's ubiquitous background (elevator) music provider. Were one to postulate a single individual at that time with the engineering education, understanding of technology, and military background to appreciate the potential of wireless, George Squier would have been that person. If anyone had the vision to recognize what wireless could mean to military operations it was he. Unfortunately we don't know what he told the committee or what questions he was asked. If they asked him whether there was a method to prevent wireless from being overheard he would have said no. If they had further asked him whether this was an insuperable problem preventing the use of wireless his answer would have been an emphatic no.

The committee's recommendation did not prevent the British Army from using wireless, but it certainly delayed it. Disquiet over interception continued. Once the war started a number of events occurred to reinforce that disquiet. It was also known early in the war that the Germans had exploited Russian wireless communications at Tannenburg. A myth developed that the Russians had been broadcasting in the clear while the clever Germans were encrypting their own messages. The Germans were therefore able to exploit the Russian messages and keep their own secret. Through them, the myth continues, the Germans learned that Rennenkampf's First Army was not moving to support Samsonov's Second Army, allowing them to concentrate against and destroy the Second Army. The truth, established by historians in recent years, is that both sides struggled with the use of wireless and often broadcast in the clear under the press of circumstances. "Virtually every account of the Tannenberg campaign mentions the Russian practice of sending radio messages in the clear and suggests it as another paradigm for the weaknesses of the Tsarist empire. It seems almost a shame to diminish the legend by mentioning that the Germans did not always code their messages either. Like their Russian counterparts, German military codes were simple substitution ciphers — childish by modern standards. Yet German communications officers feared loss of the code books and were under constant pressure to balance security against speed and accuracy."[2]

By a lucky stroke, however, Hindenburg had received an intercepted Russian operations order showing that the First Army was moving toward Konigsberg and could not support the Second. "During the morning of August 25 Hindenburg decided to go to François's headquarters and coordinate final plans for the attack he intended to make next day. Before he left an intercepted Russian wireless message came in from Konigsberg. It was a complete army order of the 1st Army sent in clear at 2:30 a.m. It embodied detailed instructions for the 1st Army's advance — instructions setting the limits of that advance only as far as the line Gerdauen-Allenburg-Wehlau by August 26. This meant Rennenkampf had almost no chance of reaching the new battle area in time to support the 2nd Army directly — *if* the order was genuine and not a Russian plant."[3] Mindful of the advantage that the intercept had given him and not willing to offer the same advantage to the enemy, Hindenburg had subsequently strictly limited the German use of wireless on the Eastern Front, a fact of which the British were well aware.[4]

The British had also benefited from interception of German *en clair* wireless transmission. In 1914, in retreat, the British and French were able to rely on the in-place commercial telephone and telegraph system to communicate. As the attackers the Germans could not use the in-place system of communications because the French and British destroyed telephone and telegraph wires, exchanges and power supplies as they retreated. The Germans were therefore compelled to rely on wireless telegraphy, with the following consequences: "During September–November 1914 French and British forces intercepted at least some 50 radio messages in plain language from German divisions, corps, armies and army groups. These provided otherwise unavailable insights into the collapse of enemy command and the yawning gap in its line during mid–September 1914. Victory on the Marne was no miracle. Over the next two months similar en clair transmissions (combined with solutions of encoded German traffic) warned the British Expeditionary Force (BEF) of the precise time, location and strength of six full-scale attacks on its front, each involving four or more German corps. Without this material, the BEF might well have lost the race to the sea, or even have been destroyed."[5] The British needed no better lesson on the dangers of using unencrypted wireless to support operations in the field.

The previous reference states that the Miracle of the Marne was greatly facilitated by intercepted messages. This is shown by the following account: "The cavalry corps of von der Marwitz was supposed to effect a screen between the areas of the German First and Second Armies. But what the troops tried to accomplish in carrying out their orders was utterly ruined by the German radio service, for the transmitted radiograms gave the French and English an absolutely clear picture of the situation. That gave the French and English the possibility of breaking into the above-mentioned gap on 8 September, since they knew precisely the weak places in the German front. This threatened to encircle the Army of von Kluck and to outflank the Army of von Bulow; and this circumstance was decisive for the recall of the German front. "It is not true that Hentsch ordered the retreat without cogent reasons in a situation which was favorable for the German troops, and that the Allies were surprised and followed only hesitantly; rather, the penetration by the Allies gave Hentsch occasion to recommend withdrawal to the Aisne. On the French side, the fighting units were indeed surprised by the change in situation but not the higher command, which had a precise view of events on the enemy side during the entire course of operations because of the intercepted radio traffic."[6] Thus the German Schlieffen Plan to win the war in 1914 was at least partially undone by intercepted wireless messages.

For the Admiralty, the Marconi engineer and vacuum tube designer H.J. Round had designed a network of direction finding and intercept stations to follow the movements of the High Seas Fleet. Each direction finding station could establish the azimuthal angle of arrival of a radio signal with considerable accuracy. The angle of arrival information from several direction finding stations in different locations was used to locate the geographic point of origin of the signal by triangulation. From its call sign (the call sign of a transmitter is unique to that transmitter), the location of the principle transmitter of the High Seas Fleet could therefore be determined. The intercepted signals themselves were passed on to Room 40 at the Admiralty, where the British government had established a facility to decipher the messages. In theory, therefore, the Admiralty and the British Grand Fleet should have had ample warning of any sortie by the High Seas Fleet.[7] Unfortunately there were many cases where the warning was duly given but the information was misused or misunderstood. The most famous case is that of Jutland, although the story remains controversial.[8]

The Room 40 analysts had noted that just prior to any sortie by the High Seas Fleet the call sign of the flagship was transferred ashore. On 31 May 1916, when asked by a senior Admiralty officer where the call sign was located, Room 40 replied "ashore." The officer asked for no further explanation and, because he was known to dislike having to interact at all with Room 40, none was offered. He reported to the Admiralty and the Grand Fleet that the High Seas Fleet was still in harbor. Room 40, of course, knew the High Seas Fleet was at sea. Meanwhile Admiral Jellicoe and the Grand Fleet had left their anchorage on Scapa Flow on May 30, based on information previously provided (by Room 40) that their opponents might sortie. Having been told by the Admiralty that the High Seas Fleet was in harbor Jellicoe was startled to learn of its presence 50 miles south of his position off Jutland. Because of this egregious error and other Admiralty misinterpretations of radio intelligence information during the subsequent battle, Jellicoe never trusted radio intelligence information for the balance of the war.

Throughout the course of the war exploitation of information intercepted from wireless continued. In 1915, for example, BEF intercept units in France began use of vacuum tubes to direction find enemy spark and CW signals, under Round's guidance. Through painstaking direction finding and triangulation effort these units managed to locate every enemy transmitter on the Western Front in 1916 and managed to keep track of them throughout the war.[9] The Germans were similarly active in locating and mapping British transmitters.

Concern about interception of wireless signals did not abate and was a convenient excuse for the Army's lack of interest. Curiously, though, other means of communications were not secure either. Telephones were surprisingly bad. Telephone wires were usually laid below ground. As the war went on this burial took place at depths up to 6 feet. Initially this connection was a single wire with a ground return. This meant that telephone signals propagated into the ground and could be picked up by suitably sensitive equipment. The Germans exploited this by enlisting the both the Nobel Laureate physicist Arnold Sommerfeld and the mathematician Richard Courant to design and install a number of intercept facilities to exploit information passing over the telephone network.[10] (Courant was one of the great mathematicians of the 20th century and completed a distinguished academic career at New York University where the Courant Institute of Mathematical Sciences bears his name.)

The devices which performed the intercept function were located in close proximity to the front. "These devices were installed in a dug-out in the front line and from here insulated wires radiated out which ended in the so-called 'search grounds'; these search grounds consisted of metal stakes which were driven into the ground as close as possible to the enemy system of trenches. Where a single telephone line was used the currents passing through the soil would encounter one or more of these search grounds, and after being amplified by the attached apparatus were rendered audible. Thus, as if with a magnet, conversations carried forward over the telephone net of the enemy were attracted, and by using a switchboard, any number of search grounds could be thrown in selectively to eavesdrop on a definite sector of the front. In the German army these listening posts, which by the beginning of 1916 were installed everywhere along the front, were called 'Arendt Stations' or 'Polyps.'"[11]

Since, under static warfare conditions, the British were heavily dependent on the telephone system, this became a serious problem for them. A new British unit entering the line might be greeted by their regimental march played by a German band or record player.[12] Shouted calls from the other side might refer to their officers by name. Comments would be made on their previous performance elsewhere at the front. More seriously, information on planned operations such as trench raids or offensives was intercepted and exploited. An egregious example of telephone insecurity had occurred at the Somme. A British officer dictated an entire set of divisional orders verbatim on forward area telephones. The orders were intercepted and the enemy was thoroughly prepared for the division's operation, leading to high casualties with little to show for it.[13] Once it was understood that the telephone system was insecure, drastic communications discipline was imposed. In October 1916, a memorandum entitled "Indiscreet use of telephones near the Front" was issued, which contained, among other items, the following rules: Information on the following points will neither be given nor asked for by telephone or "buzzer" near the frontline trenches:

(a) Names of commanders, officers, headquarters, units, places, positions, map references. (This covers all references to observation posts, machine gun emplacements, headquarters, dumps, railways, trench mortar emplacements.)
(b) Movements of troops, such as patrols, reliefs, transport, batteries, aeroplanes, etc., arrival of reinforcements.
(c) Royal Engineers indents, ammunition returns, casualty returns, burial returns, situation reports, strength of units.
(d) Positions of our troops, rest billets, training schools. Special care must be taken when repeating Corps or G.H.Q. situation reports.
(e) Impending operations such as *raids, artillery* or *trench mortar bombardment (retaliatory or otherwise), aeroplanes, mines, gas* [italics in original].
(f) Effect of the enemy's artillery fire, trench mortar fire, hand grenades or gas; in fact, any effect of the enemy's operations against us.
(g) Observations of the enemy's movements, any references to prisoners or deserters, or statements made by them.
    In addition to this, all unnecessary gossip and communication by telephone or "buzzer" must be stopped. If unnecessary conversations are permitted, time is wasted; our listening apparatus become jammed, and such conversations will constantly contain information of value to the enemy.
    Absolute silence, except in cases of urgent military necessity, must be kept during the "Silent Hours"; these should be changed frequently. Adequate measures must be taken to ensure the insulation of our wires.

Any disobedience of these orders must be punished with severity, by the most rigid disciplinary measures.[14]

In some sectors the telephone was not to be used at all, to the corresponding detriment of command and control. Where possible, though with some difficulty because the lines had been buried, twisted pair shielded telephone lines replaced single wire links, thereby considerably reducing the amount of energy radiated into the ground.

Another device, the Fullerphone, was invented by a BEF signals officer in 1915 to deal with the problem of interception.[15] Despite its name the Fullerphone provided telegraph communication only, using an interrupted buzzer system over telephone wires. It was more sensitive than standard telegraph communications equipment and nearly immune to interception. The initial issues of Fullerphones were made up from converted field telephone sets. This type, however, was not the most successful and purpose-built designs were issued later. Towards the end of 1916, the Fullerphone was firmly established, and by 1918 most divisions had adopted Fullerphones for all their forward communication circuits. The Fullerphone required a wire connection between sender and receiver (usually over existing telephone wires) so the connection was as vulnerable to shellfire as telephone connections. The Fullerphone was used by the British Army through World War II.

The power buzzer (ground telegraph) used the earth itself as a transmission medium, providing a communications link invulnerable to shellfire. The BEF used the power buzzer to carry messages during an attack; the units advancing over the top carried a transmitter and a receiver was left in the old front line, from which the message could be relayed to the rear by telephone. The manuals called for both the sending and receiving antennas, each about 5 meters in length, to be emplaced in the earth in pairs about 50 meters apart. The range was limited to 2000 to 3000 yards. It was vulnerable to interception by the enemy, who could also emplace receiving antennas in the earth. The methods developed by Sommerfeld and Courant for the interception of telephone traffic were equally applicable to the ground telegraph. Also, Courant had designed the German version of the ground telegraph system and knew its vulnerabilities. The equipment was also heavy, limiting its usefulness in supporting an assault. For example, the U.S. ground telegraph used a power buzzer (SCR-71), weighing 41 lbs. (32 lbs. of which were for the 10 volt storage battery) and a receiver (SCR-72) weighing 27 lbs.[16]

Preventing the enemy from intercepting communications or from obtaining useful information from the interception took several forms. For telephones, single wire could be replaced by twisted-pair and the wires carefully insulated and shielded. The information transmitted could be protected to a certain extent by using coded expressions and through limited, abbreviated conversations. No physical protection was available for the wireless telegraph, but when the enemy had enough time to react to the information, i.e., battle plans, troop movements, information transmitted by wireless was protected by encryption.[17]

Encryption

Encryption refers to the methods used to protect information from hostile scrutiny. Until about the 1950s encryption was used only for messages, that is, messages which are written down and transmitted by telegraph. Encryption for voice was not possible until a reliable rapid method existed to digitize voice, that is, to convert the information contained in a voice signal to the zeros and ones used by the computer. Until then other methods were used to protect voice communications, as will be discussed later in this section.

Encryption methods involve the use of codes and ciphers.[18] A code is a group of alphanumeric characters chosen to represent words or phrases in a message. A cipher replaces each letter of a message by another letter. For additional security the message could be reciphered whereby the already enciphered message is ciphered again. To provide even more security, a super enciphered code could be used, whereby a message was encoded and the code groups then enciphered. In the days before mechanical or electronic implementation of these methods they had to be performed manually. In general, the more security needed the more time it took to provide it. Encoding or single encipherment took the least time, superenciphered code, the most.

Each of these methods had strengths and weaknesses. Plain codes were easier to use and in one sense more secure, since the breaking of one encoded message would not compromise others. The breaking of one enciphered message, on the other hand, would lead to the breaking of others enciphered using the same keyword (the rule used to assign a sequence of letters to the original letter of the message). The superenciphered code was the most secure because breaking the cipher led only to the underlying code. The security of codes rests in the ability to protect the code books. In the case of diplomatic communications, code books can be securely locked in embassy safes, and access to them restricted to a small number of authorized personnel. For wartime communications, however, code books have to be widely distributed to be useful. Capture of a single code book can compromise the security of the whole communications system. When the codes are in the enemy's possession, the coded text of a message reduces to the original message and superencipherment becomes simple encipherment.

During the First World War the Russians retrieved a German naval code book from the *Magdeburg*, a cruiser sunk in the Baltic. Reasoning that their allies, the British, could make better use of it than they could, they notified the British authorities, who sent a warship to retrieve it. Possession of this codebook, and others found on sunken submarines and other warships, allowed Room 40 to read German naval messages throughout the war. The coded messages were, of course, enciphered, sometimes ingeniously, but the talented Room 40 staff stripped the cipher from the coded message and then used the captured code books to recover the original text.

Knowledge of this accomplishment reached the Germans after the war. They determined that this could not be allowed to happen in a future conflict. Their solution was to employ a commercial cipher machine called the Enigma, enhanced for military use. The enciphered output from the Enigma machine was considered unbreakable, based on the astronomically high number of potential encipherments that could be generated by the machine. Potential adversaries of Germany quickly began work on breaking the Enigma. The first success was obtained by the Poles, unfortunately too late to save their country. They passed their knowledge on to the French, who further refined the approach until they too were overrun.

The British continued the effort and finally succeeded in breaking the Luftwaffe Enigma, using electromechanical devices that were the forerunners of today's computers. The Germans were not idle and added further and further refinements to the basic Enigma machine. For the rest of World War II the British and Germans dueled, the British attacking each refinement of the machine, particularly the naval version used to control submarines. The British finally gained the upper hand but suffered shipping losses during dark periods when they could not read the German transmissions. In order to penetrate enciphered messages in time to reroute or defend the convoys, the British also needed the key lists or daily Enigma settings for a month.[19] When possible, they obtained these from a variety of methods, including attacking German weather ships and by the dangerous method of boarding disabled and sinking submarines and retrieving the key list before the submarine sank.

Voice

During World War I conversations on the telephone could not be easily protected against eavesdropping. The technology to accomplish this, the scrambler, would not be available for 20 years, and even then it would be too cumbersome to use in the field. Attempts were made to use coded references for units, locations, and times, but these usually failed, as the episodes quoted above prove. Strict disciplinary measures were instituted to minimize the use of the telephone and in some cases to prevent its use at all, which of course cut off communications between commanders and formations and between infantry and artillery and negated the reason to have a telephone in the first place. These observations apply equally to the radiotelephone.

When the United States entered the war, it took advantage of the unique languages of its Native Americans. These languages were known only to members of the tribe and impenetrable to anyone not born into the tribe. They were very hard for an outsider to learn and his accent would make his status as a non-member of the tribe instantly identifiable. "In 1918 eight Choctaws of Company D, 141st infantry transmitted orders by field telephone.... Other Indian tongues were also used."[20] During World War II the United States Marines used members of the Navajo tribe.

The question is whether the high vulnerability of radiotelephone conversations to overhearing, coupled with the impossibility of protecting such conversations in the same way that messages can be protected by encryption, means that it is useless in a military environment. Subsequent history demonstrates that such was not the case. The key factor is the time value of information. The relevant question to ask is whether the enemy has enough time to react to information obtained by overhearing a conversation. In World War II infantry platoons and companies and higher headquarters communicated with each other in the clear. At that time, the technology to accomplish voice scrambling, the alteration of voice to prevent its being understood by anyone other than the intended recipient, was still far too cumbersome to implement in the field. The primary reason why infantry units used radio communications was that the benefits associated with being in touch with other units and with their commanders outweighed the risks associated with the enemy hearing what was being said. If the enemy gathered such information but was unable to react to it in a timely way, the negative consequences were minimal.

Jamming

Jamming is the prevention of communication caused by interference from another transmitter. As discussed in Appendix A, spark transmitters transmit over a wide range of frequencies, so two spark transmitters can unintentionally jam or interfere with each other. As each tries to overcome this interference by increasing power, the level of interference rises and neither can succeed. In military communications unintentional jamming of friendly transmitters has been a problem since the beginning of radio. Intentional jamming, on the other hand, is the effort by an adversary to prevent the other side's transmitters from communicating with each other. It has been a tactic employed since the first use of radio communications in warfare.

The first instance of intentional jamming actually occurred in the commercial world. In a well known episode, Marconi hoped to repeat his successful feat of reporting on the America's Cup races in 1900 for the *New York Herald*. In 1901, however, two additional wireless companies were engaged by other newspapers to report on the race as well as Marconi. The result was a fiasco. Mutual interference appeared to prevent any of the companies from transmitting the results, and several of them fabricated stories to have something to report.[21] The truth is more intriguing.

A third company, the American Wireless Telephone and Telegraph Company, failed to get a sponsor but decided to exploit the situation in a manner hardly in keeping with the highest standards of business ethics. The AWT&T used a transmitter more powerful than its competitors, and one of its engineers, John Pickard, worked out a method which allowed him to jam signals from the other companies while at the same time reporting on the progress of the race from his boat. He evolved a simple code, whereby one 10 second dash, repeated at intervals, indicated that the US yacht *Columbia* was in the lead, two such dashes indicated that the British yacht *Shamrock* was ahead, three that they were neck and neck, and so on. Thus only the AWT&T was able to pass accurate reports on the races, and profited accordingly. Pickard's gloating account of the incident stated, "When the yachts crossed the finish line we held down the key and then continued to hold it down by the simple method of putting a weight on it. Thus, radiating waves ... we sailed for our home port, and the batteries lasted for the entire hour and a quarter that we utilized to send the longest dash ever sent by wireless."[22]

In warfare, there are benefits and disadvantages to the use of jamming. It may prevent the enemy from communicating, but it is indiscriminate in that it prevents your own side from communicating as well. Secondly, the use of jamming prevents your own side from exploiting the enemy's communications.

Very often, in fact most often, the benefits gained from listening in on enemy communications outweigh the tactical gains obtained from cutting them off.

In World War I jamming technology was very primitive. Typically it consisted of turning on a high-power spark transmitter and jamming a broad band of frequencies, effectively preventing all communications in its vicinity. Not only did this have a negative effect on friendly communications, it also could be beaten. Such a jammer, spreading its power over a broad range of frequencies, can be penetrated by a transmitter transmitting on only one frequency and concentrating its power in a narrow range of frequencies. As discussed in Chapter 1 this phenomenon had been noted as early as the Royal Navy's 1911 maneuvers, where the Blue wireless operators were able to find frequencies on which to communicate despite Red's attempts to jam. Chapter 1 notes that jamming was not much used in the naval war because of the ease of defeating it.

The radiotelephone operates on a single frequency, and therefore is difficult to jam with a barrage jammer, as the military refers to a broadband jammer. A single frequency jammer is the obvious counter, but this presents a problem for the jamming side. First, the frequency to be jammed must be found, and, second, a jammer must be tuned to this precise frequency or close enough to it to interfere with communications. The counter-countermeasure for the communicating side is simply to change frequencies. All of this takes time and is difficult to accomplish under battlefield conditions, leading to the conclusion that jamming by itself would have been ineffective in preventing the tactical use of the radiotelephone by the BEF.

World War I marked the beginning of electronic countermeasures (ECM) and electronic counter-countermeasures (ECCM) in warfare. Jamming problems similar to the one discussed above have been solved and resolved many times since then and continue to exercise the ingenuity of many engineers. It is simplistic to suggest that German jamming would have prevented the use of the radiotelephone. If the Germans had tried to jam it, talented engineers on the British side would have found a way to get around it.

Conclusion

Fear of interception was often quoted as a reason not to use radio communications. The British Army was slow to use the telephone, but when its usefulness became apparent under stalemate conditions, the Army embraced it, despite its shortcomings, which included easy interception close to the front. The British Army was similarly slow to appreciate wireless telegraphy for battlefield command and control. But when, in 1918, the conditions of mobile warfare made wireless more attractive, wireless was used, and encryption was employed to protect the information transmitted. In each case, operational requirements trumped the previously professed fear of interception.

Summing up, intercept was not a showstopper, had been dealt with for wired telephony, and, for wireless, could be prevented by encryption. (Note that the CW transmitter that supported radiotelephony could also be used for wireless telegraphy, leading to the interesting observation that if the information to be transmitted was too sensitive for radio telephony, the information could be encrypted and sent by the same transmitter.) Because the BEF depended on telephony the BEF continued to use it, even after it was compromised, but strictly controlled voice communications and installed physical protection against intercept. Eventually it replaced telephones with Fullerphones, a solution it continued to use for 30 years. Similarly, in 1918, when the BEF became dependent on wireless telegraphy, the BEF incorporated encryption to prevent interception.

CHAPTER 13

An Assessment of Wireless
as It Was Actually Employed

Constant reference has been made to the development of wireless during the war, the operational issues following from this and its position in the overall strategy adopted by the General Staff.

Through its detailed study of communications, the book has highlighted a fundamental question: Would a more perceptive and less inhibited view of the use and development of wireless have affected, radically, the overall strategic and, as a consequence, operational conduct of the war? To provide a reasoned answer to this question three aspects of its progress have to be considered. Firstly, its historical development pre-war; secondly, its increasing use during the conflict against the background of technical advances in the means available; thirdly, the changing attitude of the High Command towards its strategic and, hence, operational importance, as the war progressed. Only then is it possible to suggest answers to the fundamental question posed.

In arriving at any conclusions, however, it has been important not to move, with the benefit of hindsight, ahead of a realistic assessment of the technical progress that could have been made under demanding warfare conditions. Equally, it has not been anticipated that the High Command would leap ahead of contemporary military thinking, including that of both the German and French armies.

The first requirement, therefore, is a brief resume of the development of wireless up to the beginning of the war in which the book acknowledges the considerable value of three main sources. The first is an important primary source provided by the personal account of Majors R. Orme and C.E. Prince, RFC.[1] Two secondary sources have also been invaluable. The first is Hartcup,[2] who follows its development perceptively, and the second Hopthrow,[3] who provides useful background from the Royal Engineers' viewpoint. Chapter 4 presents the RFC's development of the radiotelephone based on these and other sources. The discussion in this chapter is not intended to include technical detail other than that considered essential to make sense of the historical significance of the means employed.[4]

Before following the development of wireless throughout the war it is necessary to deal, briefly, with its alternate as a form of communication not using cable — the power buzzer-amplifier set. Its availability, paradoxically, may well have been a contributory factor in inhibiting more rapid development of wireless. However, although while on occasions it provided invaluable service, its potential as a revolutionary means of communication was severely limited.

In early 1915 the first experiments with earth induction were carried out at the Signal Service Training Center. They involved the transmission of signals by buzzers picked up and amplified to telephone receivers connected to widely separated grounds. Their first effective use is recorded at Vermilles in 1916.[5]

At this stage in its development it was subject to a number of limitations.[6] It had a maximum effective range of 2000 yards, and could only send and not receive. If two-way communication was required, a power buzzer and amplifier needed to be installed at each end of the line. The power buzzer and separate amplifier set, with batteries, had an overall weight of 90lbs (later reduced to 72lbs when a combined set was introduced). It required three trained signalers to operate. In addition, they were vulnerable to enemy overhearing and interference from adjoining sets. Consequently, their most effective use for messages in the clear was limited to short periods when cable telephone was not available. Also, the local geology could adversely affect the efficiency of earth conductivity.

Their limitations were emphasized at the Battle of the Somme because while the buzzers and amplifiers were fairly robust, the batteries were not. Furthermore, the earths (grounds) were vulnerable in trenches and, above all, the lack of response to one-way communication limited their effectiveness and popularity. For example, H. Chaney, who first went to France with the 7th Londons in March 1915, records in his diary, much later, that "on the whole we reckoned this new-fangled wireless gadget was hardly worth troubling with, especially when there was no chance of getting a return signal."[7]

By 1917, and despite their limitations, sets were in constant use.

Indeed, many instances are recorded of their effective employment where they successfully bridged gaps and breakdowns in communications. A typical example provided by Priestley relates to their use during attacks by the Australians on the Hindenburg Line at Bullecourt in May 1917 when communications by all other signals means were severed.[8] On this occasion, two sets located in tunnel entrances remained in constant touch with the rear, enabling warnings to be given of German counterattacks, which were successfully repulsed.

By 1918 much improved contact and more portable combined sets allowing two-way communications were available. They enabled, on occasions, vital communications to be maintained and fully justified their development but were eventually replaced by the now more versatile wireless, whose development during the war is considered next.

To all intents and purposes, wireless can be disregarded so far as the Army is concerned during the opening months of the war[9] but, by early 1915, there was limited use by the artillery in conjunction with the Royal Flying Corps (RFC) for target spotting. This was its primary function at this stage, though it was also used in a limited way to intercept enemy messages for intelligence purposes.

Army wireless progressed at a slow pace owing to the clearly apparent lack of enthusiasm, from the High Command downwards,[10] with the exception of those, within the RFC and REs, with specific responsibility for its development. Consequently, while the powerful but very cumbersome Marconi Pack Set was available for use to the rear, nothing suitable was adapted for trench warfare until the summer of 1915. The available Marconi Pack Set was overpowered for use in forward positions and, as a result, subject to both jamming and overhearing by the enemy.

The breakthrough came, in August 1915, with the development of the Trench Set. Although far from the ideal solution, when linked with the more powerful and recently introduced Wilson Set, it could provide a complete wireless communications link from GHQ through to the front line. It coincided with the introduction of the new fragile but powerful Thermionic valve.[11]

However, it is necessary to place the true worth of the Trench Set in perspective, given the primitive nature of the technology and the conditions under which it operated. It was introduced on the basis that it was simple in concept, foolproof in operation and required little training to operate. Hence its original designation as the BF set but later, and more appropriately, as the British Field Set (BFS). However, as with the Wilson

Set, it relied on spark rather than continuous wave (CW) transmission, which was only experimental at this stage. This made it unreliable and more prone to interference, which the later development of CW was designed to overcome. Also available, shortly afterwards, was a smaller and simpler version in the form of the Loop or Forward Set, similarly with spark transmission, for use in the most forward positions. This was more compact, lighter and had a shorter aerial, so that it was less vulnerable within sight of the enemy when used from concealed positions. Nonetheless, the complete set required three trained wireless signallers to operate while the cumbersome BFS, with an aerial twelve feet in height, could operate only from positions of heavy concealment in dry dugouts for successful operation and survival.[12]

The first real test for both the BFS and Forward Sets arrived during the Battle of Loos in September 1915, though they had been used with limited success at Festubert in May 1915. Their value was successfully demonstrated under testing conditions and in circumstances where other means of communication had failed or were not appropriate in the prevailing circumstances of heavy enemy bombardment.[13]

Despite this success, however, operational problems were immediately apparent. Lack of security remained a problem, enabling the enemy to locate British Army positions while the available solution of codes and ciphers was both inadequate and troublesome. Technical failures were also inevitable in a new venture. The result was that commanding officers continued to resist the use of wireless.

Central to the controversy surrounding its strategic importance in the prosecution of the war, wireless had made insufficient progress, technically or in acceptability, when the Battle of the Somme opened on 1 July 1916. Crucially, it had received little attention in the overall and otherwise very detailed strategic planning for the battle. Even at this relatively untried stage in its development, the research suggests strongly that it could and should have been considered for more extensive use. This was particularly the case where cable would, inevitably, be destroyed or could not follow the advancing troops in the unparalleled and extreme conditions under which the British attack was made. Nonetheless, where wireless was used the cumbersome nature of the equipment and vulnerability of its aerials created huge difficulties for signallers with the advancing troops, although on a number of occasions it proved successful in passing urgent messages. The provision of more portable, less vulnerable and technically efficient equipment remained the key. Had this been pushed ahead with greater success, the research suggests strongly that it would have proved invaluable as battalion HQs moved ahead of the buried cable system.

The reality of the situation was that, by the close of 1916, there was still insufficient confidence, and hence enthusiasm, for wireless at the highest levels of command. Consequently resources were not made available to match the needs which the successful development of wireless required and when it was most needed. Since late 1915, however, progress had continued within the RFC. This included the establishment of a Wireless and Observers School, under Major Orme, and a Wireless Telegraphy School at Biggin Hill. The RFC was approaching the ideal organization structure in which experiments, experimental manufacture, design, testing, training and air work were in close touch.[14]

Following the early static warfare of 1917 and the return to semi-mobile conditions, first at Passchendaele and then at Cambrai, new challenges faced the Signal Service. Wireless was provided with an opportunity to play an important part, which proved to be the springboard for its more rapid development, greatly enhanced acceptability, and vastly increased its successful use in 1918.

A historic breakthrough was made during 1917 when CW wireless emerged from its experimental stage to be fully operational, though limited by the availability of sets. Its impact was immediately apparent. Until 1917 the early CW sets, because of the delicacy of the equipment, could not withstand battle conditions, were highly technical by contrast with their predecessors, difficult to operate and subject to innumerable faults. By 1917, however, sets had been greatly improved to overcome previous difficulties. Their wavelength flexibility, generally improved efficiency and range to power and weight ratio made them infinitely better suited for use in all conditions throughout the whole chain of command. This is fully endorsed, for example, in a report on the advance of the Fifth Army in February and March 1917.[15]

Spark transmission, however, continued to play an increasingly vital part in forward operations. An example, which reflects great credit on the Signal Service generally, is provided by the heroic performance of the wireless section with VI Corps Signal Company, RE during operation in the Third Army area during the Battle of Arras in April 1917.[16] On this occasion, the section was able to maintain wireless communication from several locations when other means failed entirely owing to heavy shell fire, notably around Monchy-le-Preux. On this occasion, a station worked for three weeks under heavy bombardment, sustaining numerous casualties; three Military Medals were awarded to wireless operators on this station.[17]

Wireless station in a dugout at Sailly, December 1916. (IWM No. Q-27121)

As the year progressed, so did the progress of CW wireless. This is illustrated by an example from Priestley[18] relating to communications between Corps HQ, RHA at Ecorves and its OP at Bailleul in June 1917. Two CW sets operated at distances of 12,000 yards, with the forward position using an aerial only 3 feet high and working continuously to pass messages at the rate of 50 or 60 daily.

However, the real tests for wireless during 1917 were yet to come, first at Passchendaele. The extreme ground conditions caused by rain and, subsequently, mud made cable laying almost impossible, while other means of communication proved ineffective. By this time, BFS and Forward sets were more readily available with support from CW sets, though strictly limited by supply. In addition, all types of wireless were now more popular and trusted by Signal Service personnel. The BFS proved useful and efficient as far as forward as battalion HQ. Forward Sets could be used further forward with some success and CW was able to span the full chain of command, where available.

Wireless operators attached to Corps HQ, 11 March 1919, Ham-sur-Heure, Australian Corps. (IWM No. E[AUS] 4400)

The second major challenge arrived for wireless at the Battle of Cambrai in November 1917 with the introduction of a completely new factor in, for the first time, the use of tanks in significant numbers. In the battle CW sets were used, on a limited scale, to augment visual signalling, with some success.[19]

The general concept was that CW sets would be used in signal tanks at rallying points to communicate with fixed wireless stations at appropriate HQs such as infantry brigades[20] in accordance with the then established and codified procedures in S.S. 191.[21] It was also based on excellent experimental work that had been achieved through co-operation between the Central Workshops at Erin and Tank Corps.[22]

During the battle generally, an excellent chain of wireless stations was established and used more than ever before between divisions and brigades. Even so, it could have been used more freely and exploited to better effect. Staff instructions, characterized by their insistence on the use of cipher and code, could have been relaxed with the enemy in retreat and disarray, when the opportunities for it to benefit from overhearing were greatly reduced.

By the beginning of 1918 wireless chains had been established as an alternative to cable in all divisional sectors, in preparation for the inevitable German offensive. They continued to be subject to limitations imposed by shortages of trained personnel and equipment. When the offensive opened on 21 March, many of the wireless stations were destroyed by the initial bombardment, particularly south of Arras. Nevertheless, wireless established itself now as the mainstay of communications where virtually all other means had been destroyed. Specifically, it enabled surrounded units to provide situation reports for their superior commanders.[23] They had also turned to wireless as a life-line when even rear cable communications were badly affected by the enemy's long range artillery fire. Overall, the first full indications of the value of wireless and its great flexibility, not available with any other means of communication, had become clearly apparent.[24]

During the summer of 1918, as the British Army prepared for its final advance towards the conclusion of the war, wireless grew in popularity. This was true particularly between OPS and their batteries and between battery and brigade HQs. Here its usefulness was now more fully understood and appreciated. So was the advantage of a common system operating between infantry and artillery generally. However, destruction of equipment during the German offensive had to be made up before wireless could be fully exploited. In addition, training of technically proficient operators, for which only the keenest and best signalers had the necessary aptitude, coupled with the increasing demand for wireless stations right up to the front line, imposed immense pressures on the Signal Service. To its great credit, it had been generally able to deal with demands created by the momentum of the British Army's advance, as it accelerated.

By this stage of the war, the corps main route was now firmly established as the principal line of communication. Wireless was, equally, fully accepted as the main reinforcement for cable with a directing station at corps HQ controlling all forward stations. It had become of major operational importance and value throughout the whole chain of command.

However, its full acceptance by the High Command at this very late stage in the conflict was by far the most significant factor influencing its development and more general use. Though this acceptance was still tinged by the fear of overhearing, it was now tacitly agreed that cipher and code could be relaxed with the enemy in retreat. The massive benefits which transmission in the clear provided for the speed and clarity with which orders and other vital information could be passed, particularly in a fast moving and rapidly changing situation, was recognized. Moreover, the speed of the BEF's advance required wireless sets to operate over ever increasing distances. As the number of CW sets increased this provided the solution to the problem.

In summary, as the war drew to a close, the availability, range, quality and general acceptability of wireless communication had reached the point where it had emerged as the most effective and flexible means of communication, particularly for mobile warfare. Against this background, it is possible to address the fundamental question, which has imposed itself constantly upon the research. Would a more perceptive and less inhibited view of the use and development of wireless have affected, radically, the overall strategic and, as a consequence, the operational conduct of the war?

This issue will be dealt with as the concluding part of this part of the book. It is also a vitally important part of the answer to the more wide ranging question posed in the Introduction that seeks to evaluate the overall effectiveness of communications during the war. This also will be covered in the Conclusion to the book.

In the first instance, it is necessary to consider two overriding factors. They are not only incontrovertible but are also the areas in which an entirely different philosophy and attitude towards the use of wireless would have had the most marked effect. Firstly, as the war progressed, the greater majority of a vastly increasing number of Signal Service personnel, heavily supported by infantry, were engaged in creating and maintaining the vital link between transmission and reception points. The work was almost always carried out in circumstances of extreme difficulty and danger and often during the heat of battle. Two examples alone will illustrate this. The first by Bourne at the Battle of the Somme, where the Signal Service laid no less than 50,000 miles of cable, 7,000 at a 10 foot bury, up to the British front line.[25] The second, and very specific, example is provided by Terraine.[26] It relates to the Canadian Corps which, in the Kemmel area between 1 April–30 June 1916, laid 420 miles of cable and, despite a 6 foot bury, had to repair up to 50 breaks a day—a dangerous and arduous duty calling for immense courage and skill. Given greater availability and increased use of effective wireless communication, the larger part of this effort might have been drastically reduced or eliminated, with massive savings of Signal Service and other personnel as casualties, and equipment.

Secondly, the almost total reliance on line and cable, for the greater part of the war was, more often than not, an overriding factor in decisions made by the High Command in formulating the strategy and scope of its battle plans. The increased use of a system with the flexibility of wireless might have altered this decision making process dramatically and with historic effect. There appear few doubts in the conclusions reached by influential commentators such as Van Creveld that this was the case.[27] In fact, in reviewing specifically the Battle of the Somme, he is in no doubt that, because of its limited aspiration for wireless, GHQ constructed operations in such a way as to make them controllable by wire.

However, in order to arrive at a conclusion to the fundamental question posed, it is essential to make a balanced judgment of the scope available to the High Command to make decisions on the use of wireless. This assumes, for sake of argument, the will to do so. The following factors are the most influential.

Firstly, while some progress had been made, prior to the war, in the development and use of wireless, this received a substantial setback. This was the inevitable result of the decision made by the committee set up in 1912 to decide on its future not to recommend its further development. It arrived at this conclusion firstly, because of its existing lack of progress with wireless in the Army and secondly, because of the dangers of enemy overhearing. The second appears to have some historical justification. However the first reinforced a reluctance throughout the Army as a whole, apart from those particularly concerned with signals communication, towards innovation and change in this specific area. During the early days of the war this was exemplified by considerable antipathy towards the use of telephone. However, it is acknowledged that a similar reluctance was not so apparent in other areas of rapid and massive change. Artillery provides the outstanding example, where the immediate benefits were readily apparent and, more importantly, easily understood; tanks and aircraft are others.

Secondly, during the war, under the extreme pressures and on the immense scale that it was conducted, the immediately tried and available, with some justification, overtook the use of experimental or untried means of communication. In fact when, in the exigencies of the moment, wireless became the only viable available option it tended to make rapid progress forward in both acceptability and development.

Thirdly, the most difficult area in which to make a balanced judgment is that of the available technology, and specifically its development. This was influenced, to such a high degree, by the changing attitude of the

High Command as the war progressed. There appears little doubt that the expertise was at hand to make far greater progress during the early years of the war. For example, it appears that, with adequate resources and sufficient determination and enthusiasm, earlier development of effective CW wireless could have been achieved. It would have been of inestimable value being lighter, less cumbersome, eventually more robust, less visible and with a hugely increased power to weight ratio. It would have provided the solution more quickly to the problem created by the operational limitations of the early spark sets, which did little to recommend their use, particularly towards the front line. In the event, its first faltering employment did not take place until early 1917.

Overall, the issue rests on a paradox. Before the High Command could entertain the use of a means of communication as radical in concept as wireless it had, first, to reach an appreciation that its objectives and those of the Signal Service were entirely interdependent. Once this had become fully apparent then the progress and development of wireless was a natural sequel.

It is beyond doubt, however, that for the majority of the war, with the existing mindset of the High Command, in which cable communication absolutely predominated, it was inevitable that its overall strategy should have been limited by the facilities it had decided should form the backbone of its command systems. It therefore appears logical that with a greater acceptance of a means of communication with the flexibility of wireless, this would have substantially increased its strategic options.

Conclusion

In the introduction, the book posed three fundamental questions for which the research has been designed to provide answers: (1) To what extent did the High Command have a clear understanding of the requirement for a comprehensive policy for signal communications throughout the whole of the war? (2) To what degree was the Signal Service successful in meeting the extensive demands placed upon it to provide an effective system of communications during the war? (3) Specifically, did the Signal Service exploit wireless technology to its fullest capability, recognizing its potentially revolutionary impact on command and control?

The questions were posed against the background of a generally held, and basically accurate, historical perception of a fragmented communications system which fully justified the well documented epithets of non-existent, chaotic, blurred, inadequate, or unreliable on numerous occasions. However, this by no means presents the full picture. The reality was much more complex, reflecting varying degrees of success and failure. What is beyond doubt, and an absolutely key issue for influential commentators, such as Griffith,[1] for example, is that where success in battle was achieved, particularly when fought on the massive scale of 1917 onwards, this was heavily dependent upon effective communications. Its absence, equally, would be a, more or less, guaranteed recipe for failure.

Relative success or failure was influenced by a number of factors among which the attitude of the High Command, contemporary military conventions and thinking, inexperience in modern warfare, massive scale, hugely destructive weaponry, limited although emerging technology and Signal Service leadership and direction all played a crucial part.

In fact, the basic and generally recognized requirements for a successful communications system, supported by Staff Instructions of the day,

192

demanded reliability, speed of transmission and the ability to meet constantly changing conditions.[2] However, these simple though fundamental concepts were overlaid by the extreme conditions of the First War battlefields. Given the inexperience of the High Command in a conflict of this magnitude, exacerbated by traditional military doctrine, the provision of an effective communications system to meet even basic requirements proved extremely difficult and, on occasions, impossible to achieve.

The above does not imply that the High Command was unreceptive to new developments in communications. Indeed their papers, at the highest levels, illustrate no lack of support for innovation. Both Haig and Rawlinson displayed, on occasions, real enthusiasm for the progress made with wireless, for example.[3]

This was equally true of other new developments as, for example, in artillery, airplanes and tanks. However, their impact was of a dramatic nature and the benefits usually more readily apparent and understood. Developments in communications tended to be viewed at an incremental level, in which the Director of Army Signals was a constant and unremitting advocate. Unfortunately, the exigencies of the moment, more often than not, demanded an immediate and well-tried solution to communication problems; the circumstances in which an innovative approach might have been tried were readily overtaken by events. The book argues that this was very much the case where wireless might have been developed and used more extensively, at an earlier stage in the war, when the means to do so were certainly available. It argues, with equal force, that this was a highly influential factor in much of the High Command's strategic decision making, where cable predominated as the preferred medium of communication. Van Creveld's example of the Battle of the Somme, although controversial, is almost irrefutable.[4]

This book argues that it was not technical immaturity that prevented wireless from achieving its full potential on the Western Front. The remarkable achievements of C.E. Prince and the RFC engineers at Brooklands prove that effective wireless was not just beyond reach, as Keegan and other commentators have maintained, but was well within the capability of contemporary technology. Shortly after the beginning of the war CW wireless technology had advanced to the point where it could have been exploited more fully by the BEF. The availability of the technology, however, in no way guaranteed that these advantages could be gained. What was missing was both the vision to see that CW wireless would revolutionize command and control and the will to concentrate the engineering talent necessary to design and manufacture reliable, durable CW sets to realize that vision. If just a fraction of the resources devoted to the development of artillery, tanks and aircraft had been applied to providing the BEF with wireless communications, the CW radiotelephone in particular, the whole complexion of the war would have changed. More flexible and transportable communications would have increased the strategic and tactical options available to the BEF with a corresponding and dramatic impact on combat effectiveness and, as important, a huge reduction in loss of life.

What was eventually required and achieved, through powerful advocacy at the highest levels within the Signal Service, was an entire change in attitude by the High Command. When it became clearly apparent that effective communication could be achieved only through a well-coordinated communications policy, in which the High Command and the Signal Service were inextricably linked, then it emerged as an indispensable element for success in modern warfare. As this understanding was not fully reached until 1917, the difficulties posed for the Signal Service in the intervening period were extreme and could only be even partially overcome by strong leadership at the highest level within the Service and dedicated application to duty within its ranks. Numerous citations, from the Commander-in-Chief downwards, pay tribute to this and the final Official Dispatch of January 1919, covering the advance to victory, provides a fitting memorial to all within the Signal Service who strove to provide a tenuous communications link in the most demanding circumstances imaginable.

> The constant movement of the line and shifting of headquarters has again imposed an enormous strain upon all ranks of the Signal Service. The depth of our advance, and the fact that during the latter part of it, the whole of the British armies were simultaneously involved, made the maintenance of communications most difficult. The fact that in such circumstances the needs of the armies were met reflects the highest credit upon the zeal and efficiency of all ranks.[5]

Appendix A: Wireless Technology

At the beginning of the war, wireless meant Wireless Telegraphy (W/T) only, using Morse code. The technology did not support wireless telephony (voice). W/T used inefficient spark gap transmitters, which created a spark by interrupting the flow of current in a coil, just as an ignition coil works in an automobile. The spark gap transmitter is very inefficient; a low percentage of input power is actually radiated from the antenna. The receivers used a coherer, which was a glass tube full of iron filings that became a conductor of current in the presence of the electromagnetic field radiated by the transmitting antenna. The coherer was later supplanted by a magnetic and then a crystal detector. Reflecting the inefficiency of the spark gap transmitter, the Marconi Company's field W/T set issued to the BEF in 1914 weighed 150–500 lbs (mostly lead-acid battery weight) and was transported by horse drawn wagon and later by truck.[1]

Inefficiency wasn't the principal problem of spark gap technology, though. Mutual interference between transmitters was the fundamental and inescapable problem. It is the reason spark gap transmitters have been illegal throughout the world since the late 1920s. In the episode discussed in Chapter 12, in 1901 Marconi was prevented from repeating his 1900 feat of reporting on the America's Cup races for the *New York World*. At the time it was thought that inadvertent interference from two additional wireless companies engaged by other newspapers to report on the race prevented Marconi from reporting.[2] As recounted in chapter 12, the truth was more sinister.

In order to reduce mutual interference from spark gap transmitters, Marconi and others used the principle of syntony meaning an oscillation in the receiver's circuit which is induced by an oscillation of the same frequency in the transmitter's circuit. The term syntony is taken from the sympathetic vibration induced in a tuning fork resonant at one tone, e.g., the note "A" on the piano (440 cycles per second), when a second tuning fork resonant at the same tone is struck in close proximity. Syntony between transmitter and receiver was the technical concept at the heart of Marconi's four sevens patent (British patent number 7,777 issued on 26 April 1900) which was the principal technical basis for the success of the Marconi Company.

Like the tuning fork, the spark gap transmitter excites a resonant circuit tuned for a certain frequency and the receiving circuit is tuned to the same frequency. The electromagnetic wave radiated by the transmitter from a single discharge of the spark looks like the acoustic wave radiated by the tuning fork, and is shown in Figure 1. It is called a damped sine wave since the amplitude of the oscillation decreases with time while the frequency of oscillation (the number of cycles per second) remains the same. It can be shown mathematically and experimentally that such a wave contains higher frequencies than the single resonant frequency of the transmitting and receiving circuits.[3] This spillover of higher frequencies is the reason spark gap transmitters interfere with each other. It is fundamental

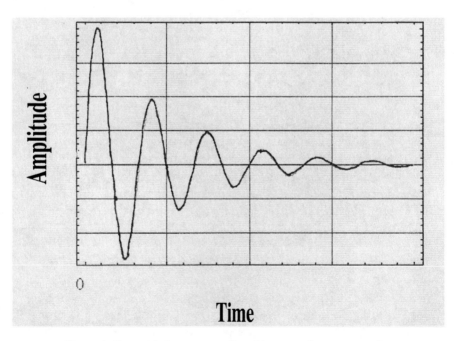

Figure 1. Damped sine wave radiated by a spark gap transmitter.

to their operation to emit a series of damped sine waves, one for each discharge of the spark. Clever design can minimize the effect but cannot eliminate it. The system Marconi used for the America's Cup race used syntony to reduce mutual interference but, as shown from the results quoted above, could not reduce it enough.[4]

Mutual interference severely limits the number of communication channels (transmitter-receiver pairs) that can be used simultaneously. During World War I, with spark gap technology, multiple transmitter-receiver pairs interfered with each other if they were less than 3000 yards apart, despite the use of syntony to reduce interference. This was the major restriction on World War I wireless in an environment that required significant communication capacity. Said another way, a World War I division occupying 1000–3000 yards of front (not atypical) had one wireless communications channel available for the entire division, if that. Clearly, wireless based on spark gap technology was grossly inadequate for command and control.

Before the war another technology which virtually eliminated the problem of mutual interference had been invented. Not only did the technology improve wireless telegraphy, it also offered the promise of wireless telephony. This was continuous wave (CW) transmission which used a single frequency (called the carrier) for each communication channel, like today's AM or FM broadcast radio. Use of a single frequency for transmission, rather than a damped sine wave, eliminated the spillover of extraneous frequencies from one channel to another and prevented mutual interference. Rather than the 3000 yard separation required of spark gap transmitters, many CW transmitters using different frequencies could be operated in close proximity, as the widespread use of walkie-talkie sets showed in World War II. This fact was well known to radio engineers before 1914, but could not be exploited until a compact source of CW was available.

CW wireless depends on having a reliable single frequency oscillator. It also requires devices to modulate (add information to) and amplify the signal. All three of these functions can be performed by electrical circuits containing three element (cathode, grid, and anode) vacuum tubes, called triodes. The cathode, when heated, emits electrons into the vacuum; they travel to the anode, which is at a much higher voltage than the cathode. The grid is placed between the cathode and anode; the voltage on the grid accelerates or inhibits the electron flow. A small change in grid voltage leads to a much larger change in anode voltage, thus amplifying the grid voltage. Vacuum tubes were available before the war. Dr. Ambrose Fleming, of Marconi, patented a two element vacuum tube, or diode, in 1904, calling it a valve. (Britain continued to use this nomenclature for all vacuum tubes in the twentieth century.) Building on Fleming's diode, Lee DeForest patented a three element triode in 1906, calling it the audion. (America did not continue to use this name.). Using the triode, Howard Armstrong patented the oscillator and regenerative amplifier in 1912.[5]

The availability of vacuum tubes was crucial to the timely application of this technology to World War I wireless. The triode is essential for: 1. Transmission, because in the appropriate circuit it is the source of sustained continuous oscillation, the carrier frequency of modern radio. It also is the only means of amplification of the signal to be delivered to the antenna; 2. Reception, because any high frequency signal detected by a crystal or other means is weak, and must be amplified in order to be heard; and 3. Weight reduction, because the CW transmitter is much more efficient than a spark gap transmitter and uses less power, i.e., smaller, lighter batteries.

The Marconi Company was the only supplier of wireless equipment to the BEF, so the company's awareness and application of CW technology to wireless was crucial if it was to be used by the BEF during the war. The Marconi Company understood the significance of the triode; Fleming and Marconi sued DeForest in 1908, claiming that DeForest's invention depended on Fleming's tube. Before the war Marconi engineers H.J. Round, C.E. Prince and R. Orme conducted experiments with and developed inventions based on the vacuum tube. In addition, after the regeneration circuit was patented, priority disputes and well publicized patent litigation over the regeneration circuit began in 1914. Marconi was also a litigant in these suits.[6]

Summing up, the status of wireless technology in 1914 to 1918 was that the spark gap wireless was inadequate for military requirements and CW wireless promised to overcome the spark gap's inadequacies. The regenerative circuit, which allowed transmission and reception of continuous waves, was invented in 1912. This achievement was well known to the Marconi Company. The technology for building and deploying CW radiotelegraph and radiotelephone sets, therefore, was available to the British Army early in World War I.

Appendix B:
Signal Service Units, 1914

Regular Units

Name of Unit	Establishment Offr's.	Men	No. of Units in E.F	Total nos. Offr's.	Personnel Men
"L" Signal Company	5	263	1	5	263
G.H.Q. Signal Coy.	5	75	1	5	75
Army Corps H.Q. Sig. Coy.	4	63	2	8	126
Divl. Signal Coy	5	157	6	30	942
Cable Section.	1	35	8	8	280
Airline Section.	1	57	5	5	285
Cavalry Sig. Squadron.	8	198	1	8	198
Sig. Troop with Cavalry Bde.	1	23	3	3	69
Sig. Trp. with Independent Cav. Bde.	1	42	1	1	42
Wireless Section (incl. Motor W/T Det.)	2	66	1	2	66

4 August 1914.   **Grand Total A.S.S. with E.F.**   75   2346

Territorial Units

Name of Unit	Establishment Offr's.	Men	No. of Units in E.F	Total nos. Offr's.	Personnel Men
Divl. Telegraph Coy.	2	57	14	28	798
Army W/T Telegraph Coy.	3	66	5	15	330
Army Cable Telegraph Coy.	6	159	5	30	795
Army Airline Telegraph Coy.	6	194	5	30	970
4 August 1914. Grand Total A.S.S. with T.F. in U.K.				**103**	**2893**

N.B.— *In addition to the above should be considered the Indian Telegraph units of the Indian Army and the Divisional Signal Company of the 7 Division which was then concentrating before completing its training with the Division.*

Appendix C:
Signal Service Units
Later in the War

Unit	Number.	Estab.	Total.	Total.
G.H.Q.				
"L" Signal Battn.		3665	3665	3665
Pigeon Service				
Signal Depot				
Cavalry Corps Signals		899	899	899
Tank Corps Signals		436	436	436
Army Signals H.Q.	(5)	274	1370	
Airline Sections	(15)	61	915	
Cable Sections	(15)	38	570	
Area Signal Detachments	(40)	16	640	
A.F.A. Bde. Sig. Sub-sections	(47)	20	940	
Extra for Corps above 3			50	
Construction Company	(5)	117	585	
Light Rly. Sig. Sections	(5)	41	205	
Intelligence W/T Groups	(6)	47	282	5557
Corps Signals H.Q.	(20)	140	2800	
Airline Sections	(20)	61	1220	
Cable Sections	(64)	38	2432	
Corps H.A. Sections	(20)	37	740	
H.A. Group Sub-sections	(90)	27	2430	
Extra for Divisions above 3			154	9776
Divisional Signals	(62)	289	17918	17918
Grand Total				**38,251**

Chapter Notes

Preface

1. R.E. Priestley, *The Signal Service in the European War of 1914 to 1918 (France)* (Chatham: Mackay, 1921).

Introduction

1. R.E. Priestley, *The Signal Service in the European War of 1914 to 1918 (France)* (Chatham: Mackay, 1921), p. 5.

2. J.H. Boraston, ed., *Sir Douglas Haig's Despatches (December 1915–April 1919)* (London: Dent & Sons, 1919) pp. 334–5.

3. S. Bidwell and D. Graham, *Fire Power. British Army Weapons and Theories of War 1904–1915* (London: George Allen & Unwin, 1982).

4. M. Van Creveld, *Command in War* (Cambridge, MA: Harvard University Press, 1985).

5. T. Travers, *How the War Was Won: Command and Technology in the British Army on the Western Front, 1917–1918* (London: Routledge, 1992).

6. R. Prior and T. Wilson, *Command on the Western Front: The Military Career of Sir Henry Rawlinson, 1914–1918* (Oxford: Blackwell, 1992).

7. P. Griffith, *Battle Tactics of the Western Front* (New Haven, CT: Yale University Press, 1994).

8. *Ibid.*, p. 103.

9. *Ibid.*, p. 120.

10. I.M. Brown, *British Logistics on the Western Front, 1914–1918* (Westport, CT, and London: Praeger, 1998); M. Cook, "Evaluating the Learning Curve: 38th (Welsh) Division on the Western Front 1916–1918" (Unpublished M.Phil. thesis, Birmingham University, 2006); C.B. Hammond, "The Theory and Practice of Tank Co-operation with the other arms on the Western Front during the First World War" (Unpublished Ph.D. diss., Birmingham University, 2006); G. Sheffield and D. Todman, eds., *Command & Control on the Western Front: The British Army's Experience 1914–1918* (Staplehurst: Spellmount, 2004); and R. Prior and T. Wilson, *The Somme* (New Haven, CT, and London: Yale University Press, 2005).

11. Priestley, *Signal Service in the European War of 1914 to 1918 (France)*.

12. This is not to overlook John Ferris' important study, *The British Army and Signal Intelligence During the First World War* (London: Blackwell 1992), which, however, makes only passing reference to the day-to-day role of the Signal Service.

13. B. Bond, ed., *The First World War and British Military History* (Oxford: Clarendon Press, 1991).

14. General Staff Instruction No S.S. 191 *Inter-Communication in the Field—November 1917*.

15. Van Creveld, *Command in War*, p. 158.

16. J. Terraine, *White Heat: The New Warfare 1914–1918* (London: Sedgwick & Jackson, 1982), p. 129.

17. Van Creveld, *Command in War*, p. 186.

18. Priestley, *The Signal Service in the European War of 1914 to 1918 (France)*, p. ix.

19. Griffith, *Battle Tactics of the Western Front*, p. 169.

20. *Ibid.*, p. 174.

21. Prior and Wilson, *Command on the Western Front*, p. 40.

22. T. Travers, *The Killing Ground* (London: Unwin Hyman, 1986), p. 55.

23. *Ibid.*, p. 169.

24. Priestley, *The Signal Service in the European War of 1914 to 1918 (France)*, Appendices 1–4.

25. R. Raines, *Getting the Message Through* (Washington, D.C.: Office of the Chief of Military History, U.S. Army, 1996), p. 186.

26. J. Keegan, *The First World War* (New York: Knopf, 1999), p. 22.

Chapter 1

1. "Statement of Capt. Jackson's claims as regards the invention of wireless telegraphy" appended in a letter from Capt. F.T. Hamilton to the Commander-in-Chief Devonport 28 January 1899, ADM 116/523, quoted in R. Burns, *Communications: An International History of the Formative Years* (London: Institution of Electrical Engineers History of Technology, Series No. 32, 2004), p. 291.

2. H.B. Jackson, letter to G. Marconi, 15 September 1896, Marconi file HIS 64, quoted in Burns, *Communications: An International History of the Formative Years,* p. 295.

3. N. Lambert, "Strategic Command and Control for Maneuver Warfare: Creation of the Royal Navy's 'War Room' System, 1905 to 1915" *Journal of Military History* 69 (April 2005), p. 373.

4. Burns, *Communications: An International History of the Formative Years*, p. 343.

5. T. P. Sarkar, et al., *History of Wireless* (Hoboken, NJ: John Wiley & Sons, 2006) pp. 393–394.

6. Sarkar et al., *History of Wireless*, p. 394. Also, Marconi might have received the signal at a different frequency without knowing it, due to the characteristics of the Poldhu transmitter, see http://www.antiquewireless.org/otb/marconi1901a.htm.

7. Lambert, "Strategic Command and Control for Maneuver Warfare: Creation of the Royal Navy's 'War Room' System, 1905 to 1915" p. 379.

8. *Ibid.*, pp. 381–384.

9. *Ibid.*, pp. 382–383.

10. *Ibid.*, p. 390.

11. "Final report of the Norman Committee" WO 32/8879, PRO, p. 8, quoted in Burns, *Communications: An International History of the Formative Years*, p. 403.

12. *Ibid.*

13. *Ibid.*

14. *Ibid.*, p. 404.

15. *Ibid.*

16. G. Hartcup, *The War of Invention: Scientific Developments, 1914–18* (London: Brassey's, 1988), p. 15, emphasis in the original.

17. A. Hezlet, *The Electron and Sea Power* (London: Peter Davies, 1975), p. 39.

18. *Ibid.*, p. 51.

19. *Ibid.*, pp. 51–52.

20. *Ibid.*, p. 63.

21. *Ibid.*, p. 64.

22. *Ibid.*, p. 75.

Chapter 2

1. Lt. Col. F.T. Stear (Ret.), *Development of Signalling in the Corps* (Royal Engineers Historical Society, 1968).

2. R.E. Priestley, *The Signal Service in the European War of 1914 to 1918 (France)* (Chatham: Mackay, 1921), p. 4.

3. "Early Days of the Signal Service" *Royal Engineers' Journal* (date unknown).

4. Priestley, *The Signal Service in the European War of 1914 to 1918 (France)*, p. 5. There is no other record of this committee or that of the 1911 committee mentioned below.

5. "A Story of Lt. Gen. Sir John Fowler" *Royal Signals Institution Journal* (date unknown).

6. Priestley, *The Signal Service in the European War of 1914 to 1918 (France)*, p. 6.

7. *Brigade Signal Sections Instructions* (Dimoline Papers, Liddell Hart Centre for Military Archives, Kings College, London: 1915).

8. Priestley, *The Signal Service in the European War of 1914 to 1918 (France)*, Tables IIA and IIB p. 11.

9. *Ibid.*, p. 12.

10. R.T Foley, "Assessing the Enemy: German Intelligence and German War Plan-

ning Before the Great War" Centre for First World War Studies, War & Society Seminar 2004.

11. TNA: PRO, WO95/57 War Diary of the Director of Army Signals, Circular Memoranda Nos. 1 and 5, August 1914, illustrate cooperation with the French, including a diagram of the lines available.

12. TNA: PRO, WO 95/57 War Diary of the Director of Army Signals, August 1914, records a further meeting with French GHQ to arrange the use of their line circuits and existing telegraph and telephones.

13. Priestley, *The Signal Service in the European War of 1914 to 1918 (France)*, p. 22.

14. TNA: PRO, WO 95/57 War Diary of the Director of Army Signals, Circular Memoranda Nos. 4 and 6, August 1914, illustrate his involvement with important issues concerning wireless at this time. They include wavelength arrangements between cavalry and the RFC, interception of enemy signals and the use of code and cipher.

Chapter 3

1. J.C. Craven, "A Signaller in France 1914–1918" *Royal Engineers Journal* (date unknown), p. 28.

2. TNA: PRO, WO 256/1 War Diary of Field Marshal Sir Douglas Haig, Part I, §2, pp. 111–2, 124. This also records that he intervened personally to ask for five extra wireless sets at Corps HQ!

3. The war diary of the GHQ Carrier Pigeon Service indicates that carrier pigeons were first utilized in September 1914 by the "I" (b) Branch, General Staff, GHQ, BEF and with its rapid development the service was transferred to the Royal Engineers as a branch of the Signal Service on 28 July 1915.

4. R.E. Priestley, *The Signal Service in the European War of 1914 to 1918 (France)* (Chatham: Mackay, 1921), p. 42.

5. Lt. Col. F.S. Garwood, as a major commanding 7 Signal Company, 7th Division, IV Corps at the First Battle of Ypres, records in his diary that the cables were cut continually by enemy shells and linemen had to repair them under the most hostile of conditions (IWM 91/23/1). It was at this at this early stage of the war that the enemy used 8" guns for the first time. These were to prove a massive obstacle to maintaining communications despite the use of 6 foot and even 8 foot buries.

6. Priestley, *The Signal Service in the European War of 1914 to 1918 (France)*, Plate IV.

7. TNA: PRO, WO 95/57 War Diary of the Director of Army Signals.

8. *Ibid.*, Circular Memorandum No. 25, December 1914, seeks to clarify the responsibilities and duties of officers I/C Signals at this time.

9. Priestley, *The Signal Service in the European War of 1914 to 1918 (France)*, p. 53.

10. The General Staff, *Forward Inter-Communication in Battle. S.S. 148* March 1917, which was included and revised in *InterCommunication in the Field. S.S. 191* November 1917.

11. TNA: PRO, WO 95/57 War Diary of the Director of Army Signals, Circular Memorandum No. 29, September 1914.

12. TNA: PRO, WO 95/57 War Diary of the Director of Army Signals, September 1914.

13. *Ibid.*, Circular Memoranda Nos. 10/22/24, August, November and December 1914, deal with the establishment of the signals depot, the supplies for it and the excessive demands made upon it.

14. TNA: PRO, WO 95/57 War Diary of the Director of Army Signals makes constant reference to this.

15. By 1918 the pigeon service had become a very well established branch of the Signal Service, with 90,000 men in battalions and other units trained to care for and fly pigeons.

16. Churchill College, Cambridge: The Journals of Sir Henry Rawlinson, 1/1, p. 33, record his attendance at wireless experiments in early 1915, which "achieved good results."

17. In fact, by 1916, the Signal Service had official responsibility for the artillery signals system as far forward as brigade HQs.

18. Priestley, *The Signal Service in the European War of 1914 to 1918 (France)*, p. 55.

19. TNA: PRO, WD 256/1 War Diary of Field Marshal Sir Douglas Haig, § 2, p. 28, provides the specific illustration of the interception of a message conveying orders of XXVIII German Reserve Corps in early 1915 using wireless.

20. TNA PRO, AIR 1/131/15/40/221 Instructions for the Guidance of OCs' detachments RFC, April 1916.

21. TNA: PRO, WO95/288 War Diary of Deputy Director of Signals, Second Army, January 1915.

22. J.W. Palmer (IWM P257) in his diary written while serving as a signaller with 26 Brigade RFA in early 1915 makes constant reference to the extreme difficulties of maintaining communication by wire both during and immediately after enemy action. The journals of Sir Henry Rawlinson, Churchill College, Cambridge 1/1 p. 33 record that "the news that comes back from the actual trenches is much delayed owing to the difficulties of passing messages — always the case in trench warfare and the source of constant misunderstanding."

23. LHCMA: Dimoline Papers: *Brigade Signal Sections*, p. 2. Visual Signalling — "Visual signalling has fallen on evil times at present."

24. Priestley, *The Signal Service in the European War of 1914 to 1918 (France)*, p. 69.

25. Colonel H.L.F. Dimmock (IWM 78/15/1) records in his diary for 17 May 1915 notes of a speech delivered during a scheme of training for signallers in the front line covering the educational matters referred to above.

26. TNA: PRO, WO 95/57 War Diary of the Director of Army Signals records that large quantities of cable were lost or destroyed north of Ypres.

27. *Ibid.*, Circular Memorandum No. 52, August 1915, provides comprehensive instructions for visual signalling with electric lamps.

28. TNA: PRO, WO 95/57 War Diary of the Director of Army Signals, 18 June 1915, records his visit to 5th Division in June to witness successful experiments with Sterling wireless sets. During the same period, he sent his Assistant Director of Army Signals to inspect wireless for use with 27th Division and also issued Circular Memorandum 17A on wireless procedure.

29. Priestley, *The Signal Service in the European War of 1914 to 1918 (France)*, p. 86.

30. *Ibid.*, p. 88.

31. TNA: PRO, WO 95/57 War Diary of the Director of Army Signals, Circular Memorandum No. 47, July 1915, provides guidance on methods and devices for retaining communication with trenches, including pigeons, and the spread of best practice, in their use.

32. *Ibid.*, Circular Memoranda 46 and 48, July 1915, illustrate the establishment of the Pigeon Service with notes on its organizational structure — issued to Armies.

33. *Ibid.*, 27 August 1915, records visits by him to First and Second Army HQs to discuss serious problems of enemy overhearing, particularly in front line trenches.

34. Priestley, *The Signal Service in the European War of 1914 to 1918 (France)*, p. 99.

35. TNA: PRO, WO 256/5 War Diary of Field Marshal Sir Douglas Haig, Part I, §2, pp. 96–97, 9 September 1915, records that very strict orders were given that *no* messages of importance be transmitted by telephone if the wire ran close to the enemy's trenches in contact with the ground.

36. TNA: PRO, WO 95/57 War Diary of the Director of Army Signals, December 1915, recognized the importance of this and comments that the band could be removed in sight of the enemy — worn on both arms, by DRs!

37. Priestley, *The Signal Service in the European War of 1914 to 1918 (France)*, p. 94.

38. TNA: PRO, WO 95/57 War Diary of the Director of Army Signals, Circular Memorandum No. 58, November 1915.

39. TNA: PRO, WO 95/57 War Diary of the Director of Army Signals, December 1915, for example, he was now able to intervene, with Signal Service requirements as a priority, in the siting of HQs, either actual or proposed.

40. TNA: PRO, 256/6 War Diary of Field Marshal Sir Douglas Haig, Part I, § 1, p. 53, 7 November 1915, refers to training at Corps level, signals being fundamentally a Corps function — a significant recognition.

41. TNA: PRO, WO 95/57 War Diary of the Director of Army Signals, Circular Memoranda Nos. 57 and 59, November 1915, cover stores requirements and economy.

42. TNA: PRO, WO 95/288 War Diary of the Deputy Director of Signals, Second Army, April 1915, clearly indicates, however, Army's view, at least, that the Signal Service had tacit responsibility.

43. TNA: PRO, WO 95/57 War Diary of the Director of Army Signals, 1916.

44. TNA: PRO, WO 95/1072 War Diary of the Canadian Corps HQ Signal Co. RE, May 1916, illustrates the laying of huge

quantities of cable hampered by heavy shelling, insufficient labor and cable shortages.

45. Priestley, *The Signal Service in the European War of 1914 to 1918 (France)*, p. 120.

Chapter 4

1. It is worthy of mention that during the early part of the war the telephone was subject to similar skepticism that was fairly rapidly overcome in the face of events and, in fact, resulted in an over-dependence.

2. TNA: PRO, AIR/1/733/183/1 History of RFC Wireless from the outbreak of War.

3. *Ibid.* Prince and Orme record that "under Dowding's energetic guidance, a period of great wireless activity was inaugurated which was the genesis of all subsequent aircraft wireless work in the RFC at home."

4. *Ibid.*

5. G. Hartcup, *The War of Invention: Scientific Developments, 1914–18* (London: Brassey's, 1988), p. 152.

6. TNA: PRO, AIR/1/733/183/1 records "an undefined opposition to experimental work at Brooklands was becoming evident at the War Office." Later, after some prevarication, the High Command ordered that no experimental work should be carried out at Brooklands, only testing.

7. TNA: PRO, AIR/1/2217/209/33/6 "Memorandum of the use of wireless in the RAF" quoted in R. Burns, *Communications: An International History of the Formative Years* (London: Institution of Electrical Engineers History of Technology, Series No. 32, 2004), p. 407.

8. C.E. Prince, "Wireless Telephony on Aeroplanes" in G. Shiers, ed., *The Development of Wireless to 1920* (New York: Arno Press, 1977), p. 377.

9. Italics by the authors for emphasis. If the carrier frequency from a CW transmitter is modulated by a microphone, it will transmit voice. If, instead, the microphone is replaced by a telegraph key, the CW transmitter will transmit Morse code. In modern terms this is called on-off keying, the simplest form of Amplitude-Shift Keying (ASK).

10. Prince, "Wireless Telephony on Aeroplanes" pp. 377–378.

11. *Ibid.*, p. 378. Italics by the authors for emphasis.

12. Burns, *Communications: An International History of the Formative Years*, p. 414.

13. J. F. C. Fuller, *Tanks in the Great War 1914–1918* (New York: Dutton, 1920), p. 18.

14. Hartcup, *The War of Invention: Scientific Developments 1914–1918*, p. 83.

15. C. R. M. F. Cruttwell, *A History of the Great War 1914–1918* (Oxford: Clarendon), p. 271.

16. Fuller, *Tanks in the Great War 1914–1918*, p. 21.

17. *Ibid.*, p. 26.

18. Hartcup, *The War of Invention: Scientific Developments 1914–1918*, p. 88.

19. *Ibid.*, p. 146.

20. *Ibid.*, p. 147.

21. *Ibid.*, p. 156.

22. L. Kennett, *The First Air War 1914–1918* (New York: Macmillan, 1991), p. 34.

23. E. Lawson and J. Lawson, *The First Air Campaign* (Conshohocken, PA: Combined Books, 1966), pp. 74–76. The book also shows an example of the card. It shows concentric circles centered on the target, labeled Y, Z, A, B, C, D, at increasing distances from the target. When the card was oriented so 12 o'clock pointed north, the distance and orientation of the burst from the target was communicated to the battery as, say, 8C, meaning at 8 o'clock, at a distance of 200 yards, the radius of circle C.

24. Prince, "Wireless Telephony on Aeroplanes" p. 378.

25. *Ibid.*

26. *Ibid.*, p. 379.

27. Burns, *Communications: an International History of the Formative Years,* p. 417.

Chapter 5

1. TNA: PRO, WO 95/57 War Diary of the Director of Army Signals, Circular Memorandum No. 61, December 1916.

2. R.E. Priestley, *The Signal Service in the European War of 1914 to 1918 (France)* (Chatham: Mackay, 1921), p. 121.

3. *Ibid.*, p. 135.

4. A. Surfleet, (IWM P126) in his diary, July 1916, p. 37, kept while serving with 13th Battalion, East Yorkshire Regiment, 31st Division as a signals linesman records, with

considerable understatement, that "this linesman business is hard work" after he put down a new system of trench telephone from battalion HQ down the communication trench, along the front line, in and out of every bay, through supports and back to battalion HQ.

5. *Ibid.*, p. 37, reports that the signals officer had arranged for lamp signals to be sent from the front line to battalion HQ, "a fairly hot spot."

6. *Ibid.*, p. 48, reports that he had good contact signalling with some airplanes using huge ground sheets which were changed from red to white by pulling a string making a dot and dash alphabet possible.

7. *Ibid.*, p. 37, reports that "if this job is not so cushy as generally supposed, it is a very great improvement on the fire step life of the ordinary soldier."

8. Priestley, *The Signal Service in the European War 1914 to 1918 (France)*, p. 145.

9. The General Staff, *Forward Inter-Communication in Battle* S.S. 148 March 1917, which was included and revised in *Inter-Communication in the Field* S.S. 191 November 1917.

10. TNA: PRO, WO 95/57 War Diary of the Director of Army Signals, January 1916, records his visit to witness successful demonstrations of power buzzer-amplifiers — he recommended the purchase of 1000 sets, on the strength of this.

11. The British term for battery in 1914 and, to some extent today, is accumulator. For consistency, we employ the American term.

12. TNA: PRO, WO 95/57 War Diary of the Director of Army Signals, Circular Memorandum No. 154 Army Wireless Cos. & Listening Set Organization, November 1916.

13. TNA: PRO, WD 256/14 War Diary of Field Marshal Sir Douglas Haig, Part II, § 2, p. 65, November 1916, records, during a visit to the RFC at Doullens, "The progress with wireless is wonderful. We can telephone between two machines in the air at the same time using wireless."

Chapter 6

1. R. Raines, *Getting the Message Through*, (Washington, D.C.: Office of the Chief of Military History, U.S. Army, 1996), p. 187.

2. R.E. Priestley, *The Signal Service in the European War of 1914 to 1918 (France)* (Chatham: Mackay, 1921), p. 226.

3. A. Hezlet, *The Electron and Sea Power* (London: Peter Davies, 1975), p. 64.

4. M. Van Creveld, *Command in War* (Cambridge, MA: Harvard University Press, 1985), p. 158.

5. P. Hart, *The Somme* (New York: Pegasus Books, 2008), p. 114ff. Hart presents an exceptionally clear description of the battle, in particular the experiences of each division involved. The account presented here closely follows his description.

6. Hart, *The Somme*, p. 533.

7. *Ibid.*, p. 184.

8. *Ibid.*, p. 116.

9. *Ibid.*, p. 132.

10. *Ibid.*, p. 135.

11. *Ibid.*, p. 140.

12. *Ibid.*, p. 144.

13. *Ibid.*, p. 149.

14. *Ibid.*, p. 161.

15. *Ibid.*, p. 162.

16. *Ibid.*, p. 167.

17. *Ibid.*, p. 175.

18. *Ibid.*, p. 179.

19. *Ibid.*, p. 184.

20. *Ibid.*, p. 186.

21. *Ibid.*, p. 197.

22. *Ibid.*, p. 203.

23. *Ibid.*, p. 204.

24. *Ibid.*, p. 223.

25. *Ibid.*, p. 262.

26. *Ibid.*, p. 264.

27. *Ibid.*, p. 272.

28. *Ibid.*, p. 287.

29. *Ibid.*, p. 304.

30. *Ibid.*, p. 306.

Chapter 7

1. R.E. Priestley, *The Signal Service in the European War of 1914 to 1918 (France)* (Chatham: Mackay, 1921), p. 106.

2. TNA: PRO, WO 95/57 War Diary of the Director of Army Signals, Circular Memorandum No. 164, November 1916.

3. Priestley, *The Signal Service in the European War 1914 to 1918 (France)*, p. 109.

4. TNA: PRO, WO 95/57 War Diary

of the Director of Army Signals, Circular Memorandum No. 167, November 1916, Allocation of Cable for Corps heavy artillery.

5. *Ibid.*, Circular Memorandum No. 155, November 1916, War Establishments of Army, Corps & Divisional Signal Cos.

6. The General Staff, *Inter-Communication in the Field,* S.S. 191, November 1917, p. 53.

7. *Ibid.*, p. 66 describes this apparatus in detail; in summary, it was a Morse instrument which buzzed its output into the earth via two earth terminals and, without the use of cable, connected to an amplifier similarly earthed by means of induction current for distances of up to a mile. H.L. Harris, *Signals Venture* (Aldershot: Gale & Polden, 1951), p. 42, describes how during his experience in the Messines sector in 1917 the instrument was temporarily abandoned for use at the front line because of its susceptibility to enemy overhearing.

8. Harris, *Signals Venture*, p. 43, describes how risk of interception of signals by the enemy led to the introduction of the Fullerphone again in the Messines sector in 1917. He describes it, succinctly, as operating with small direct currents instead of comparatively high-voltage, high frequency currents used with field telephones, which made it almost immune from interception. The Liddle Archives. The General Staff, *The Fullerphone — Its Action & Use 40/W.O./3941* March 1917 provides full details of its inception.

9. G. Hartcup, *The War of Invention: Scientific Developments, 1914–1918* (London: Brassey's, 1988), p. 78.

10. TNA: PRO, WO 95/57 War Diary of the Director of Army Signals, Circular Memorandum No. 192, March 1917.

11. The General Staff, *Forward Inter-Communication in Battle* S.S. 148 March 1917.

12. The General Staff, *Inter-Communication in The Field* S.S. 191 November 1917.

13. TNA: PRO, WO 95/57 War Diary of the Director of Army Signals, March 1917.

14. At this point of the war, wireless was still not regarded as a primary means of message transmission but was gaining considerable ground as a vital medium for gathering intelligence. It was based in a series of intelligence gathering centers that greatly improved the overall picture of enemy dispositions compared with the previously fragmented picture. In addition, as well as constantly listening in to enemy communications, it also monitored British Army wireless for indiscretions in procedure that might be of value if overheard by the enemy; an increasingly important role as the use of wireless reached something approaching its full potential in 1918.

15. Priestley, *The Signal Service in the European War of 1914 to 1918 (France)*, p. 198.

16. The General Staff, *Forward Inter-Communication in Battle* S.S. 148 March 1917; and The General Staff, *Inter-Communication in the Field* S.S. 191 November 1917.

17. Priestley, *The Signal Service in the European War of 1914 to 1918 (France)*, p. 212.

18. The General Staff, *Inter-Communication in the Field* S.S. 191 November 1917, p. 56.

19. Royal Corps of Signals Library and Museum: *I Corps Signal Communications Instructions No. 5,* dated 6 April 1917, p. 7, makes it explicit that unnecessary changes of HQ locations away from the main communications route should be avoided.

20. H. Cheney (IWM 77/47/1) in his memoirs "A Lad goes to War" (a shortened version of which has been published in Moynihan's *People at War 1914–1918*), describes, during his service as a signals NCO with the 7th Londons, the miles of armored cable buried in the ground before attacks having their weak points and being entirely dependent for their repair on human agencies; and the heroic part played by linesmen with their wires and pliers who mended breaks in peril of their lives.

21. Cheney again describes runners as being the most dependable means of communication, who in the face of the barrage and dense fighting showed qualities of courage, resource and hardihood.

22. W.T. Manns (IWM 77/182/1) during his service with the 1/1 Welsh Heavy Battery TF at Arras and Ypres in 1917, describes how in locating his unit he spotted the wireless mast and tracked down the combined map, telephone exchange and wireless room and also makes reference to difficulties experienced in moving wireless masts.

23. TNA: PRO, WO 158/318 IV Corps Report, October 1917; TNA: PRO, WO

95/98 Tank Corps HQ 1st Brigade War Diary, November 1917; TNA: PRO, WO 95/408 Third Army Signal Co. War Diary, November 1917; TNA: PRO, WO 158/318 IV Corps Report, October 1917.

24. TNA: PRO, WO 95/2856 War Diary of 51st (Highland) Division Signal Co RE, November 1917.

25. The General Staff, *Inter-Communication in the Field* S.S. 191, November 1917 section 8, p. 50.

26. TNA: PRO, WO 95/2846 War Diary of 51st (Highland) Division Signal Co. RE, November 1917.

27. TNA: PRO, WO 95/2856 War Diary of 51st (Highland) Division Signal Co. RE, November 1917, records that "shutter and lamp were used with great success."

28. *Ibid.*, records that "a far better use of wireless was obtained than ever before. Over 80 important messages were sent and received during three days working."

29. TNA: PRO, WO95/2852 War Diary of 51st (Highland) Division Signal Co. RE, November 1917.

30. TNA: PRO, WO95/2856 War Diary of 51st (Highland) Division Signal Co. RE, November 1917, records that runners proved invaluable in the prevailing conditions.

31. TNA: PRO, WO 95/57 War Diary of the Director of Army Signals, Circular Memorandum No. 194, March 1917, provides instructions on the movement of lofts at this time. The diary also records his personal comments that "pigeons proved a great disappointment in the misty conditions and poor results were achieved."

32. Priestley, *The Signal Service in the European War of 1914 to 1918 (France)*, p. 242.

33. *Ibid.*

34. TNA: PRO, WO 95/2846 War Diary of 51st (Highland) Division Signal Co. RE, December 1917, Notes on lessons learned from the Battle of Cambrai.

35. The way in which tank signals communications were organized are very well described, in detail, in The General Staff, *Signal Organization for Heavy Branch Machine Gun Corps* S.S. 167, June 1917. J.F.C. Fuller, *Tanks in the Great War* (London: Murray, 1920) Chapter 24 — Tank Signalling Organization.

36. Priestley, *The Signal Service in the European War of 1914 to 1918 (France)* Table 5, p. 252 — see Appendix B.

Chapter 8

1. L. Wolff, *In Flanders Fields* (New York: Time, 1963) pp. 147–153.

2. *Ibid.*, p. 105.

3. *Ibid.*, p. 36.

4. *Ibid.*, p. 183.

5. *Ibid.*, p. 209.

6. *Ibid.*, p. 196.

7. *Ibid.*, p. 214.

8. *Ibid.*, pp. 229–239.

9. *Ibid.*, p. 262.

10. Keegan, *The First World War* (New York: Knopf, 1999), p. 366.

11. *Ibid.*

12. *Ibid.*, p. 368.

13. *Ibid.*, p. 371.

14. J. F. C. Fuller, *Tanks in the Great War 1914–1918* (New York: Dutton, 1920), p. 151.

15. *Ibid.*, p. 152.

Chapter 9

1. H.A.J Lamb (IWM PP/MCR/187) reports in his diaries while serving as a second lieutenant with the 40 Division Signal Company at Arras that, following the initial German attack, signal communications throughout were, more or less, badly damaged and in retreat. H.L. Harris. *Signals Venture* (Aldershot: Gale & Polden, 1951), p. 45, endorses Lamb's experiences.

2. R.E. Priestley, *The Signal Service in the European War of 1914 to 1918 (France)* (Chatham: Mackay, 1921), p. 260.

3. *Ibid.*, p. 260.

4. J.C. Craven, "A Signaller in France 1914–1918" *Royal Engineers Journal* (date unknown), p. 186, endorses the complete uselessness of visual during the offensive.

5. Priestley, *The British Army Signal Service in the European War of 1914 to 1918 (France)*, p. 269.

6. The General Staff, *Inter-Communication in the Field* S.S. 191 November 1917.

7. Priestley, *The Signal Service in the European War 1914 to 1918 (France)*, p. 272.

8. *Ibid.*, p. 271.

9. *Ibid.*, p. 274.

10. Journals of Sir Henry Rawlinson 1/9 p. 118 Churchill College, Cambridge.

11. Priestley, *The Signal Service in the European War 1914 to 1918 (France)*, p. 275.

12. H.A.J. Lamb reports again on 17 April 1918 that Signals began a period of complete re-organization.

13. Priestley, *The Signal Service in the European War of 1914 to 1918 (France)*, p. 282.

14. *Ibid.*, p. 287.

15. TNA: PRO, WO95/57 War Diary of the Director of Army Signals, 1917, contains a comprehensive document covering the importance issues affecting wireless development at this time.

16. Priestley, *The Signal Service in the European War of 1914 to 1918 (France)*, p. 298 Table XI.

17. *Ibid.*, p. 301.

18. *Ibid.*, p. 306.

19. *Ibid.*

20. *Ibid.*, p. 309.

21. The General Staff, *Inter-Communication in the Field* S.S. 191 November 1917, pp. 81–85.

22. A letter dated 3 February 1967 from the Royal Engineers Historical Society in reply to an enquiry, held at the Royal Engineers Library, Chatham, pays tribute to a selection of gallantry awards presented during this period.

23. Priestley, *The Signal Service in the European War of 1914 to 1918 (France)*, p. 313.

24. *Ibid.*, p. 319. The only exception was during the temporary pause around the Hindenburg Line which had been occupied by the British Army during the summer and winter of 1917; here buried cable existed which had not been destroyed by either the British or German armies. Cable re-discovered here was in a reasonable state of repair. It was salvaged and used prior to the final rapid success of the attack on 29 September, which quickly carried the British Army's advance well ahead of the Hindenburg Line.

25. Priestley, *The Signal Service in the European War of 1914 to 1918 (France)*, p. 323. On the night before the battle for the Hindenburg Line, 300 yards were cut from the main divisional route, by a cavalry squadron, to create a picket line for horses. The same infantry of a brigade whose line had been cut (above) used part of their own cable route to make bivouacs. On the evening before the crossing of the Sambre–Oise canal, all the signals poles of a divisional route were removed by Australian troops for making bivouacs.

Chapter 10

1. B. Pitt, *1918 The Last Act* (New York: Norton, 1962), p. 50.

2. M. Middlebrook, *The Kaiser's Battle: 21st March 1918: The First Day of the German Spring Offensive* (London: Allen Lane, 1971), p. 80.

3. *Ibid.*, p. 76 presents a diagram of the British defensive positions.

4. *Ibid.*, pp. 51–54.

5. *Ibid.*, pp. 54–55.

6. *Ibid.*, p51.

7. M. Thompson, *The White War* (New York: Basic Books, 2009), pp. 295–296.

8. E. Rommel, *Infantry Attacks* (London: Greenhill Books, 2006), p. 168ff.

9. Thompson, *The White War*, p. 294.

10. Middlebrook, *The Kaiser's Battle: 21st March 1918: The First Day of the German Spring Offensive*, p. 147.

11. *Ibid.*, pp. 266–268.

12. *Ibid.*, p. 340.

13. *Ibid.*, p. 340.

14. *Ibid.*, p. 84.

15. Pitt, *1918 The Last Act*, p. 197.

16. *Ibid.*, p. 205.

17. *Ibid.*, p. 206.

18. J. Keegan, *The First World War* (New York: Knopf, 1999), p. 411.

19. *Ibid.*, 413.

Chapter 11

1. J. Terraine, *White Heat: The New Warfare 1914–1918* (London: Sedgwick & Jackson, 1982), p. 148. General Sir Hubert Gough expressed it thus: "The problem is controlling events when you have gone beyond the plans which are cut and dried and once troops are committed to the attack, all control is lost." See also Terraine, *White Heat*, pp. 48, 149, 150.

2. M. Van Creveld, *Command in War* (Cambridge, MA: Harvard University Press, 1985), p. 186.

3. P. Griffith, *British Battle Tactics on the Western Front 1916–1918* (New Haven, CT: Yale University Press, 1994), p. 170.

4. R.E. Priestley, *The Signal Service in the European War of 1914 to 1918 (France)* (Chatham: Mackay, 1921), Plate XVIII.

5. Lt. Gen. Sir John Fowler, who was Director of Army Signals on the Western Front throughout the whole of the war.

6. Van Creveld, *Command in War*, p. 156.

7. J. Charteris, *At GHQ* (London: 1931), p. 208.

8. J.F.C. Fuller, *Generalship: Its Diseases and their Cure* (London: 1937), p. 61.

9. Van Creveld, *Command in War*, p. 158.

10. The General Staff, *Forward Inter-Communication in Battle* S.S. 148, March 1917.

11. The General Staff, *Inter-Communication in the Field* S.S. 191, November 1917.

12. T. Travers, *How the War Was Won: Command and Technology in the British Army on the Western Front—1917–1918* (London: Routledge 1992), p. 54.

13. *Ibid.*

14. The General Staff, *Inter-Communications in the Field* S.S. 191 November 1917.

Chapter 12

1. G. Hartcup, *The War of Invention: Scientific Developments, 1914–18* (London: Brassey's, 1988), p. 15 also TNA: PRO WO2/ 8876/ 8878/ 8879.

2. D. Showalter, *Tannenberg* (Hamden, CT: Shoe String Press, 1991), p. 169.

3. *Ibid.*, pp. 229–230.

4. R.E. Priestley, *The Signal Service in the European War of 1914 to 1918 (France)* (Chatham: Mackay, 1921), p. 151.

5. J. Ferris, *The British Army and Signals Intelligence During the First World War* (Wolfeboro Falls, NH: Sutton, 1992), p. 5.

6. W. Flicke, *War Secrets in the Ether*, Vol. 1 (Laguna Hills, CA: Aegean Park Press, 1977), p. 24.

7. Hartcup, *The War of Invention: Scientific Developments, 1914–18*, pp. 123–125.

8. C. Andrew, *Secret Service* (London: Guild, 1985), p. 104.

9. R. Burns, *Communications: An International History of the Formative Years* (London: Institution of Electrical Engineers History of Technology, Series No. 32, 2004), p. 406.

10. Hartcup, *The War of Invention: Scientific Developments, 1914–18*, p. 77. Also http://homepage.ntlworld.com/lapthorn/earthmode.htm.

11. Flicke, *War Secrets in the Ether*, Vol. 1, p. 28.

12. Hartcup, *The War of Invention: Scientific Developments, 1914–18*, p. 77.

13. Priestley, *Work of Royal Engineers in the European War, 1914–1919, the Signal Service (France)*, pp. 105–106.

14. Ferris, *The British Army and Signals Intelligence During the First World War*, pp. 28–29.

15. Hartcup, *The War of Invention: Scientific Developments, 1914–18*, p. 78, photographs available at *http://home.wxs.nl/meuls003/fullerphone/fullerphone.html.*

16. E. H. Hinricks, *Intercepting German Trench Communications in World War I* (Shippensburg, PA: White Mane Publishing, 1996), pp. 129–132.

17. Priestley, *Work of Royal Engineers in the European War, 1914–1919, the Signal Service (France)*, p. 29.

18. An excellent discussion of codes and ciphers, from which this description is taken, is given in Ferris, *The British Army and Signals Intelligence During the First World War*, pp. 7–8.

19. D. Kahn, *Seizing the Enigma* (Boston: Houghton Mifflin, 1991), p. 152.

20. D. Kahn, *The Codebreakers* (New York: Scribner, 1967, 1996), p. 549.

21. H. G. J. Aitken, *Syntony and Spark: The Origins of Radio* (New York: Wiley, 1970), p. 246.

22. A. Price, *The History of US Electronic Warfare*, Vol. 1 (Westford, MA: Murray, 1984), p. 3.

Chapter 13

1. TNA: PRO, AIR/1/733/183/1 History of RFC Wireless from the outbreak of War.

2. G. Hartcup, *The War of Invention: Scientific Developments, 1914–18* (London: Brassey's, 1988), pp. 14–16.

3. Brig. H.E. Hopthrow, *The Use of Wireless Technology by the Royal Engineers in the 1914–1918 War* (Chatham, 1983), occasional paper No. 2.

4. TNA: PRO, AIR/1/733/189/1 A paper entitled Wireless in the Royal Air Force, delivered to the Institute of Electrical Engineers, Wireless Section on 14 May 1919, by Major Erskine–Murray, summarizes wireless use in the RAF, with useful technical information.

5. R.E. Priestley, *The Signal Service in the European War of 1914 to 1918 (France)* (Chatham: Mackay, 1921).

6. The General Staff, *Inter-Communication in the Field*. S.S. 191 Section 11, p. 66.

7. H. Chaney, "A Lad Goes to War" (IWM 77/47/1), p. 130.

8. Priestley, *The Signal Service in the European War of 1914 to 1918 (France)*, p. 229.

9. TNA: PRO, AIR/1/2217/209/33/6 History of Wireless Telegraphy from August 1914–November 1918 does, however, record the first real cooperation between the artillery and the RFC, at the Battle of the Marne, using wireless which is described as being "very successful" and was followed by a great demand, from field battery commanders, for enhanced facilities.

10. TNA: PRO, AIR/1/733/183/1 records "an undefined opposition to experimental work at Brooklands was becoming evident at the War Office." Later, after some prevarication, the High Command ordered that no experimental work should be carried out at Brooklands, only testing.

11. TNA: PRO: AIR/1/2217/209/13/6 History of Wireless Telegraphy from August 1914–November 1918.

12. The General Staff, *Inter-Communications in the Field* S.S. 191 pp. 64/65.

13. TNA: PRO, AIR/ 1/2217/209/33/6 quotes Field Marshal Sir John French: "The RFC has become, more and more, an indispensable factor in combined operations — particularly in cooperation with artillery, due to wireless."

14. TNA: PRO, AIR /1/733/183/1.

15. LHCMA: The Uniacke Papers.

16. *War Diary* (Wireless Section, 6 Corps Signal Company, RE: April 1917).

17. TNA: PRO, AIR1/2217/209/33/6 illustrates 2nd Wing RFC cooperation with 38 HA Group, 55th Divisional Artillery and 187 Heavy and Siege Batteries when huge damage was caused to the enemy at the Battle of Arras using 30 aircraft simultaneously over a seven mile front with *no* wireless failures.

18. Priestley, *The Signal Service in the European War of 1914 to 1918 (France)*, p. 227.

19. E.F. Churchill, "Memories 1914 to 1918 of a Signal Officer" (IWM 83/23/1).

20. The General Staff, *Signal Organization for Heavy Branch Machine Gun Corps* S.S. 167 June 1917, p. 4.

21. The General Staff, *Inter-Communication in the Field S.S. 191* November 1917, Section VI.1.(c).

22. J.F.C. Fuller, *Tanks in the Great War* (London: Murray, 1920), pp. 180-181.

23. Soon after midnight on the first day of the offensive, Fifth Army in retreat lost communication by wire but re-established it by wireless and on one occasion, at least, a German concentration was broken up by interception of their orders by a British Army wireless station in their area and artillery alerted.

24. TNA: PRO, AIR/1/733/183/1 On 1 April 1918 when the Royal Air Force was established, the RAF and Army Wireless Co-operation School was also set up "and thus from the small wireless section collected by Major Dowding in 1915, it sprang in direct line of descent of the Wireless Experimental Establishment, the Wireless School, and the Wireless Telegraphy School. At last, there was a coherent and workable organization." TNA: PRO, WO 95/1050 Australian Corps Wireless Section War Diary, June 1918.

25. J.M. Bourne, *Britain and the Great War 1914–1918* (London: Edward Arnold, 1989), p. 167.

26. J. Terraine, *White Heat: The New Warfare 1914–1918* (London: Sedgwick & Jackson, 1982), p. 148.

27. M. Van Creveld, *Command in War* (Cambridge, MA: Harvard University Press, 1985), p. 158.

Conclusion

1. P. Griffith, *Battle Tactics of the Western Front* (New Haven, CT: Yale University Press, 1994), p. 11.

2. The General Staff, *Inter-Communication in the Field*, S.S. 191 November 1917.

3. PRO: WO 256/14 War Diary of Field Marshal Sir Douglas Haig; Churchill College, Cambridge: The Journals of Sir Henry Rawlinson, 1/1, p. 33.

4. M. Van Creveld, *Command in War* (Cambridge, MA: Harvard University Press, 1985), p. 158.

5. R.E. Priestley, *The Signal Service in the European War of 1914 to 1918 (France)* (Chatham: Mackay, 1921), p. 307.

Appendix A

1. R. E. Priestley, *Work of Royal Engineers in the European War, 1914–1919, The Signal Service (France)* (Chatham: Mackay, 1921), p. 29–30.

2. H. G. J. Aitken, *Syntony and Spark: the Origins of Radio* (New York: Wiley, 1970), p. 246.

3. J. Mills, *Radio Communication Theory and Methods* (New York: McGraw-Hill, 1917), p. 63–65.

4. Aitken, *Syntony and Spark: the Origins of Radio*, p. 246.

5. S. Hong, *From Marconi's Black-Box to the Audion* (Cambridge, MA: MIT Press, 2001), p. 155–156.

6. *Ibid.*, pp. 184–189.

Bibliography

Unpublished Sources

Imperial War Museum, London

MANUSCRIPT PERSONAL
ACCOUNTS

Abbott, A. Diary of a signaller in the Royal RGA IWM 86/77/1.

Acklam, W.R. Diary of a signaller with "B" Battery, 190 Brigade, RFA (41 Division) IWM 83/23/1.

Atkinson, A.R. Diary of a wireless operator in the RFC IWM 89/12/1.

Barlow, G.R. Diary of a private with the 31 Divisional Signal Company, RE IWM 86/40/1.

Bedford, W. Diary of a signaller with the 2/10 Battalion (201 Brigade, 67 Division) IWM 78/51/1.

Best, O.H. Copies of letters as a DR/RE attached to 2 Division Signals Office on the Western Front IWM 87/56/1.

Bishop, E.D. Diary of a signaller with the RFA 62 Division IWM 77/111/1.

Bradbury, S. Diary of a signaller with the 3/4 Battalion, Cameron Highlanders IWM 81/35/1.

Brookes, B.J. Diary of a signaller with the Queen's Westminster Rifles (1/16 Battalion, London Regiment) IWM PP/MCR/283.

Brooks, H.G. Diary of a signaller, RE IWM 87/62/1.

Brown, G. Diary of a signaller with "M" Signal Company, RE IWM 85/11/1.

Brundskill-Reid, M. (Mrs.) Diary of her service with the Women's Signallers Territorial Corps IWM 78/39/1 & 1A.

Bryan, G. Diary of a signaller with the RGA IWM 80/28/1.

Carey, F. Diary of a signaller with the 196 Siege Battery RGA IWM 85/43/1.

Carus-Williams, L.C. Diary whilst serving as an RE officer with the 2 Army Signals Corps IWM 77/184/1.

Chandley, S. Diary of a signaller with the 6 Battalion, Cheshire Regiment IWM 77/184/1.

Chaney, H. Diary of a signaller with the 7 London Territorial Battalion IWM 77/47/1.

Christian, J.H. An outline history of the Cavalry Corps Signals Squadron, 1914–1916 IWM 90/28/1.

Churchill, E.F. Memories 1914–1919 IWM 83/23/1.

Dennis, G.V. Extracts from the Diary of a yeoman rifleman and signaller with the 21 KRRS IWM 78/58/1.

Dimmock, H.L.F. A speech delivered during a scheme of training for Artillery Signallers IWM 78/15/1.

Drury, J.W. Diary of a signaller with the 3 Grenadier Guards, 2 Guards Brigade, Guards Division IWM P434.

Fergusson, V.M. First World War letters relating to the inadequacies of communications systems in the trenches IWM PP/MCR/111.

Garwood, F.S. A Diary of the 7 Divisional Signal Company during the Third Battle of Ypres IWM 91/23/1.

Lamb, H.A.J. Diaries of a signaller with the

40 Signal Company, RE IWM PP/MCR/ 187.

Manns, W.T. Diaries of a wireless operator attached to the 1/1 Welsh Heavy Battery TA IWM 77/182/1.

Outen, C.R. Numerous photographs relating to wireless operations 1915–1918 whilst giving assistance to RA shoots IWM Reference Unknown.

Palmer, J.W. Diaries of his service with 26 Brigade RFA IWM P257.

Patterson, W. Diary of a signaller with the 6 Seaforth Highlanders IWM 89/7/1.

Rawnsley, F. Diary of a signaller in the 16 West Yorkshire Regiment IWM 80/40/1.

Riley, A. Diary of a signaller with the 42 Divisional Signal Company IWM 68/8/1.

Surfleet, A. Diary of a signaller with the 13 Battalion, East Yorkshire Regiment (31 Division) IWM P126.

Thomas, A. Diary of a signaller with the 2/4 Battalion, Ox & Bucks Light Infantry (61 Division) IWM P457.

Thomas, W.R. Diary of a signaller with the 1 & 14 Battalions, the Royal Welch Fusiliers (7 & 35 Divisions) IWM 77/121/1.

The National Archives: Public Record Office, Kew

AIR/1/32/15/1/169 Tactical Use of Wireless Telephony. Recommendations of Conference in France, 18 July–30 September.

AIR/1/131/15/40/221 Instructions for the Guidance of OCs Detachments RFC when co-operating with Columns of All Arms, April 1916.

AIR/1/733/183/1 "History of RFC Wireless from the Outbreak of War" by R. Orme and C.E. Prince.

AIR/1/733/189/1 Wireless in the Royal Air Force by Major Erskine-Murray.

AIR/1/2217/209/33/6 History of Wireless Telegraphy from August 1914–November 1918.

WO 95/57 War Diary. Director of Army Signals.

WO 95/98 Tanks Corps. War Diary. HQ 1st Brigade, November 1917.

WO 95/288 War Diary. Deputy Director of Signals, Second Army.

WO 95/408 War Diary. Third Army Signal Company, April 1915–February 1919.

WO 95/1010 War Diary. Australian Corps Wireless Section, June 1918.

WO 95/1072 War Diary. Canadian Army Corps HQ Signal Company RE.

WO 95/2846 War Diary. 51st (Highland) Division General Staff (III Corps), November 1917.

WO 95/2852 War Diary. HQ RE 51st (Highland) Division, November 1917.

WO 95/2856 War Diary. 51st (Highland) Division, November 1917.

WO 158/318 IV Corps Report Havricourt-Bourlon Operations, 20 November–1 December 1917.

WO 256/1–18 War Diary. Field Marshal Sir Douglas Haig.

Royal Corps of Signals Library & Museum, Blandford Forum

Field Service Manuals — Signal Service — Signal Company (with Division) Expeditionary Force 1913 & 1915.

1 Corps Signal Communications Instructions 6 April 1917.

Forward Inter-communication in Battle S.S.148 1917.

Handbook of Procedure (Wireless Telegraphy) 1918.

Handbook of Procedure for use with Wireless Signal Service in the Army 1914.

Instruction in Army Telegraphy and Telephony — Provisional Field Cables 1915.

Inter-communication in the Field S.S.191 1917.

Manual of Army Signal Service — War (Provisional) 1914.

Notes in Communication during recent operations on the Front of the Second Army (Provisional) 1917.

Notes on Army Signalling for Signallers 1914.

Notes on Signalling Communication in the Second Army 1916.

Signal Organisation for Heavy Branch Machine Gun Corps 1917.

Signal Training Manual 1917.

Signalling — Morse, Semaphore, Station Work, Despatch Riding, Telephone Cables, Map Reading —1914 & 1915.

A Story of Lt. Gen. Sir John Fowler (*Royal Signals Institution Journal*: date unknown).

Training Manual — Signalling (Provisional) 1915.

Royal Engineers Library, Chatham

A Signal Company, formerly 1 Division Telegraph Battalion (formerly C Troop) Royal Engineers.

Craven, J.C. "A Signaller in France 1914–1918" *Royal Engineers' Journal*: date unknown.

Early Days of the Signal Service (*Royal Engineers' Journal*: date unknown).

1 Division Telegraph Battalion — Royal Engineers.

Hopthrow, Brigadier H.E., *The Use of Wireless Technology by the Royal Engineers' in the 1914–1918 War* (Chatham, 1983).

Stear, F.T. Lt. Col. (Ret.). *Development of Signalling in the Corps*. Royal Engineers Historical Society, 1968.

Sundry Records

Brigade Signal Sections (Dimoline Papers, Liddell Hart Center for Military Archives, King's College, London University).

The General Staff, The Fullerphone — Its Action and Use 40 / W.O. / 3941 March 1917 (The Liddle Archives, Leeds University).

Journals of Sir Henry Rawlinson (Churchill College, Cambridge).

The Uniacke Papers (Liddell Hart Center for Military Archives, King's College, London University).

Published Sources

General Works and Special Studies

Aitken, Hugh G.J. *Syntony and Spark: The Origins of Radio*. New York: Wiley, 1970.

Andrew, Christopher. *Secret Service*. London: Guild Publishing, 1985.

Ascoli, David. *The Mons Star: The British Expeditionary Force 5th August–22nd November 1914*. London: Harrap, 1982.

Barrie, Alexander. *War Underground—The Tunnellers of the Great War*. London: Tom Donovan, 1988.

Bidwell, Shelford, and Dominick Graham. *Fire Power. British Army Weapons and Theories of War 1904–1945*. London: George Allen & Unwin, 1982.

Blake, Robert, ed. *The Private Papers of Sir Douglas Haig: 1914–1918*. London: Eyre & Spottiswoode, 1952.

Bond, Brian, ed. *The First World War & British Military History*. Oxford: Clarendon Press, 1991.

Boraston, J.H., ed. *Sir Douglas Haig's Despatches (December 1915–April 1919)*. London: J.M Dent & Sons, 1919.

Bourne, John M. *Britain and the Great War 1914–1918*. London: Edward Arnold, 1988.

Bowyer, Chaz. *Albert Ball VC*. London: William Kimber, 1977.

Brown, Ian M. *British Logistics on the Western Front 1914–1918*. Westport, CT, & London: Praeger, 1998.

Burns, Russell W. *Communications: An International History of the Formative Years*. London: The Institution of Electrical Engineers History of Technology Series No. 32, 2004.

Callwell, Charles E. *Field Marshal Sir Henry Wilson: His Life and Diaries*. 2 vols. London: Cassell, 1927.

Cassar, George H. *The Tragedy of Sir John French*. London: Associated University Press, 1985.

Charteris, John. *At GHQ*. London: Cassell, 1931.

_____. *Field Marshal Earl Haig*. London: Cassell, 1929.

Clayton, C.P., and Michael Clayton. *The Hungry One*. Llandysul: Gomer, 1978.

Cooper, Bryan. *Tank Battles of World War I*. London: Ian Allan, 1974.

Cousins, Geoffrey. *The Defenders: A History of the British Volunteer*. London: Muller, 1969.

Cruttwell, Charles R.M.F. *A History of the Great War 1914–1918*. Oxford: Clarendon Press, 1934.

Doughty, Robert A. *Pyrrhic Victory: French Strategy and Operations in the Great War*. Cambridge, MA: Harvard University Press, 2005.

Farrar-Hockley, Anthony H. *Ypres 1914: Death of an Army*. London: Arthur Barker, 1967.

Ferris, John R. *The British Army and Signals Intelligence during the First World War*. London: Blackwell, 1992.

Flicke, Wilhelm F. *War Secrets in the Ether*.

2 vols. Laguna Hills, CA: Aegean Park, 1977.

Fuller, John F.C. *Generalship: Its Diseases and Their Cure*. London: Murray, 1937.

_____. *Tanks in the Great War*. London: Murray, 1920, and New York: E.P. Dutton, 1920.

Gardner, Brian. *The Big Push: A Portrait of the Battle of the Somme*. New York: William Morrow, 1963.

Gilbert, Martin. *The First World War: A Complete History*. New York: Henry Holt, 1994.

_____. *The Somme*. New York: Henry Holt, 2006.

Gladden, E. Norman. *Ypres 1917*. Abingdon: William Kimber, 1967.

Graves, Robert. *The Assault Heroic, 1895–1926*. London: Weidenfeld & Nicolson, 1986.

_____. *Goodbye to All That*. Harmondsworth: Penguin, 1960.

Griffith, Paddy. *British Battle Tactics on the Western Front 1916–1918*. New Haven, CT: Yale University Press, 1994.

Harfield, A.G., and Alan Harfield. *Pigeon to Packhorse*. Chippenham: Picton, 1989.

Hart, Peter. *The Somme*. New York: Pegasus Books, 2008.

Hartcup, Guy. *The War of Invention: Scientific Developments, 1914–1918*. London: Brassey's, 1988.

Hezlet, Arthur R. *The Electron and Sea Power, 1914–2007*. London: Peter Davies, 1975.

Hinricks, Ernest H. *Intercepting German Trench Communications in World War I*. Shippensburg, PA: White Mane, 1996.

Holmes, Richard. *Firing Line*. Harmondsworth: Penguin, 1987.

Hong, Sungook. *From Marconi's Black-Box to the Audion*. Cambridge, MA: MIT Press, 2001.

Horne, Alistair. *The Price of Glory: Verdun 1916*. New York: St. Martin's, 1963.

James, Robert R. *Gallipoli*. London: B.T. Batsford, 1965.

Kahn, David. *The Codebreakers*. New York: Scribner, 1967, 1996.

_____. *Seizing the Enigma*. Boston: Houghton Mifflin, 1991.

Keegan, John. *The Face of Battle*. London: Jonathan Cape, 1976.

_____. *The First World War*. New York: Knopf, 1999.

Kennett, Lee. *The First Air War, 1914–1918*. New York: Macmillan, 1991.

Lawson, Eric, and Jane Lawson. *The First Air Campaign*. Conshohocken, PA: Combined Books, 1966.

MacDonald, Lynn. *They Called It Passchendaele*. London: Michael Joseph, 1978.

Marble, Sanders. *The Infantry Cannot Do with a Gun Less*. New York: Columbia University Press, 2008.

Middlebrook, Martin. *The First Day on the Somme*. New York: Norton, 1972.

_____. *The Kaiser's Battle: 21st March 1918: The First Day of the German Spring Offensive*. London: Allen Lane, 1971.

Moorehead, Alan. *Gallipoli*. London: Hamish Hamilton, 1956.

Nalder, R.F.H. *The Royal Corps of Signals*. London: Royal Signals Institution, 1958.

Pitt, Barrie. *1918: The Last Act*. New York: Norton, 1962.

Price, Alfred. *The History of US Electronic Warfare*. Westford, MA: Murray, 1984.

Prior, Robin, and Trevor Wilson. *Command on the Western Front. The Military Career of Sir Henry Rawlinson, 1914–1918*. Oxford: Blackwell, 1992.

_____. *The Somme*. New Haven, CT, and London: Yale University Press, 2005.

Raines, Rebecca. *Getting the Message Through*. Washington, D.C.: Office of the Chief of Military History, U.S. Army, 1996.

Robertson, John. *Anzac and Empire: The Tragedy and Glory of Gallipoli*. London: Leo Cooper, 1990.

Rommel, Erwin. *Infantry Attacks*. London: Greenhill Books, 2006.

Sarkar, Tapan K., et al. *History of Wireless*. Hoboken, NJ: John Wiley & Sons, 2006.

Scrivenor, J.B. *Brigade Signals*. Oxford: Basil Blackwell, 1932.

Sheffield, Gary, and Dan Todman. *Command & Control on the Western Front: The British Army's Experience, 1914–1918*. Staplehurst: Spellmount, 2004.

Sheldon, Jack. *The German Army on the Somme, 1914–1916*. Barnesly: Pen and Sword Books, 2005.

Showalter, Dennis E. *Tannenberg*. Hamden, CT: Shoe String, 1991.

Simkins, Peter. *Kitchener's Army: The Raising of the New Armies, 1914–1916*. Manchester: Manchester University Press, 1988.

Slowe, Peter, and Richard Woods. *Fields of Death*. London: Robert Hale, 1986.

Terraine, John. *White Heat: The New Warfare, 1914–1918*. London: Sidgwick & Jackson, 1982.

Travers, Tim. *How the War Was Won: Command and Technology in the British Army on the Western Front 1917–18*. London: Routledge, 1992.

_____. *The Killing Ground*. London: Unwin Hyman, 1987.

Thompson, Mark. *The White War*. New York: Basic Books, 2009.

Van Creveld, Martin. *Command in War*. Cambridge, MA: Harvard University Press, 1985.

Wheldon, John. *Machine Age Armies*. London: Abelard-Schuman, 1968.

Wilson, Trevor. *The Myriad Faces of War*. Oxford: Basil Blackwell, 1986.

Winter, Denis. *Death's Men:. Soldiers of the Great War*. London: Allen Lane, 1978..

_____. *The First of the Few; Fighter Pilots of the First World War*. London: Allen Lane, 1982

Wolff, Leon. *In Flanders Fields*. London: Longmans Green, 1959, and New York: Time, 1963.

Contemporary Published and Printed Sources

General Staff. *Instructions for the Training of Divisions for Offensive Action [S.S. 135]* (originally published December 1916).

General Staff. *Instructions for the Training of Platoons for Offensive Action [S.S. 143]* (originally published February 1917).

Priestley, Raymond E. *The Signal Service in the European War of 1914 to 1918 (France)*. Chatham: MacKay, 1921.

Autobiographies and Memoirs

Ashurst, George. *My Bit: A Lancashire Fusilier at War, 1914–18*. Marlborough: Crowood, 1987.

Blunden, Edmund. *Undertones of War*. Harmondsworth: Penguin, 1982.

Bridges, Lt.-Gen. Sir Tom. *Alarms and Excursions*. London: Longman, 1938.

Coppard, George. *With a Machine Gun to Cambrai*. London: HMSO, 1969.

Douie, Charles. *The Weary Road: Recollections of a Subaltern of Infantry*. London: John Murray, 1988.

Graham, Stephen. *A Private in the Guards*. London: Macmillan, 1919.

Greenwell, Graham H. *An Infant in Arms: War Letters of a Company Officer*. London: L. Dickson & Thompson, 1935.

Griffiths, Llewelyn W. *Up to Mametz*. London: Faber & Faber, 1931.

Harris, Lionel H. *Signal Venture*. Aldershot: Gale & Polden, 1951.

Hawkinsg, Frank. *From Ypres to Cambrai*. Morley: Elmfield, 1974.

Hitchcock, F.C. *Stand To: A Diary of the Trenches*. London: Hurst & Blackett, 1937.

Liveing, Edward G.D. *Attack on the Somme: An Infantry Subaltern's Impressions of July 1st, 1916*. Stevenage: Spa Books, 1986.

May, Ernest. *Signal Corporal*. London: Johnson, 1972.

Mellersh, Harold E.L. *Schoolboy at War*. London: Kimber, 1978.

Murray, Joseph. *Call to Arms: From Gallipoli to the Western Front*. London: William Kimber, 1980.

Onions, Maude. *A Woman at War*. London: C.W. Daniel, 1928.

Owen, Edward. *1914: Glory Departing*. London: Buchan & Enright, 1986.

Richards, Frank. *Old Soldiers Never Die*. London: Faber & Faber, 1933.

Shephard, Ernest. *A Sergeant-Major's War*. Marlborough: Crowood, 1987.

Tyndale-Biscoe, J. *Gunner Subaltern, 1914–1918*. London: Leo Cooper, 1971.

Wade, Aubrey. *Gunner on the Western Front*. London: Batsford, 1959.

Watson, William H.L. *Adventures of a Despatch Rider*. London: William Blackwood, 1917.

Wood, Gordon. *I Was There*. Devon: Arthur H. Stockwell, 1984.

Relevant Articles

Lambert, Nicholas A. "Strategic Command and Control for Maneuver Warfare: Creation of the Royal Navy's 'War Room' System, 1905 to 1915." *Journal of Military History* 69 (April 2005).

Prince, Charles E. "Wireless Telephony on Aeroplanes." In G. Shiers, ed., *The Development of Wireless to 1920*. New York: Arno Press, 1977.

Unpublished Dissertations and Theses

Bruton, Elizabeth. "Marconi Wireless Telegraphy in the British Army in World War One." Unpublished M.Sc. thesis, Oxford University, 2005.

Clark, Paul W. "Major General George Owen Squier: Military Scientist." Unpublished Ph.D. diss., Case Western Reserve University, 1974.

Cook, Mark N. "Evaluating the Learning Curve: 38th (Welsh) Division on the Western Front 1916–1918." Unpublished M.Phil. thesis, Birmingham University, 2006.

Hammond, Bryn. "The Theory and Practice of Tank Co-operation with the Other Arms on the Western Front during the First World War." Unpublished Ph.D. diss., Birmingham University. 2006.

Index

wagons 70, 137
walkie-talkies 197
warships 11, 19, 176
waves 1, 15–16, 20–22, 46, 54, 55, 105, 139,
146, 184, 185, 196–197, 205
weather 9, 18, 33, 36, 45, 109, 148, 177
weight (of communications apparatus) 17,
21, 32, 52, 58, 76, 98, 166, 179, 182, 185,
191, 195, 198
Westmorland and Cumberland Yeomanry
53
Wilson, Adm. Sir Arthur 20
Wilson, Trevor 4, 10, 47, 203–204, 219
Wilson transmitter set 47, 183
wire 10–11, 15–16, 58–59, 67, 78, 84, 110,
122, 148, 172, 174–175, 206, 213, 216–218

wireless 1, 7–13, 15–24, 27, 29, 33, 35, 42–
44, 46–49, 53–57, 59–63, 65, 68–72,
75–76, 78, 87–89, 97–99, 102–105, 107,
111–113, 116–118, 121–122, 126–128, 130,
135, 138–141, 145–146, 149, 153, 155–157,
159–172, 175, 178–195, 197–199, 204–213,
215–216, 219–220
wireless telegraphy (W/T) 23, 195, 199–201
workshops 187

Ypres 12, 36–37, 43, 45, 51–52, 87, 91, 108,
154, 157, 205, 209, 215, 217–219
Ypres-Armentières 154

Zulu War 25